BETTER HOMES AND GARDENS®

Spectacular

DESSERTS

BETTER HOMES AND GARDENS® BOOKS
Des Moines

WE CARE!

All of us at Better Homes and Gardens® Books are dedicated to providing you with the information and ideas you need to create tasty foods. We welcome your comments or suggestions. Write us at: Better Homes and Gardens® Books, Cookbook Editorial Department, LS-348, 1716 Locust Street, Des Moines, IA 50309-3023

If you would like to order additional copies of any of our books, call 1-800-678-2803 or check with your local bookstore.

SPECTACULAR DESSERTS

Editors: Shelli McConnell, Mary Jo Plutt, Mary Major Williams
Associate Department Editor: Elizabeth Woolever
Graphic Designer: Neoma Thomas
Publishing Systems Text Processor: Paula Forest
Test Kitchen Product Supervisor: Marilyn Cornelius
Food Stylists: Rick Ellis, Pat Godsted, Janet Herwig
Contributing Food Photographers: Tim Schultz, Mark Thomas

Illustration adapted from a Hallmark Cards gift wrap design (pages 9, 43, 81, 105, 135, 165, and 203).

BETTER HOMES AND GARDENS® BOOKS

An Imprint of Meredith® Books
President, Book Group: Joseph J. Ward
Vice President and Editorial Director: Elizabeth P. Rice
Executive Editor: Connie Schrader
Food and Family Life Editor: Sharyl Heiken
Art Director: Ernest Shelton
Managing Editor: David A. Kirchner
Prepress Production Manager: Randall Yontz
Test Kitchen Director: Sharon Stilwell

On the cover: Honey-Almond Pie (see recipe, page 55)

Our seal assures you that every recipe in **Spectacular Desserts** has been tested in the Better Homes and Gardens® Test Kitchen. This means that each recipe is practical and reliable, and meets our high standards of taste appeal. We guarantee your satisfaction with this book for as long as you own it.

Spectacular Desserts

Calling all dessert lovers! Better Homes and Gardens® Books brings you the ultimate feast in sweets. With *Spectacular Desserts* let yourself go and indulge in irresistible temptations that are a cut above the ordinary dessert. Each and every extraordinary dessert featured here is a sinfully delicious extravagance and also a visually stunning treat. With almost every recipe, you receive a "Special Touch" tip on how to enhance your show-stopping presentations. There's also a chapter on Dessert Artistry with more clever and practical advice on creating dessert masterpieces. So when you are searching for that truly unique dessert to be the grand finale to a fine meal, or something sweetly unusual for a special celebration, turn to *Spectacular Desserts*—you may receive a round of applause.

▼ ▼ ▼

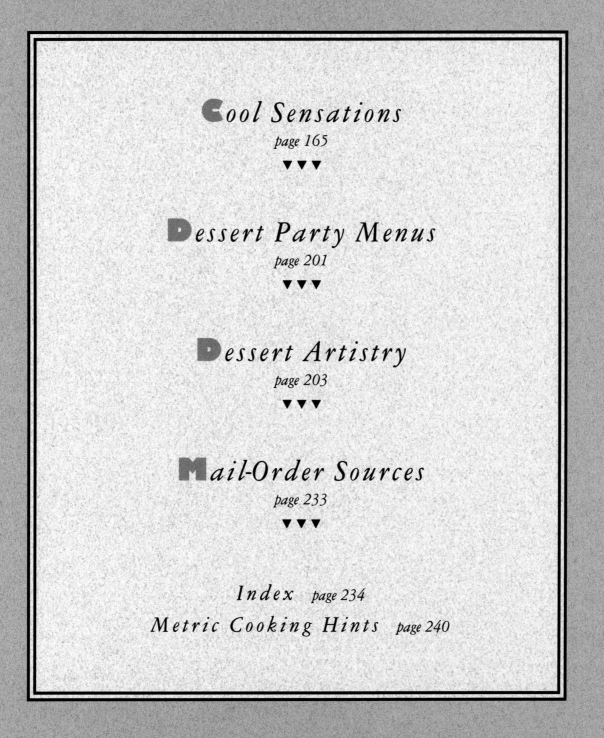

Desserts in this Book

Betties, Cobblers, and Crisps

Cakes

Candies

Cheesecakes

Cookies

Chocolate Fantasies

Whether it's poured over a cake, layered in a pie, chunked in a cookie, or drizzled over a soufflé, the wonderful flavor of chocolate exceeds the imagination. Take this chance to treat yourself to true chocolate decadence in recipes such as Triple-Chocolate Chunk Cookies, Bittersweet Chocolate Torte with Raspberries, White Chocolate Lemon-Almond Truffles, Double-Chocolate French Silk Pie, and Duo Chocolate Fondue.

▼ ▼ ▼

Chocolate Chip Éclairs

SPECIAL TOUCH

▼ ▼ ▼

For a fanciful display of these tasty chocolate-filled pastries, pipe or drizzle some additional Chocolate Glaze onto each dessert plate. Then top the plates with the éclairs and place a few nectarine slices or fresh strawberries on the side.

1   *recipe for 2 cups Chocolate Pastry Cream (see page 209)*
½   *cup whipping cream*
1   *recipe for Cream Puff Pastry (see page 205)*
2   *tablespoons semisweet* **or** *bittersweet chocolate, finely chopped,* **or** *miniature semisweet chocolate pieces*
½   *cup Chocolate Glaze (see recipe, page 211)*

Chill a small mixing bowl and the beaters of an electric mixer in the refrigerator. Meanwhile, prepare Chocolate Pastry Cream as directed, then set aside to cool slightly. (*Do not stir*).

In the chilled bowl beat whipping cream with chilled beaters on low speed till soft peaks form. Fold the whipped cream into the slightly cooled pastry cream, then cover and chill well.

Grease a large baking sheet. Set baking sheet aside. Prepare the Cream Puff Pastry as directed, *except* after adding all of the eggs, stir in the chopped chocolate or miniature chocolate pieces (*do not overstir* or the chocolate will melt). Spoon the dough into a decorating bag fitted with a large plain round tip (about ½-inch opening). Slowly pipe strips of dough 3 inches apart on the prepared baking sheet, making 12 éclairs, each about 4 inches long, 1¼ inches wide, and about ¾ inch high. Bake in a 400° oven for 30 to 35 minutes or till golden brown and puffy. Remove the éclairs and cool on a wire rack.

To assemble, horizontally cut off the tops of the éclairs. Remove any soft dough from the insides. Spoon about ¼ *cup* of the chilled pastry cream mixture into *each* éclair. Replace tops. Spoon the Chocolate Glaze over the top of éclairs. If desired, chill in the refrigerator for up to 2 hours. Makes 12 servings.

PER SERVING
358 CALORIES
7 g PROTEIN
27 g CARBOHYDRATES
26 g TOTAL FAT
9 g SATURATED FAT
180 mg CHOLESTEROL
225 mg SODIUM

Chocolaty Pecan Strudel

¼ *cup sugar*
¼ *cup orange juice*
¼ *cup honey*
 1 *teaspoon ground cinnamon*
 2 *cups pecans* or *walnuts, finely chopped*
 9 *ounces semisweet* or *bittersweet*
     chocolate, finely chopped, or *1½ cups*
     miniature semisweet chocolate pieces
     All-purpose flour
12 *sheets frozen phyllo dough, thawed*
 ½ *cup margarine* or *butter, melted*
 1 *cup Sweetened Whipped Cream*
     (see recipe, page 210) (optional)

For filling, in a small saucepan stir together the sugar, orange juice, honey, and cinnamon. Heat and stir till the sugar is dissolved and the mixture is smooth. Cool to room temperature. Stir in the pecans or walnuts and chocolate.

Lightly grease a 15x10x1-inch baking pan. Set the baking pan aside.

To assemble strudel, cover a large surface with a cloth. Sprinkle some flour over the cloth. Unfold the sheets of phyllo dough. Stack *2 sheets* of phyllo on the floured cloth. Brush the stack with some of the melted

margarine or butter. Arrange another stack of 2 sheets of phyllo on the cloth, overlapping the stacks as necessary and brushing them with margarine. Add 4 more stacks of 2 sheets of phyllo, brushing each stack with melted margarine and forming a rectangle about 40x20 inches (stagger the stacks of phyllo so all seams are not down the middle). Trim the rectangle to make it 40x20 inches. To assemble strudel, beginning 4 inches from a short side of the rectangle, spread the filling in a 4-inch-wide band across the dough, leaving 1 inch uncovered at each end. Using the cloth underneath the dough as a guide, gently lift the 4-inch-wide edge of dough and lay it over the filling. Then slowly and evenly lift the cloth and roll up the dough and filling, jelly-roll style, into a tight roll. Fold the ends under to seal.

Carefully transfer the strudel roll and place it diagonally on the prepared baking pan. Slightly curve the roll to fit the pan. Brush the top of the roll with the remaining melted margarine or butter. Bake in a 350° oven for 35 to 40 minutes or till golden. Carefully remove strudel from baking pan and cool on a wire rack. If desired, serve strudel with Sweetened Whipped Cream. Serves 12.

PER SERVING
432 CALORIES
6 g PROTEIN
42 g CARBOHYDRATES
31 g TOTAL FAT
5 g SATURATED FAT
14 mg CHOLESTEROL
169 mg SODIUM

White Chocoladamia Brownie Pie à la Mode

Flaky Pie Pastry for a single crust
  (see recipe, page 205)
¼ cup unsalted butter
3 ounces white baking bar, grated
1 cup all-purpose flour
¼ teaspoon baking powder
3 eggs
¾ cup sugar
1 teaspoon vanilla
1 cup chopped macadamia nuts **or**
  chopped pecans **or** almonds, toasted
3 ounces white baking bar, chopped
  Chocolate ice cream
  White Chocolate Sauce

For piecrust, on a lightly floured surface, use your hands to slightly flatten Flaky Pie Pastry dough. Roll dough from center to edges, forming a 12-inch circle. Wrap pastry around the rolling pin. Then unroll pastry onto a 9-inch pie plate. Ease pastry into pie plate, being careful not to stretch it. Trim pastry to ½ inch beyond edge of pie plate. Fold under extra pastry. Crimp edge. *Do not prick pastry.* Set pastry shell aside.

For filling, in a medium saucepan melt the butter. Remove from heat and cool. In a small mixing bowl stir together the 3 ounces grated white baking bar, flour, and baking powder; set aside. Stir the eggs, sugar, and vanilla into the melted butter in the saucepan. Using a wooden spoon, lightly beat the egg mixture *just till combined.* Then stir in the flour mixture, nuts, and 3 ounces chopped white baking bar.

Spread the filling into the unbaked pastry shell. Bake in a 350° oven for 50 to 55 minutes or till a wooden toothpick inserted near the center comes out clean. Serve warm or cooled with chocolate ice cream and White Chocolate Sauce. Makes 8 servings.

White Chocolate Sauce

In a heavy medium saucepan bring ⅔ cup *whipping cream* and 1 teaspoon *vanilla* just to boiling, stirring frequently. Remove saucepan from heat. In a bowl beat 1 *egg yolk,* ⅓ cup *sugar,* and *2 to 4 tablespoons* of the hot whipping cream mixture with an electric mixer on medium speed for 2 to 3 minutes or till thick and lemon-colored.

Gradually stir about *half* of the remaining whipping cream mixture into the egg yolk mixture. Return all of the mixture to the saucepan. Cook and stir over medium heat just till mixture returns to boiling, then remove from heat. Stir in 2 ounces (½ cup) grated *white baking bar.* Continue stirring till bar is melted. Cover surface and cool for 15 minutes. Stir before serving. Makes ¾ cup.

PER SERVING
791 CALORIES
11 g PROTEIN
81 g CARBOHYDRATES
49 g TOTAL FAT
20 g SATURATED FAT
160 mg CHOLESTEROL
162 mg SODIUM

Chocolate-Walnut Supreme Pie

Flaky Pie Pastry for a single crust
  (see recipe, page 205)
1 cup chopped walnuts or pecans, toasted
6 ounces semisweet or bittersweet
    chocolate, chopped, or one 6-ounce
    package (1 cup) semisweet chocolate
    pieces
½ cup caramel ice-cream topping
1 8-ounce package cream cheese, softened
1 8-ounce carton dairy sour cream
½ cup sugar
1 teaspoon vanilla
3 eggs
2 cups Sweetened Whipped-Cream
    Frosting (see recipe, page 210)
  Grated semisweet or bittersweet
    chocolate
  Broken walnuts or pecans, toasted
  Caramel ice-cream topping

For piecrust, on a lightly floured surface, use your hands to slightly flatten Flaky Pie Pastry dough. Roll dough from center to edges, forming a 12-inch circle. Wrap pastry around the rolling pin. Then unroll pastry onto a 9-inch pie plate. Ease pastry into pie plate, being careful not to stretch it. Trim pastry to ½ inch beyond edge of pie plate. Fold under extra pastry. Crimp edge, making a high flute edge. *Do not prick pastry.*

Sprinkle the 1 cup walnuts or pecans evenly in the bottom of the unbaked pastry shell. Then sprinkle with the chocolate and drizzle with the ½ cup caramel topping. Set the pastry shell aside.

For filling, in a medium mixing bowl beat the cream cheese, sour cream, sugar, and vanilla with an electric mixer on medium speed till smooth. Add the eggs and beat on low speed *just till combined.*

Pour the filling over the caramel topping layer in the pastry shell. Bake in a 350° oven about 45 minutes or till the center appears set. Cool pie on a wire rack.

Spoon Sweetened Whipped-Cream Frosting into a decorating bag fitted with a large star tip (about ½-inch opening). Pipe stars on top of the filling to cover pie. Chill in the refrigerator for 1 hour before serving.

Just before serving, sprinkle grated chocolate and broken walnuts or pecans on pie. Drizzle with additional caramel topping. Cover and refrigerate to store. Makes 10 servings.

SPECIAL TOUCH
▼ ▼ ▼

A pie so elaborate and rich your guests will savor every bite. Just dish it up on your favorite dessert plates, serve it along with cups of espresso, and then sit back and wait for the oohs and ahs.

PER SERVING
648 CALORIES
10 g PROTEIN
57 g CARBOHYDRATES
46 g TOTAL FAT
17 g SATURATED FAT
132 mg CHOLESTEROL
250 mg SODIUM

▼▼▼
With chocolate in the filling and chocolate in the topping, this *Double-Chocolate French Silk Pie* is sinfully delicious.

Double-Chocolate French Silk Pie

Flaky Pie Pastry for a single crust
(see recipe, page 205)
3 *ounces unsweetened chocolate, chopped*
1 *cup sugar*
¾ *cup butter*
1 *teaspoon vanilla*
3 *eggs (see tip, page 175)**
3 *ounces white baking bar, chopped*
1 *cup whipping cream*

For piecrust, on a lightly floured surface, use your hands to slightly flatten Flaky Pie Pastry dough. Roll dough from center to edges, forming a 12-inch circle. Wrap pastry around the rolling pin. Then unroll pastry onto a 9-inch pie plate. Ease pastry into pie plate, being careful not to stretch it.

Trim pastry to ½ inch beyond edge of pie plate. Fold under extra pastry. Crimp edge. Using the tines of a fork, prick bottom and sides of pastry generously. Line pastry shell with a double thickness of foil. Bake in a 450° oven for 8 minutes. Remove foil. Bake for 5 to 6 minutes more or till golden. Cool pastry on a wire rack.

For filling, melt the unsweetened chocolate according to the directions on page 225, cool. In a medium mixing bowl beat the sugar and butter with an electric mixer on medium speed about 4 minutes or till fluffy. Stir in the melted chocolate and the vanilla. Add the eggs, one at a time, beating on high speed after each addition and scraping the sides of the bowl constantly. Spoon the filling into the baked pastry shell. Cover and chill in the refrigerator for 5 to 24 hours or till set before serving.

Just before serving, spread White Chocolate Whipped Topping evenly over the chocolate filling. Use a hot knife to cut the pie. Makes 10 servings.

White Chocolate Whipped Topping

Melt 3 ounces chopped *white baking bar* with ¼ cup *whipping cream* according to the directions on page 225; cool. In a small mixing bowl beat ¾ cup *whipping cream* with an electric mixer on low speed till soft peaks form. Add the baking bar mixture. Continue beating on low speed just till stiff peaks form. Makes about 2 cups.

*If you wish, replace the eggs with ¾ cup thawed, frozen *egg substitute.* Just beat the product in the same way as the eggs, using ¼ cup at a time.

SPECIAL TOUCH
▼ ▼ ▼
For the true chocoholic, turn this double-chocolate pie into a triple-chocolate pie. Simply make another recipe of the White Chocolate Whipped Topping using semisweet or bittersweet chocolate instead of the white baking bar. Then two-tone pipe the toppings on the pie, top with white baking bar curls, and dust with cocoa powder.

PER SERVING
500 CALORIES
5 g PROTEIN
39 g CARBOHYDRATES
38 g TOTAL FAT
18 g SATURATED FAT
134 mg CHOLESTEROL
230 mg SODIUM

White Chocolate Cake Laced with Lemon

5 egg whites
2¼ cups all-purpose flour
1 tablespoon baking powder
¼ teaspoon salt
4 ounces white baking bar, chopped
1 cup half-and-half, light cream, or milk
½ cup butter
1¼ cups sugar
1 teaspoon vanilla
5 egg yolks
1 recipe for 4 cups Sweetened Whipped-Cream Frosting (see page 210)
6 ounces white baking bar, chopped
2 cups Citrus Curd (using lemon or orange) (see recipe, page 215)

In a large mixing bowl let egg whites stand at room temperature for 30 minutes. Meanwhile, grease and lightly flour two 9x1½-inch round baking pans; set aside. In a small mixing bowl stir together the flour, baking powder, and salt. Set the flour mixture aside.

Melt the 4 ounces white baking bar with ⅓ cup of the half-and-half according to the directions on page 225. Stir in the remaining half-and-half, then set aside to cool.

In a large mixing bowl beat butter with an electric mixer on medium to high speed about 30 seconds or till softened. Add the sugar and vanilla and beat till combined. Then add egg yolks, one at a time, beating till combined. Alternately add the flour mixture and white baking bar mixture, beating on low to medium speed after each addition just till combined.

Thoroughly wash beaters. In a large mixing bowl beat the egg whites till stiff peaks form (tips stand straight). Gently fold the egg whites into the batter.

Spread the batter in the prepared pans. Bake in a 350° oven for 30 to 35 minutes or till a wooden toothpick inserted near the centers of the cakes comes out clean. Cool cakes in pans on wire racks for 10 minutes. Then remove cakes; cool completely on the racks.

For frosting, prepare the Sweetened Whipped-Cream Frosting as directed, except melt the 6 ounces white baking bar with ¼ cup of the whipping cream according to the directions on page 225; cool. Beat the remaining 1¾ cups whipping cream from the Sweetened Whipped-Cream Frosting with the sugar and dissolved gelatin till soft peaks form. Add the cooled baking bar-whipping cream mixture to the beaten whipped cream mixture. Then continue beating till stiff peaks form.

To assemble, cut each cake horizontally into two even layers. Place first cake layer on a large serving plate. Spread with half of the Citrus Curd. Top with second cake layer, then spread with about 1 cup of the frosting. Top with third cake layer, then spread with remaining curd. Finally, top with the remaining cake layer and spread sides and top of the cake with remaining frosting. Cover and refrigerate to store. Serves 12.

PER SERVING
693 CALORIES
9 g PROTEIN
77 g CARBOHYDRATES
41 g TOTAL FAT
22 g SATURATED FAT
278 mg CHOLESTEROL
324 mg SODIUM

Buttermilk-Chocolate Cake

3 ounces unsweetened chocolate, chopped
2¼ cups sifted cake flour
1¾ cups sugar
1 teaspoon baking powder
1 teaspoon baking soda
¼ teaspoon salt
1⅓ cups buttermilk
½ cup butter, softened
1 teaspoon vanilla
2 eggs
3 cups Chocolate Buttercream
   (see recipe, page 211)
¾ cup crushed Glazed Nuts
   (see recipe, page 216)
¾ cup finely chopped Glazed Nuts
   (see recipe, page 216)

Grease and lightly flour two 9x1½-inch round baking pans. Melt chocolate according to directions on page 225; cool. Set pans and chocolate aside.

In a large mixing bowl stir together the cake flour, sugar, baking powder, baking soda, and salt. Add buttermilk, softened butter, and vanilla. Beat with an electric mixer on low to medium speed about 30 seconds or till combined. Then beat on medium to high speed for 2 minutes, scraping sides of bowl occasionally. Add the melted chocolate and eggs and beat for 2 minutes more.

Spread batter in the prepared pans. Bake in a 350° oven for 30 to 35 minutes or till a wooden toothpick inserted near the centers of the cakes comes out clean. Cool cakes in pans on wire racks for 10 minutes. Then remove cakes; cool completely on the racks.

In a small mixing bowl stir together *1 cup* of the Chocolate Buttercream and ¾ cup crushed Glazed Nuts.

To assemble, place first cake layer on a large serving plate. Spread with the buttercream-nut mixture. Top with the remaining cake layer. Frost the sides and top with the remaining Chocolate Buttercream, smoothing surface with narrow-bladed metal spatula. Press ¾ cup finely chopped Glazed Nuts on sides of cake. Cover and refrigerate to store. Makes 12 servings.

SPECIAL TOUCH
▼ ▼ ▼
There are no extra fancies needed for this cake—the rich layers of buttercream and crushed pralines are enough. Perch the cake on a pedestal cake plate and it will shine with the best.

PER SERVING
749 CALORIES
9 g PROTEIN
78 g CARBOHYDRATES
49 g TOTAL FAT
21 g SATURATED FAT
226 mg CHOLESTEROL
284 mg SODIUM

Chocolate Petits Fours

SPECIAL TOUCH
▼ ▼ ▼
Top these little cakes with Candied Flowers or a drizzle of melted white baking bar and they'll look just as cute as can be.

2 ounces unsweetened chocolate, chopped
1⅓ cups all-purpose flour
1 cup sugar
¾ teaspoon baking powder
½ teaspoon baking soda
¼ teaspoon salt
1 cup water
½ cup shortening
1 teaspoon vanilla
1 egg
½ cup apricot preserves
Chocolate Petits Fours Glaze
Candied Flowers (see recipe, page 219)
(optional)

Grease and lightly flour a 9x9x2-inch baking pan. Melt chocolate according to the directions on page 225; cool. Set the pan and chocolate aside.

In a medium mixing bowl stir together the flour, sugar, baking powder, baking soda, and salt. Add the water, shortening, and vanilla. Beat with an electric mixer on low to medium speed about 30 seconds or till combined. Then beat on medium to high speed for 2 minutes, scraping sides of bowl occasionally. Add the melted chocolate and egg and beat for 2 minutes more.

Spread batter evenly in the prepared pan. Bake in a 350° oven for 30 to 35 minutes or till a wooden toothpick inserted near the center of the cake comes out clean. Cool

cake in pan on wire rack for 10 minutes. Remove cake; cool completely on the rack.

Cut cake horizontally into *two* even layers. Place first cake layer on a cutting board. Stir preserves to soften; cut up any large pieces. Spread preserves on top of the first cake layer. Top with second cake layer.

Trim sides of the cake to make the edge smooth and straight. Cut the cake into 1½-inch squares, diamonds, hearts, and/or circles. Brush off crumbs. Place cake pieces on wire racks with waxed paper underneath the wire racks.

Carefully spoon Chocolate Petits Fours Glaze over cakes, spreading evenly to glaze tops and sides completely. If desired, decorate tops of cakes with Candied Flowers. Refrigerate to store. Makes about 36.

Chocolate Petits Fours Glaze

In a medium saucepan, melt 4 ounces chopped *unsweetened chocolate* with ⅓ cup *margarine* or *butter* according to the directions on page 225. Remove from heat. Stir in 4 cups sifted *powdered sugar* and 1½ teaspoons *vanilla*. Stir in 5 tablespoons *hot water* till blended. Stir in about 2 tablespoons *hot water*, 1 teaspoon at a time, till glaze is pouring consistency. (If icing gets too thick to pour, beat in an additional few drops *hot water*.) Makes 2 cups.

PER CAKE
159 CALORIES
1 g PROTEIN
24 g CARBOHYDRATES
7 g TOTAL FAT
1 g SATURATED FAT
6 mg CHOLESTEROL
56 mg SODIUM

Candy-Topped Brownie Torte

3 ounces unsweetened chocolate, chopped
¾ cup margarine or butter
1½ cups packed brown sugar
3 eggs
1 teaspoon vanilla
1 cup all-purpose flour
½ cup coarsely chopped almonds
5 ounces white baking bar with almonds, chopped
2 tablespoons shortening
½ ounce semisweet or bittersweet chocolate, chopped
¼ teaspoon shortening

Grease and lightly flour the bottom and 1 inch up the sides of an 8-inch springform pan. Set pan aside.

Melt the chocolate with margarine or butter according to the directions on page 225; cool slightly. In a large mixing bowl stir together the melted chocolate mixture and the brown sugar. Add the eggs and vanilla. Using a wooden spoon, lightly beat *just till combined.* (Do not overbeat or torte will rise during baking, then fall and crack.) Stir in the flour and almonds.

Spread the batter in the prepared springform pan. Then place on a shallow baking pan on the oven rack. Bake in a 350° oven about 45 minutes or till the top gently springs back when lightly touched. Cool cake in the springform pan on a wire rack for 5 minutes. Loosen the cake from the sides of the pan. Remove sides of the springform pan. Cool completely.

Melt the white baking bar with almonds with 2 tablespoons shortening according to the directions on page 225. Place cake on a wire rack with waxed paper underneath the rack. Pour the melted baking bar over the cake, spreading as necessary to glaze the top and sides completely.

Melt the semisweet or bittersweet chocolate with ¼ teaspoon shortening according to the directions on page 225. Drizzle the chocolate over the top of cake.

Chill cake in the refrigerator for 4 to 24 hours before serving. Just before serving, bring the cake to room temperature. Makes 12 to 14 servings.

SPECIAL TOUCH
▼ ▼ ▼

To present these chocolaty wedges artistically, drizzle or pipe melted semisweet or bittersweet chocolate in a zigzag pattern on each dessert plate. Then place wedges of the torte on top and serve a fanned strawberry or two alongside of each.

PER SERVING
422 CALORIES
6 g PROTEIN
44 g CARBOHYDRATES
27 g TOTAL FAT
5 g SATURATED FAT
55 mg CHOLESTEROL
167 mg SODIUM

▼ ▼ ▼

Bring on the pièce de résistance—this *Bittersweet Chocolate Torte with Raspberries* is a fudgy cake meant especially for true chocolate enthusiasts.

Bittersweet Chocolate Torte with Raspberries

14 ounces bittersweet **or** semisweet
    chocolate, chopped
½ cup margarine **or** butter
¼ cup milk
5 eggs
1 teaspoon vanilla
½ cup sugar
¼ cup all-purpose flour
¼ cup seedless red raspberry jam
1½ to 2 cups raspberries
    Powdered Sugar (optional)

Grease the bottom only of an 8-inch heart-shaped pan with a removeable bottom or an 8-inch springform pan. Set pan aside.

Melt chocolate with margarine or butter and milk according to the directions on page 225; cool for 20 minutes.

In a large mixing bowl beat eggs and vanilla with an electric mixer on low speed till well combined. Add the sugar and flour. Then beat on high speed for 10 minutes. Stir chocolate mixture into egg mixture.

Spread batter evenly in the prepared pan. Then place on a shallow baking pan on the oven rack. Bake in a 325° oven about 30 minutes or till cake is slightly puffed on outer one-third of the top. (If using a springform pan, bake about 35 minutes.)

Remove heart-shaped or springform pan from baking pan. Cool cake in the pan on a wire rack for 20 minutes. Loosen cake from sides of pan, then remove sides of pan. Cool for 2 to 3 hours more or till completely cooled. Remove the cake from the bottom of the pan. Wrap cake in foil and chill in the refrigerator for 6 to 48 hours before serving.

Just before serving, bring the cake to room temperature. In a small saucepan heat raspberry jam till melted; cool. Spread the jam over the top of cake. Place raspberries, hole sides down, on top of jam layer. If desired, sift the powdered sugar over the raspberries. Makes 16 servings.

SPECIAL TOUCH
▼ ▼ ▼
To make this torte even grander, place heart-shaped white paper doilies on your finest dessert plates. Then top each plate with a piece of this berry-covered torte.

PER SERVING
246 CALORIES
4 g PROTEIN
28 g CARBOHYDRATES
16 g TOTAL FAT
2 g SATURATED FAT
67 mg CHOLESTEROL
90 mg SODIUM

Double-Chocolate and Orange Torte

SPECIAL TOUCH
▼ ▼ ▼
Add some pizzazz to the sides of this torte by lightly pressing lots of chocolate curls or finely chopped chocolate into the icing.

3 ounces unsweetened chocolate, chopped
½ cup margarine or butter
1 cup sugar
¾ cup all-purpose flour
½ cup water
2 tablespoons orange liqueur
    or orange juice
1 tablespoon finely shredded orange peel
1½ teaspoons baking powder
½ teaspoon baking soda
½ teaspoon salt
4 eggs
1 tablespoon orange liqueur
    or orange juice
1 tablespoon orange juice
½ cup orange marmalade
    Bittersweet Chocolate Icing

Grease an 8x8x2-inch baking pan. Line the bottom of the baking pan with waxed paper. Grease the paper, then lightly flour the pan. Set pan aside.

Melt the chocolate according to the directions on page 225; cool. In a large mixing bowl beat margarine or butter with an electric mixer on medium to high speed about 30 seconds or till softened. Add the sugar, flour, water, 2 tablespoons orange liqueur or juice, orange peel, baking powder, baking soda, and salt. Beat on medium speed till combined. Then beat on high speed for 2 minutes. Add melted chocolate and eggs; beat for 2 minutes more.

Pour the batter into the prepared pan. Bake in a 350° oven for 30 to 40 minutes or till a wooden toothpick inserted near the center of the cake comes out clean. Cool cake in pan on a wire rack for 10 minutes. Then remove cake from pan and peel off waxed paper. Cool cake completely.

If using liqueur, combine the 1 tablespoon orange liqueur and 1 tablespoon orange juice. Or, if using juice, use the 2 tablespoons. Cut the cake horizontally into two layers. Sprinkle each cut side with half of the orange liqueur-juice mixture. Place first cake layer on a large serving plate. Spread orange marmalade evenly on top of cake layer. Top with remaining cake layer.

Frost sides and top of cake with the Bittersweet Chocolate Icing. Serves 10 to 12.

Bittersweet Chocolate Icing

In a heavy small saucepan combine ¼ cup whipping cream and 1 tablespoon light corn syrup. Bring just to boiling, stirring constantly. Remove from heat; stir in 4 ounces finely chopped semisweet or bittersweet chocolate, or ⅔ cup semisweet chocolate pieces till chocolate is melted and smooth. Cool to room temperature. Stir icing before using. Makes ¾ cup.

PER SERVING
398 CALORIES
5 g PROTEIN
50 g CARBOHYDRATES
22 g TOTAL FAT
4 g SATURATED FAT
93 mg CHOLESTEROL
335 mg SODIUM

Bittersweet Espresso Torte

Unsalted butter
Unsweetened cocoa powder
10 ounces bittersweet or semisweet
    chocolate, chopped
¾ cup sugar
¾ cup espresso or very strong coffee
⅔ cup unsalted butter
4 eggs
4 egg yolks
½ cup Chocolate Glaze
    (see recipe, page 211)
1 cup Sweetened Whipped-Cream
    Frosting (see recipe, page 210)

Remove sides from an 8-inch springform pan. Line the bottom of the pan with parchment paper or plain brown paper, extending the paper over edges of bottom. Then attach sides to the bottom of the springform pan, making sure paper is securely under bottom of pan. Grease paper and sides of pan with unsalted butter, then dust with cocoa powder. Set pan aside.

In a heavy medium saucepan heat and stir the chocolate, sugar, espresso or strong coffee, and ⅔ cup butter over medium heat just till chocolate is melted. Remove from heat and cool slightly.

In a medium mixing bowl beat the whole eggs and egg yolks with an electric mixer on high speed about 6 minutes or till light and foamy. Using a wire whisk, *gradually* stir the chocolate mixture into the eggs.

Pour batter into the prepared springform pan. Then place the springform pan on a shallow baking pan on the oven rack. Bake in a 325° oven for 35 to 45 minutes or till the edges puff and crack slightly.

Remove springform pan from baking pan. Completely cool cake in springform pan on a wire rack. Loosen cake from sides of pan. Remove sides of springform pan. Invert cake onto a large serving plate. Remove bottom of pan. Peel off the paper.

Pour Chocolate Glaze over cake, spreading as necessary to glaze the top and sides completely. Spoon Sweetened Whipped-Cream Frosting into a decorating bag fitted with a large star tip (about ½-inch opening). Pipe a shell border around top edge of cake. Cover and refrigerate to store. Makes 12 to 16 servings.

SPECIAL TOUCH
▼ ▼ ▼
Turn this rich chocolate torte from special to spectacular by garnishing the top shell border with chocolate-covered coffee beans and a dusting of grated chocolate.

PER SERVING
385 CALORIES
6 g PROTEIN
31 g CARBOHYDRATES
29 g TOTAL FAT
12 g SATURATED FAT
194 mg CHOLESTEROL
32 mg SODIUM

Chocolate, Mascarpone, and Fruit Shortcakes

SPECIAL TOUCH
▼ ▼ ▼

All wonderful hearts are overflowing with goodness and 'tis the same with these heart-shaped shortcakes. For a spilling-over effect, place the bottom half of each shortcake on a dessert plate. Then spoon on the cheese mixture, arrange the fruit, and place the top half of the shortcake at an angle on top.

1½ cups all-purpose flour
¼   cup packed brown sugar
3   tablespoons unsweetened cocoa powder
2   teaspoons baking powder
    Dash salt
¼   cup margarine or butter
3   ounces semisweet or bitterweet chocolate, finely chopped, or 1 cup miniature semisweet chocolate pieces
1   beaten egg
¼   cup half-and-half, light cream, or milk
⅔   cup whipping cream
12 ounces mascarpone cheese
¾   cup sifted powdered sugar
1   teaspoon vanilla
3   medium nectarines, pitted and sliced, or 3 medium peaches peeled, pitted, and sliced
1   cup raspberries, blackberries, and/or blueberries

Chill a medium mixing bowl and the beaters of an electric mixer in the refrigerator while preparing the shortcakes.

For shortcakes, in a medium mixing bowl stir together flour, brown sugar, cocoa powder, baking powder, and salt. Cut in margarine or butter till the mixture resembles coarse crumbs. Add the chopped chocolate or chocolate pieces, then toss till mixed. Make a well in the center of the dry mixture.

In a small mixing bowl stir together beaten egg and half-and-half. Then add the egg mixture all at once to the dry mixture. Using a fork, stir *just till moistened.*

Turn the dough out onto a lightly floured surface. Gently knead dough for 10 to 12 strokes or till *nearly* smooth. Pat or lightly roll dough to ½-inch thickness. Using a floured 3-inch heart-shaped cookie cutter, cut dough into hearts, dipping cutter into flour between cuts.

Place shortcakes 1 inch apart on an ungreased baking sheet. Bake in a 375° oven for 12 to 15 minutes or till a wooden toothpick inserted near the centers of the shortcakes comes out clean. Remove shortcakes and cool slightly on a wire rack.

Meanwhile, for cheese mixture, in the chilled mixing bowl beat the whipping cream with an electric mixer on low speed just till soft peaks form. Add the mascarpone cheese, powdered sugar, and vanilla and beat till fluffy. (Mixture will thicken as it is beaten.)

To serve, split shortcakes horizontally in half. Assemble by spooning the cheese mixture, nectarines, and berries between shortcake layers and over top. Makes 8 servings.

PER SERVING
526 CALORIES
9 g PROTEIN
51 g CARBOHYDRATES
34 g TOTAL FAT
16 g SATURATED FAT
104 mg CHOLESTEROL
313 mg SODIUM

Chocolate, Almond, and Raspberry Cheesecake

1 teaspoon margarine or butter
1 cup ground almonds
1 pound milk chocolate, chopped
4 8-ounce packages cream cheese, softened
½ cup margarine or butter, softened
⅓ cup milk
2 tablespoons raspberry liqueur, amaretto, or milk
4 eggs
1 egg yolk
1 cup raspberries
½ cup sliced almonds, toasted
1 ounce white baking bar or milk chocolate, chopped

Grease the bottom of a 9-inch springform pan with the 1 teaspoon margarine or butter. Press the ground almonds onto the bottom of the greased springform pan. Melt the 1 pound milk chocolate according to the directions on page 225; cool. Set pan and chocolate aside.

For filling, in a large mixing bowl beat the melted chocolate, cream cheese, ½ cup margarine or butter, ⅓ cup milk, and liqueur or milk with an electric mixer on medium to high speed till combined. Add whole eggs and egg yolk all at once. Beat on low speed just till combined.

Pour filling into the nut-lined springform pan. Then place on a shallow baking pan on the oven rack. Bake in a 350° oven about 55 minutes or till 1 to 2 inches of outside edges appear set when shaken.

Remove springform pan from baking pan. Cool cheesecake in springform pan on a wire rack for 15 minutes. Loosen cheesecake from sides of pan and cool for 30 minutes more. Remove sides of the springform pan. Cool completely, then chill in the refrigerator for 4 to 24 hours before serving.

Just before serving, gently toss together the raspberries and sliced almonds. Mound the raspberry mixture in the center of the cheesecake. Melt the 1 ounce white baking bar or milk chocolate according to the directions on page 225. Then drizzle over the raspberry mixture in a zigzag pattern. Makes 12 to 16 servings.

SPECIAL TOUCH
▼ ▼ ▼

Carefully dip the tines of your dessert forks into melted chocolate and place the forks on waxed paper to dry. Then delight your guests by arranging a fork alongside each piece of this creamy cheesecake.

PER SERVING
682 CALORIES
14 g PROTEIN
33 g CARBOHYDRATES
57 g TOTAL FAT
20 g SATURATED FAT
179 mg CHOLESTEROL
381 mg SODIUM

▼ ▼ ▼
Here is just one pretty idea for decorating the *Berry-Glazed White Chocolate Cheesecake.* Create your own personalized look by shaping different decorations using our easy-to-mold chocolate clay on page 231.

Berry-Glazed White Chocolate Cheesecake

2 teaspoons *margarine* or *butter*
¾ cup *ground almonds*
16 ounces *white baking bar, chopped*
4 *8-ounce packages cream cheese, softened*
½ cup *margarine* or *butter, softened*
3 tablespoons *milk*
1 tablespoon *vanilla*
4 *eggs*
1 *egg yolk*
3 cups *Chocolate Modeling Clay (using white vanilla-flavored candy coating) (see recipe, page 231) (optional)*
½ cup *desired butter frosting (optional)*
   Berry Glaze
   Food coloring (optional)
   Powdered sugar (optional)

Grease the bottom and sides of a 9-inch springform pan with the 2 teaspoons margarine or butter. Press the ground almonds onto the bottom of the greased springform pan. Set pan aside.

For cheesecake filling, melt the white baking bar according to the directions on page 225. In a large mixing bowl beat melted baking bar, cream cheese, ½ cup margarine or butter, milk, vanilla, and dash *salt* with an electric mixer on medium to high speed till combined. Add whole eggs and egg yolk all at once. Beat on low speed *just till combined.*

Pour filling into the crust-lined springform pan; place on a shallow baking pan on the oven rack. Bake cheesecake on a shallow baking pan in a 350° oven for 50 to 55 minutes or till the cheesecake appears *nearly* set in the center when shaken.

Remove springform pan from baking pan. Cool on a rack for 15 minutes. Loosen crust from sides of pan; cool 30 minutes more. Remove sides of pan. Cool, then chill for at least 4 hours. To serve, loosen cheesecake from pan bottom. Transfer to a plate.

If desired, to decorate with modeling clay, roll *1 cup* of the clay into two 14-inch-long strips, each about 2½ inches wide and ⅛ inch thick. Measure height of the cake; cut strips to match the height plus ¼ inch. Spread edges of cake with a butter frosting; press the ribbons around the cake. Trim off overlapping ends; smooth seams with a hot knife. Spread Berry Glaze on top. For a lattice and bow, roll another *1 cup* of the clay to ⅛-inch-thickness. Cut ⅜-inch-wide strips for the lattice and ½-inch-wide strips for the bow. Arrange strips on cake to make a lattice and bow. Tint remaining clay with food coloring; mold flowers and leaves to garnish cake.

Or, if not using clay, spread Berry Glaze on top of cheesecake. Then sift powdered sugar over top. Makes 16 servings.

Berry Glaze

In a saucepan stir together 2 tablespoons *sugar* and 1 tablespoon *cornstarch.* Add 2 cups fresh *or* frozen *raspberries, blueberries,* or *blackberries.* Gently toss. Cook and stir mixture till thickened and bubbly. Cook and stir for 2 minutes more. If desired, press mixture through a sieve; discard seeds. Cool glaze, then cover and chill in the refrigerator before using. Makes ¾ cup.

PER SERVING
483 CALORIES
9 g PROTEIN
24 g CARBOHYDRATES
40 g TOTAL FAT
19 g SATURATED FAT
129 mg CHOLESTEROL
285 mg SODIUM

Creamy, Fudgy, and Nutty Brownies

SPECIAL TOUCH
▼ ▼ ▼
This is the ultimate
brownie. Just add a dollop
of whipped cream and a
sprinkling of grated
chocolate and you have
pure decadence.

4 ounces unsweetened chocolate, chopped
½ cup margarine or butter
1 cup all-purpose flour
½ cup chopped walnuts or pecans, toasted
¼ teaspoon baking powder
1½ cups sugar
3 eggs
1 teaspoon vanilla
3 ounces semisweet or bittersweet chocolate, chopped
2 3-ounce packages cream cheese
1 egg
¼ cup sugar
1 tablespoon milk
½ teaspoon vanilla

Grease and lightly flour an 8x8x2-inch baking pan; set aside. Melt the unsweetened chocolate with margarine or butter according to the directions on page 225; set aside to cool slightly. In a medium mixing bowl stir together the flour, walnuts or pecans, and baking powder; set aside.

In a large mixing bowl stir together the melted chocolate mixture and the 1½ cups sugar. Add the 3 eggs and 1 teaspoon vanilla. Using a wooden spoon, lightly beat the mixture *just till combined.* (Do not overbeat or brownies will rise during baking, then fall and crack.) Stir in the flour mixture. Spread the batter in the prepared pan. Bake in a 350° oven for 40 minutes.

Meanwhile, for topping, in a small saucepan melt semisweet or bittersweet chocolate according to the directions on page 225; cool slightly. In a medium mixing bowl beat the cream cheese with an electric mixer on medium speed about 30 seconds or till softened. Add the melted semisweet or bittersweet chocolate, 1 egg, ¼ cup sugar, 1 tablespoon milk, and ½ teaspoon vanilla. Beat till combined.

Carefully spread topping evenly over hot brownies. Bake in the 350° oven about 10 minutes more or till the topping is set. Cool brownies in pan on a wire rack. Cover and chill in the refrigerator for at least 2 hours before serving. To serve, cut into bars. Cover; refrigerate to store. Makes 12 to 16.

PER BROWNIE
402 CALORIES
6 g PROTEIN
45 g CARBOHYDRATES
25 g TOTAL FAT
5 g SATURATED FAT
87 mg CHOLESTEROL
161 mg SODIUM

Fudgy Brownies with Chocolate-Orange Glaze

4 ounces *unsweetened chocolate, chopped*
½ cup *margarine* or *butter*
1 cup *sugar*
2 *eggs*
2 teaspoons *finely shredded orange peel*
1 teaspoon *vanilla*
¾ cup *all-purpose flour*
½ cup *broken walnuts* or *pecans*
    Chocolate-Orange Glaze

In a medium saucepan melt unsweetened chocolate with the margarine or butter according to the directions on page 225. Remove from heat. Stir in sugar, eggs, orange peel, and vanilla. Using a wooden spoon, lightly beat the mixture *just till combined.* Stir in the flour and nuts.

Spread the batter in an ungreased 8x8x2-inch baking pan. Bake in a 350° oven for 30 minutes. Cool the brownies in the pan on a wire rack.

Pour Chocolate-Orange Glaze over cooled brownies, spreading as necessary to glaze top evenly. Let stand at room temperature till glaze is set. Makes 9.

Chocolate-Orange Glaze

In a small heavy saucepan, bring ⅓ cup *whipping cream* to a gentle boil over medium-low heat, stirring constantly. Remove from heat. Add 3 ounces finely chopped *semisweet* or *bittersweet chocolate* and 1 teaspoon finely shredded *orange peel.* Let stand for 1 minute. Using a wire whisk or wooden spoon stir mixture till chocolate is melted. Cool for 5 minutes before using. Makes ½ cup.

SPECIAL TOUCH
▼ ▼ ▼
For a refreshing touch, top off these simply divine brownies with a scoop of orange sherbet.

PER BROWNIE
404 CALORIES
6 g PROTEIN
40 g CARBOHYDRATES
28 g TOTAL FAT
4 g SATURATED FAT
59 mg CHOLESTEROL
137 mg SODIUM

Triple-Chocolate Chunk Cookies

SPECIAL TOUCH
▼ ▼ ▼
In the world of wonderful cookies, these would be rated topnotch. Make them even more spectacular by drizzling them with a luscious, chocolate glaze. To make the glaze, melt 4 ounces white baking bar or semisweet or bittersweet chocolate and 1 tablespoon shortening according to the directions on page 225.

2 ounces unsweetened chocolate, chopped
1 cup margarine or butter
2 cups all-purpose flour
¾ cup sugar
¾ cup packed brown sugar
2 eggs
1 teaspoon baking soda
1 teaspoon vanilla
6 ounces white baking bar, cut into ½-inch pieces
6 ounces semisweet or bittersweet chocolate, cut into ½-inch pieces
1 cup chopped black walnuts or pecans (optional)

Grease a cookie sheet; set aside. Melt the unsweetened chocolate according to the directions on page 225; set aside to cool.

In a large mixing bowl beat the margarine or butter with an electric mixer on medium to high speed about 30 seconds or till softened.

Add about *half* of the flour and all of the melted chocolate, sugar, brown sugar, eggs, baking soda, and vanilla to the margarine. Beat till thoroughly combined, scraping the sides of bowl occasionally. Then beat or stir in the remaining flour. Stir in the white baking bar, semisweet or bittersweet chocolate, and, if desired, nuts.

Drop ¼ *cup* of dough at a time 4 inches apart on the prepared cookie sheet. Bake in a 350° oven for 12 to 14 minutes or till edges are firm. Cool on cookie sheet for 1 minute. Then remove the cookies and cool on a wire rack. Makes about 22.

PER COOKIE
264 CALORIES
3 g PROTEIN
32 g CARBOHYDRATES
15 g TOTAL FAT
3 g SATURATED FAT
19 mg CHOLESTEROL
149 mg SODIUM

Chocolate Cookie Hearts with Raspberry Sauce

1¾   cup all-purpose flour
⅓   cup unsweetened cocoa powder
1½   teaspoons baking powder
⅔   cup margarine or butter
¾   cup sugar
1   teaspoon vanilla
1   egg
½   cup dairy sour cream
2   cups Chocolate Buttercream (see recipe, page 211)
1   cup Raspberry Sauce (see recipe, page 213)

In a small mixing bowl stir together the flour, cocoa powder, and baking powder. Set flour mixture aside.

In a large mixing bowl beat the margarine or butter with an electric mixer on medium to high speed about 30 seconds or till softened. Add the sugar and vanilla and beat till combined. Then add the egg, beating till combined. Alternately add the flour mixture and sour cream, beating on low to medium speed after each addition *just till combined.* Divide dough in half. Cover; chill in the refrigerator 2 hours or till easy to handle.

Grease a cookie sheet. Set cookie sheet aside. On a lightly floured surface, roll *each* half of dough to about ¼-inch thickness. Using a 3-inch heart-shaped cookie cutter, cut dough into hearts. Place 1 inch apart on the prepared cookie sheet.

Bake in a 350° oven for 6 to 8 minutes or till edges are firm. Cool cookies on cookie sheet for 1 minute. Then remove cookies and cool on a wire rack.

To assemble cookie sandwiches, spoon Chocolate Buttercream into a decorating bag fitted with a medium star tip (about ¼-inch opening). Pipe stars onto the bottoms of *half* the cookies, completely covering each bottom. *Or,* spread buttercream on the bottoms. Then top each with the remaining unfrosted cookies, bottom sides down. Cover and refrigerate to store.

To serve, spoon some Raspberry Sauce onto each dessert plate. Then place cookie sandwiches on top of the sauce. Makes 12 to 15 servings.

SPECIAL TOUCH
▼ ▼ ▼
Highlight each cookie with a decorative dusting of powdered sugar. For a lacy pattern, place a paper doily on the cookie and sift powdered sugar on top. Then remove the doily.

PER SERVING
505 CALORIES
5 g PROTEIN
51 g CARBOHYDRATES
33 g TOTAL FAT
13 g SATURATED FAT
135 mg CHOLESTEROL
175 mg SODIUM

For that very special person, show your love with a gift of these lavishly rich *Rum Truffles* and almondy *Marzipan Treasures* (page 104).

Rum Truffles

6 *ounces semisweet* or *bittersweet chocolate, chopped*
¼ *cup margarine* or *butter*
3 *tablespoons whipping cream*
1 *beaten egg yolk*
3 *tablespoons rum* or *brandy*
1 *pound semisweet* or *bittersweet chocolate* or *chocolate-flavored candy coating, chopped*
White or *pink vanilla-flavored candy coating, melted (optional)*

Melt 6 ounces chocolate with the margarine or butter and whipping cream according to the directions on page 225. Gradually stir about *half* of the hot mixture into the beaten egg yolk. Return all of the egg mixture to saucepan. Cook and stir over medium heat till mixture *just begins to bubble.* This should take about 2 minutes. Remove saucepan from heat.

Stir in the rum or brandy. Transfer the chocolate mixture to a medium mixing bowl. Chill in the refrigerator about 1 hour or till the chocolate mixture is completely cool and smooth, stirring occasionally.

Beat the cooled chocolate mixture with an electric mixer on medium speed about 2 minutes or till slightly fluffy, scraping the sides of the bowl constantly. Chill about 15 minutes or till the mixture holds its shape.

Line a baking sheet with waxed paper. Drop mixture from a rounded teaspoon onto the prepared baking sheet. Chill about 30 minutes more or till firm.

If desired, use your hands to shape truffles into smooth balls, working quickly so the truffles don't get too soft.

To dip the truffles, if using the 1 pound chocolate, quick-temper it according to the directions on page 226. If using chocolate-flavored candy coating, melt it according to the directions on page 225.

Dip truffles, one at a time, into the chocolate or chocolate-flavored candy coating, turning to coat. Using a 2- or 3-prong long-handled fork, lift the truffle out; draw fork across rim of bowl or pan to remove excess chocolate. Invert onto the waxed-paper-lined baking sheet, twisting fork slightly as candy falls to form a swirl on top. Let dipped truffles dry.

If desired, to decorate truffles, melt white or pink candy coating according to the directions on page 225. Spoon the melted white or pink candy coating into a decorating bag fitted with a small round tip (about ⅛-inch opening). Pipe coating in a design on top of truffles. *Or,* drizzle coating on top of truffles with a spoon. Let stand till dry. Tightly cover and store truffles in a cool, dry place. Makes about 30.

PER TRUFFLE
123 CALORIES
2 g PROTEIN
12 g CARBOHYDRATES
9 g TOTAL FAT
1 g SATURATED FAT
9 mg CHOLESTEROL
19 mg SODIUM

White Chocolate Lemon-Almond Truffles

SPECIAL TOUCH

▼ ▼ ▼

For a special gift, place a
few of these extraordinary
truffles in colorful candy
cups. Then package them in
a decorative gift box or
antique tin.

8 *ounces white baking bar, chopped*
¼ *cup whipping cream*
2 *tablespoons finely snipped Candied
   Citrus Peel (using lemons) (see
   recipe, page 217)*
1 *tablespoon amaretto or whipping cream
   Finely chopped toasted almonds or
   coconut, or sifted powdered sugar*

Line a baking sheet with waxed paper; set
aside. Melt 8 ounces white baking bar with
whipping cream according to the directions
on page 225. Add the Candied Citrus Peel
and amaretto or whipping cream. Then pour
the mixture into a small metal bowl.

Place the small bowl in a larger bowl of *ice*
and *water.* Using a wooden spoon, beat the
mixture till thickened, being *very careful* not
to splash any water into the mixture.

Drop the mixture by *rounded teaspoons* onto
the prepared baking sheet. Chill in the
refrigerator about 30 minutes or till firm.

Then use your hands to shape truffles into
balls, working quickly so the truffles don't
get too soft. Roll each ball into almonds,
coconut, or powdered sugar. Tightly cover
and store truffles in a cool, dry place for up
to 1 week. Makes about 20.

White Chocolate Orange-Pecan Truffles

Prepare White Chocolate Lemon-Almond
Truffles as directed above, *except* substitute
Candied Citrus Peel (using oranges) (see
recipe, page 217) for the Candied Citrus
Peel (using lemons), *orange liqueur* for the
amaretto, and finely chopped toasted *pecans*
for the almonds.
Per Truffle: Same as main recipe, except 89 calories.

PER TRUFFLE
90 CALORIES
1 g PROTEIN
9 g CARBOHYDRATES
6 g TOTAL FAT
3 g SATURATED FAT
4 mg CHOLESTEROL
11 mg SODIUM

Triple-Nut and Date Dacquoise

4 egg whites
1 teaspoon vanilla
½ teaspoon cream of tartar
¾ cup sugar
3 tablespoons unsweetened cocoa powder
⅔ cup pitted whole dates, finely snipped
⅓ cup very finely chopped toasted almonds
⅓ cup very finely chopped toasted hazelnuts (filberts)
⅓ cup very finely chopped toasted walnuts
2 cups Chocolate Buttercream (see recipe, page 211)*
2 cups Flavored Whipped Cream (using cocoa plus sugar) (see recipe, page 210)
Powdered sugar

In a large mixing bowl, let egg whites stand at room temperature for 30 minutes. Meanwhile, line 2 baking sheets with parchment paper or plain brown paper. Draw three 7-inch circles 2 inches apart on the paper. Set baking sheets aside.

For meringues, add vanilla and cream of tartar to the egg whites. Beat with an electric mixer on medium to high speed about 3 minutes or till soft peaks form (tips curl). Gradually add sugar, 1 tablespoon at a time, beating on high speed about 1½ minutes or till very stiff peaks form (tips stand straight) and sugar is almost dissolved. Then beat in cocoa powder just till combined. Fold in the almonds, hazelnuts, and walnuts.

Using a spoon or a spatula, spread one-third of the meringue mixture evenly over each circle on the prepared baking sheet. Bake in a 300° oven for 30 minutes. Turn off oven. Then let meringue shells dry in oven with door closed for 1 hour. (Do not open oven.)

Peel paper from meringues. To assemble, spread about 1 tablespoon Chocolate Buttercream in the center of a large serving plate. (The buttercream on the plate will help prevent the meringue from sliding.) Place 1 meringue layer on top of the buttercream. Spoon 1 cup of buttercream into a decorating bag fitted with a large star tip (about ½-inch opening). (Store remaining buttercream, covered, in the refrigerator for up to 3 days or in the freezer for up to 2 months; use it to spread on a one-layer cake or on cookies.) Pipe a shell border around the top outside edge of the meringue on the plate, forming a rim about 1 inch high.

Fold the dates into chocolate Flavored Whipped Cream. Spread half of the cream mixture in center of buttercream rim. Top with second meringue; repeat piping buttercream in a border and spreading with remaining cream mixture. Top with remaining meringue. Sift powdered sugar over top. Finally, pipe a border around edge of top meringue. Cover loosely. Chill in the refrigerator about 8 hours to slightly soften meringue before serving. Makes 8 servings.

*If desired, prepare Chocolate Buttercream as directed using 2 teaspoons hazelnut liqueur or amaretto.

PER SERVING
694 CALORIES
8 g PROTEIN
62 g CARBOHYDRATES
49 g TOTAL FAT
23 g SATURATED FAT
210 mg CHOLESTEROL
48 mg SODIUM

Coffee-Spiked Pudding with Figs and Pecans

    ¾ cup sugar
    2 tablespoons cornstarch or ¼ cup
       all-purpose flour
  2⅔ cups milk
    3 ounces unsweetened chocolate, chopped
    4 beaten egg yolks
    2 tablespoons coffee liqueur (optional)
    1 tablespoon margarine or butter
  1½ teaspoons vanilla
    ⅔ cup snipped Mission (dark) dried figs
    2 tablespoons coffee liqueur or warm
       water
    ½ cup coarsely chopped toasted pecans or
       black walnuts

In a heavy medium saucepan stir together
sugar and cornstarch or flour. Stir in milk
and chocolate. Cook and stir over medium
heat till thickened and bubbly. Cook and stir
for 2 minutes more. Remove from heat.

Gradually stir about *1 cup* of the hot mixture
into the egg yolks. Return all of the egg yolk
mixture to saucepan. Bring to a gentle boil,
then reduce heat. Cook and stir for 2
minutes more. Remove from heat. Stir in the
2 tablespoons coffee liqueur (if desired),
margarine or butter, and vanilla till
margarine melts. Pour pudding into a bowl.
Cover surface with plastic wrap. Chill in the
refrigerator before serving. (*Do not stir.*)

About 30 minutes before serving, soak the
snipped figs in 2 tablespoons coffee liqueur
or warm water, stirring occasionally. Drain
figs and discard liqueur or water. Gently fold
the figs and pecans or walnuts into the
pudding. Makes 6 servings.

Bread Pudding with Irish Crème Anglaise

2 *cups milk*

8 *ounces semisweet* or *bittersweet chocolate, chopped*

4 *cups dry French bread cubes*

4 *beaten eggs*

½ *cup sugar*

2 *tablespoons margarine* or *butter, melted*

½ *teaspoon ground cinnamon*

¼ *teaspoon salt*

⅔ *cup whipping cream*

1 *recipe for 1 cup Crème Anglaise (see page 212)*

1 *tablespoon Irish cream liqueur*

Lightly grease a 1½-quart soufflé dish; set aside. In a medium saucepan heat and stir milk and chocolate over low heat just till chocolate is melted.

In a large mixing bowl combine the milk mixture and the bread cubes. Let stand for 15 to 20 minutes or till bread is completely softened, stirring occasionally.

In a medium mixing bowl stir together the eggs, sugar, margarine or butter, cinnamon, and salt. Add the whipping cream. Using a wire whisk, stir mixture till well combined. Pour egg mixture over the bread mixture. Stir till combined. Then pour the mixture into the prepared soufflé dish.

Bake in a 350° oven about 60 minutes or till the center is puffed and *nearly* set (if necessary, loosely cover with foil the last 20 minutes of baking to prevent overbrowning). Cool on a wire rack before serving (the bread pudding may slightly fall).

Meanwhile, prepare Crème Anglaise as directed, *except* substitute the 1 tablespoon Irish cream liqueur for the 2 teaspoons of liqueur.

To serve, spoon warm bread pudding into dessert dishes. Pour the Crème Anglaise on top. Makes 6 servings.

SPECIAL TOUCH
▼ ▼ ▼

What a wondrous delight this bread pudding is with a dusting of powdered sugar over the top and a fresh berry or two served on the side.

PER SERVING
666 CALORIES
13 g PROTEIN
66 g CARBOHYDRATES
43 g TOTAL FAT
16 g SATURATED FAT
256 mg CHOLESTEROL
343 mg SODIUM

▼ ▼ ▼
Oh so light and oh so luscious. You'll be floating on clouds when you sample this wonderfully scrumptious *Bittersweet Chocolate Pâté.*

Bittersweet Chocolate Pâté

6 *ounces bittersweet or semisweet*
   chocolate, chopped
1 *cup whipping cream*
2 *slightly beaten egg yolks*
2 *tablespoons milk*
2 *tablespoons sugar*
2 *cups Crème Fraîche or Crème Anglaise*
   (see recipes, pages 208 and 212)

Chill a small mixing bowl and the beaters of an electric mixer in the refrigerator. Meanwhile, line the bottom and sides of a 7½x3½x2-inch loaf pan or an 8x4½-inch loaf pan with rounded bottom (nut bread pan) with plastic wrap, extending plastic wrap over the edges of the pan; set aside.

Melt chocolate according to the directions on page 225; set aside to cool slightly. In the chilled mixing bowl beat whipping cream with the chilled beaters on low speed till stiff peaks form. Cover and refrigerate the whipped cream till needed.

In a heavy small saucepan stir together the beaten egg yolks, milk, and sugar. Bring to a gentle boil, stirring constantly. Reduce heat. Cook and stir for 2 minutes. Remove from heat and pour mixture into a medium bowl.

Add the melted chocolate, *2 tablespoons* at a time, to the hot mixture, beating on low speed till combined (mixture will be thick). Add ½ *cup* of the whipped cream and continue beating on low speed till smooth. Gently fold in the remaining whipped cream. Spoon the mixture into the prepared pan. Cover and freeze for at least 4 hours before serving.

To serve, invert a serving plate over the pâté, and turn pan and plate over together. Remove pan, then carefully peel off the plastic wrap. Let pâté stand at room temperature for 15 minutes. Then cut into slices. If desired, use a hot, dry knife to smooth cut surfaces on slices and return slices to freezer till serving time. Serve with Crème Fraîche or Crème Anglaise. Makes about 9 servings.

SPECIAL TOUCH
▼ ▼ ▼
Whether your style is classic or contemporary, here's a dessert with endless presentation possibilities. For a classic presentation, pool Crème Anglaise on dessert plates. Then place a slice of the pâté on top and add edible flowers or petals for a spark of color. For a contemporary design, spoon Crème Fraîche on each dessert plate and use a decorating comb to create a decorative pattern. If you like, pipe melted chocolate into the grooves for added interest.

PER SERVING
352 CALORIES
4 g PROTEIN
17 g CARBOHYDRATES
32 g TOTAL FAT
16 g SATURATED FAT
131 mg CHOLESTEROL
37 mg SODIUM

Chocolate Crème Brûlée with Berries

2 cups whipping cream
3 ounces semisweet or bittersweet
chocolate, chopped
6 slightly beaten egg yolks
¼ cup sugar
1 teaspoon vanilla
¼ teaspoon salt
2 tablespoons sugar
Whipped cream
Strawberries

In a heavy medium saucepan heat and stir the 2 cups whipping cream and chocolate over low heat till chocolate is melted. Remove from heat.

In a large mixing bowl stir together the egg yolks, ¼ cup sugar, vanilla, and salt. Using a wire whisk, gradually stir the hot cream mixture into the egg yolk mixture.

Place six ½-cup ramekin dishes or one 3½-cup soufflé dish in a baking pan. Then set pan on the oven rack. Pour the egg mixture into the ramekin dishes or soufflé dish. Pour *boiling water* or *very hot water* into the baking pan around the ramekins or soufflé dish to a depth of 1 inch. Bake in a 325° oven for 25 to 30 minutes for ramekins (50 to 60 minutes for soufflé dish) or till a knife inserted near each center comes out clean. Remove ramekins or soufflé dish from pan with water. Cool slightly on a wire rack.

Immediately after removing brûlée from oven, place 2 tablespoons sugar in a small heavy skillet or saucepan. Cook over medium-high heat till sugar just begins to melt, shaking skillet occasionally to heat sugar evenly. *(Do not stir.)* Reduce heat to low and cook and stir till sugar is melted and golden brown (watch closely as sugar melts quickly). Drizzle melted sugar in a zigzag pattern over brûlée in ramekins or soufflé dish. Cool about 1 hour before serving. *Or,* cool slightly, then cover and chill in the refrigerator for up to 6 hours. If chilled, let stand at room temperature for 1 hour before serving. Serve with whipped cream and strawberries. Makes 6 servings.

Duo Chocolate Fondue

2 teaspoons unsalted butter

¼ cup ground toasted almonds **or** pecans

6 ounces semisweet **or** bittersweet chocolate, chopped

3 ounces milk chocolate, chopped

⅓ cup whipping cream

1 tablespoon unsalted butter

1 tablespoon amaretto **or** whipping cream
Sliced almonds **or** pecan halves, toasted

4½ cups fresh strawberries, pineapple chunks, mango chunks, papaya chunks, pitted dark sweet cherries, sliced carambola (star fruit), **and/or** Calimyrna (light) dried figs

Grease six 4- to 6-ounce clear glass dessert dishes (such as sherbet dishes) or 6 individual soufflé dishes with the 2 teaspoons butter. Then sprinkle the dessert dishes with the ground nuts to coat; set aside.

For fondue mixture, in a heavy medium saucepan heat and stir the semisweet or bittersweet chocolate, milk chocolate, whipping cream, 1 tablespoon butter, and liqueur or whipping cream over low heat till chocolate is melted and mixture is blended.

To serve, carefully spoon fondue mixture into the nut-coated dessert dishes. Garnish each with toasted sliced almonds or pecan halves. Serve warm with desired fruit. Makes 6 servings.

SPECIAL TOUCH
▼ ▼ ▼
Adults and kids alike will enjoy the fun of this fondue. Place the fondue-filled dessert dishes on plates and arrange the fruit around them. Then hand out the fondue forks.

PER SERVING
376 CALORIES
6 g PROTEIN
37 g CARBOHYDRATES
26 g TOTAL FAT
6 g SATURATED FAT
29 mg CHOLESTEROL
21 mg SODIUM

Swirled Chocolate and Peanut Butter Soufflé

Margarine or butter
Sugar
2 ounces bittersweet or semisweet chocolate, chopped
3 tablespoons margarine or butter
¼ cup all-purpose flour
1¼ cups half-and-half, light cream, or milk
¼ cup creamy peanut butter
4 egg yolks
6 egg whites
⅓ cup sugar
1 cup Bittersweet Chocolate Sauce (see recipe, page 212) (optional)

Grease the sides of a 2-quart soufflé dish with margarine or butter. For a collar on the soufflé dish, measure enough foil to wrap around the top of the soufflé dish and add 3 inches. Fold the foil in thirds lengthwise. Lightly grease 1 side with margarine or butter; sprinkle with sugar. Attach the foil, sugar side in, around the outside of the dish so that the foil extends about 2 inches above the dish. Tape ends of foil together. Sprinkle sides of dish with sugar. Set the dish aside.

Melt the chocolate according to the directions on page 225; set aside. Meanwhile, in a medium saucepan melt the 3 tablespoons margarine or butter. Stir in the flour. Add the half-and-half, light cream, or milk all at once. Cook and stir over medium heat till mixture is thickened and bubbly. Remove from heat. Stir *half* of the hot cream mixture into the chocolate. Set aside.

Stir the peanut butter into the remaining hot cream mixture in the saucepan. In a medium mixing bowl, beat *two* of the egg yolks just till combined. Gradually stir the peanut butter mixture into the beaten egg yolks. Set peanut butter mixture aside.

In another bowl, beat the remaining egg yolks. Gradually stir the chocolate mixture into the remaining egg yolks. Set aside.

If necessary, thoroughly wash beaters of the electric mixer. In a large mixing bowl beat the egg whites on medium to high speed till soft peaks form (tips curl). Gradually add the ⅓ cup sugar, *1 tablespoon* at a time, beating till stiff peaks form (tips stand straight) and sugar is *completely* dissolved.

Gently fold *half* of the beaten egg white mixture into the peanut butter mixture. Transfer peanut butter mixture to the prepared soufflé dish. Gently fold the remaining egg white mixture into the chocolate mixture. Spoon chocolate mixture on top of peanut butter mixture in the soufflé dish. Using a small narrow metal spatula, gently swirl the chocolate mixture into the peanut butter mixture, using a folding technique.

Bake in a 350° oven for 45 to 50 minutes or till a knife inserted near the center comes out clean. Serve at once. If desired, serve the soufflé with the Bittersweet Chocolate Sauce. Makes 6 to 8 servings.

Bounties of the Seasons

When your fruit garden is bursting with the colors of ripeness and markets are spilling over with fresh fruits and nuts, load your baskets to the brim. Once you're home and ready to bake, feature your pickings in dessert recipes that show off the goodness of fruits and nuts. Try Gingered Rhubarb Pie, Della Robbia Fruit Tart, Peach-Almond Tart, Walnut Torte with Buttercream, or Pecan Cake with Tangerine Cream Filling, to name a few.

▼ ▼ ▼

Fresh Fruit in Coconut Puff

SPECIAL TOUCH
▼ ▼ ▼
Rely on the natural colors and various shapes of the fresh fruit to dress up this tart. For a pretty arrangement, place a circle of berries or melon balls in the center of the filling. Then arrange the sliced fruit in circles around the berries or melon balls. Sprinkle shredded coconut over the top.

½ cup coconut
½ cup margarine **or** butter
1 cup water
1 cup all-purpose flour
4 eggs
½ cup sugar
3 tablespoons cornstarch
1⅓ cups milk
2 beaten eggs
½ cup vanilla yogurt
2 teaspoons finely shredded lime peel
¼ cup lime juice
1 teaspoon grated gingerroot
  or ¼ teaspoon ground ginger
½ cup whipping cream
2 cups desired fresh fruit (such as sliced, peeled peaches; halved strawberries; raspberries; sliced plums; sliced, peeled kiwi fruit; **and/or** melon balls)

Grease a baking sheet; set aside. Place coconut in a blender container or food processor bowl. Cover and blend or process till very fine.

For coconut puff, place margarine or butter in a medium saucepan. Add water and the coconut. Bring mixture to boiling, stirring till margarine or butter melts. Then add flour all at once, stirring vigorously. Cook and stir till the mixture forms a ball that doesn't separate. Remove from heat and cool for 10 minutes.

Add the 4 eggs, one at a time, to margarine mixture, beating with a wooden spoon after each addition about 1 minute or till smooth.

On the prepared baking sheet, spread *one-third* of the dough into a 6-inch circle about ¼ inch thick. Spoon remaining dough into a decorating bag fitted with a large star tip (about ½-inch opening). Pipe remaining dough around the edge of the circle. (Dough will puff and spread as it bakes.)

Bake in a 400° oven about 35 minutes or till golden brown and puffy. Carefully remove pastry and cool on a wire rack. (Center will slightly sink as pastry cools.)

For filling, in a heavy medium saucepan stir together sugar and cornstarch. Stir in milk. Cook and stir over medium heat till thickened and bubbly. Cook and stir for 2 minutes more. Remove from heat.

Gradually stir about *half* of the hot mixture into the 2 eggs. Then return all of the egg mixture to the saucepan. Bring to a gentle boil, then reduce heat. Cook and stir for 2 minutes more. Remove from heat. Stir in vanilla yogurt, lime peel, lime juice, and ginger. Pour mixture into a bowl. Cover surface with plastic wrap. Chill in the refrigerator till serving time *(do not stir)*. Meanwhile, chill a small mixing bowl and the beaters of an electric mixer.

Just before serving, in the chilled mixing bowl beat whipping cream with the chilled beaters on low speed till soft peaks form. Fold whipped cream into the filling. Spoon mixture into the center of the cooled pastry shell. Arrange fresh fruit on top. Serves 12.

PER SERVING
261 CALORIES
6 g PROTEIN
24 g CARBOHYDRATES
16 g TOTAL FAT
6 g SATURATED FAT
122 mg CHOLESTEROL
144 mg SODIUM

Banana Cream Napoleons

1 *portion Quick-Method Puff Pastry (see recipe, page 204)* **or** *½ of a 17¼-ounce package (1 sheet) frozen puff pastry, thawed*

1 *recipe for 1 cup Pastry Cream (see page 209)*

½ *teaspoon finely shredded orange peel*

1 *ounce semisweet* **or** *bittersweet chocolate, chopped*

1 *cup sifted powdered sugar*

1 *to 2 tablespoons milk*

2 *ripe medium bananas*

2 *tablespoons orange juice*

Line 2 baking sheets with parchment paper or plain brown paper; set aside.

If using Quick-Method Puff Pastry, cut the portion of dough in half *crosswise*. (Cover and return 1 piece of dough to the refrigerator and reserve for another use.) On a lightly floured surface, roll the remaining piece of dough into a 9x8-inch rectangle. Using a sharp knife, cut off ½ inch on all 4 sides to make an 8x7-inch rectangle. *Or,* if using purchased puff pastry, unfold the sheet and trim to an 8x7-inch rectangle.

Cut the pastry rectangle into eight 3½x2-inch rectangles. Transfer pastry rectangles to the prepared baking sheets. Using the tines of a fork, prick pastry rectangles.

Bake in a 425° oven for 18 to 23 minutes or till golden. Carefully remove pastry rectangles and cool on a wire rack.

Meanwhile, prepare Pastry Cream as directed, *except* stir orange peel into the warm Pastry Cream. Set Pastry Cream aside. Melt chocolate according to the directions on page 225; set aside to cool.

For glaze, in a bowl combine powdered sugar and *1 tablespoon* of the milk. If necessary, stir in enough additional milk till glaze is of spreading consistency; set aside.

To assemble, use the tines of a fork to separate *each* pastry rectangle horizontally into *three* layers. Spread about *1 tablespoon* of Pastry Cream on *each* bottom layer. Thinly slice the bananas. Sprinkle with orange juice. Arrange a few banana slices on Pastry Cream. Top with middle pastry layers, then spread with another *1 tablespoon* of Pastry Cream and top with remaining banana slices. Finally, top with remaining pastry layers. Spoon glaze over each pastry, spreading as necessary to glaze tops. Drizzle with the melted chocolate. Serve immediately or chill in the refrigerator for up to 1 hour. Makes 8 servings.

SPECIAL TOUCH
▼ ▼ ▼

For a show-stopping finale, bring out a dazzling array of these flaky pastries. After spreading the glaze on the Napoleons, arrange them on a large rectangular serving platter. Drizzle the melted chocolate diagonally across the Napoleons, allowing the chocolate to fall on the platter between the pastries. For a bit of color, garnish the platter with a few edible violets.

PER SERVING
487 CALORIES
6 g PROTEIN
53 g CARBOHYDRATES
29 g TOTAL FAT
17 g SATURATED FAT
127 mg CHOLESTEROL
418 mg SODIUM

Apples in Phyllo

Reap the compliments
when you serve these spicy
baked apples in phyllo cups.
For bonus points, fill each
apple center with a tiny
scoop of extra-rich vanilla
ice cream. Then ladle the
rum-raisin sauce over all.

4 sheets frozen phyllo dough, thawed
¼ cup margarine or butter, melted
6 small cooking apples, peeled and cored
¼ cup sugar
1 teaspoon ground cinnamon
⅓ cup slivered almonds
½ cup packed brown sugar
1 tablespoon cornstarch
⅓ cup water
⅓ cup raisins
1 tablespoon rum or ¼ teaspoon rum
    extract

Grease six 6-ounce custard cups; set aside.
Unfold phyllo dough. Place *one* sheet of
phyllo dough on a waxed-paper-lined cutting
board, then brush with some of the melted
margarine or butter. Top with a second sheet
of phyllo, then brush with more margarine
or butter. Repeat layering remaining phyllo
and brushing with the remaining margarine.
(Keep phyllo dough covered with a damp
cloth and remove only 1 sheet at a time.)

Using a sharp knife, cut the phyllo stack
lengthwise into six 2-inch-wide strips. Then
cut the strips crosswise into thirds, forming
eighteen rectangles, about 6x2-inches.
Carefully press *three* rectangles into *each*
prepared custard cup so that the entire cup
is covered with the phyllo. Set the phyllo-
lined custard cups aside.

To cut apples, place a wooden-handled spoon
or chopstick on each side of an apple to
prevent cutting through to the bottom of the
apple. Cut the apple into thin wedges,
cutting *three-fourths* of the way to, but not
through the bottom. Repeat with the
remaining apples.

Place an apple into each phyllo-lined custard
cup. In a small mixing bowl combine the
sugar and cinnamon. Sprinkle sugar mixture
over apples, then spoon almonds into apple
cavities. Place the custard cups in a 15x10x1-
inch baking pan.

Bake in a 375° oven for 25 to 30 minutes or
till phyllo is golden and apples are tender.
Cool slightly.

Meanwhile, for rum-raisin sauce, in a small
heavy saucepan stir together brown sugar
and cornstarch. Stir in water and raisins.
Cook and stir over medium heat till sauce is
thickened and bubbly. Cook and stir for 2
minutes more. Stir in rum or rum extract.

Carefully transfer the apple desserts from
custard cups to dessert plates. Serve warm or
chilled with the rum-raisin sauce. Serves 6.

Plum Dumplings

½ of a 3-ounce package cream cheese,
   softened
¼ cup finely chopped walnuts or pecans
2 tablespoons brown sugar
½ teaspoon ground cinnamon
   Dumpling Pastry
6 medium plums, halved and pitted
2 tablespoons red raspberry preserves
2 tablespoons half-and-half, light cream,
   or milk
   Sugar

Grease a 13x9x2-inch baking dish. Set
baking dish aside. In a small mixing bowl stir
together cream cheese, walnuts or pecans,
brown sugar, and cinnamon. Set cream
cheese mixture aside.

On a lightly floured surface, use your hands
to slightly flatten the Dumpling Pastry
dough. Roll the dough to form an 18x13-
inch rectangle. Cut a 1-inch strip from 1 long
side of the rectangle; set aside. Then cut the
rectangle into six 6-inch squares. Set pastry
squares aside.

Spread the cream cheese mixture on the cut
sides of six of the plum halves. Then top
each with 1 teaspoon of the raspberry
preserves. Place remaining plum halves on
top of the filled plum halves.

Place a filled plum in the center of each
pastry square. Moisten edges of pastry with
water. Fold corners of the pastry to the center
of the plum, pinching the edges together to
seal. Place the dumplings in the prepared
baking dish. Brush dumplings with some of
the 2 tablespoons half-and-half, light cream,
or milk. Using a knife or small cookie
cutters, cut leaves from the reserved strip of
pastry. Brush leaves with the remaining
portion of half-and-half, light cream, or milk.
Place on dumplings. Lightly sprinkle
dumplings with sugar.

Bake in a 375° oven about 40 minutes or till
pastry is golden. Serve warm. Serves 6.

Dumpling Pastry

In a medium mixing bowl stir together 2
cups all-purpose flour and ½ teaspoon salt. Cut
in ⅔ cup margarine or butter till pieces are the
size of small peas. Sprinkle 1 tablespoon cold
water over the flour mixture, then gently toss
with a fork. Repeat till all the dough is
moistened, using a total of 6 to 7 tablespoons
water. Form dough into a ball.

SPECIAL TOUCH
▼ ▼ ▼

Dumplings taste great
drenched with cream.
When serving the dump-
lings, provide each diner
with a tiny pitcher filled to
the brim with half-and-half
or light cream.

PER SERVING
470 CALORIES
6 g PROTEIN
50 g CARBOHYDRATES
28 g TOTAL FAT
6 g SATURATED FAT
10 mg CHOLESTEROL
441 mg SODIUM

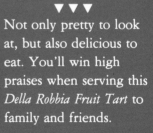
▼ ▼ ▼
Not only pretty to look at, but also delicious to eat. You'll win high praises when serving this *Della Robbia Fruit Tart* to family and friends.

Della Robbia Fruit Tart

2 recipes Rich Tart Pastry
  (see recipe, page 206)
3 ripe medium nectarines, peaches,
  apples, or pears (about 1 pound)
¼ cup sugar
1 tablespoon all-purpose flour
¼ teaspoon ground nutmeg
¼ cup chopped pecans
¼ cup dried cherries or raisins
  Pastry Paint or 1 slightly beaten
  egg yolk
1 cup Crème Anglaise (see recipe,
  page 212)

Divide the Rich Tart Pastry dough in half. Shape each half into a ball. For bottom pastry, on a lightly floured surface, use your hands to slightly flatten *one* ball of dough. Roll dough from center to edges, forming an 11-inch circle. Trim the circle to 10 inches; reserve dough scraps. Transfer pastry circle to a baking sheet; set aside.

If using peaches, apples, or pears; peel. Cut fruit in half. Remove and discard pits or seeds. With cut sides down, cut *each* fruit half into *sixteen* slices. *Do not separate slices.* Then set fruit aside.

In a small mixing bowl stir together sugar, flour, and nutmeg. Sprinkle about *half* of the sugar mixture over pastry circle on baking sheet. Then sprinkle with pecans and cherries or raisins. Arrange fruit halves, cut sides down, in a circle about 1 inch from edge on bottom pastry. Press down on the fruit halves to slightly fan out the slices. Sprinkle with remaining sugar mixture.

For top pastry, on a lightly floured surface, use your hands to slightly flatten remaining portion of dough. Roll dough from center to edges, forming a 12½-inch circle. Trim circle to 11½ inches; reserve scraps. Place top pastry on top of fruit, draping pastry over fruit and matching the edges of pastry circles. Carefully press pastry around fruit, being careful not to stretch pastry. Fold edges of top pastry under bottom pastry. Seal and crimp edge. If desired, cut a 1½-inch hole in center to form a ring.

Roll dough scraps to ⅛-inch thickness. Using a knife or small cookie cutters, cut fruit and leaf shapes from the dough. Brush pastry cutouts with a little *water.* Press cutouts onto the top pastry. If desired, brush cutouts with the Pastry Paint or a mixture of egg yolk and 1 tablespoon *water.*

Bake in a 375° oven for 30 to 40 minutes or till golden. (If necessary, to prevent overbrowning, cover with foil after 20 minutes.) Cool on baking sheet for 10 minutes. Carefully transfer tart from baking sheet to serving plate. Serve warm with Crème Anglaise. Makes 6 servings.

Pastry Paint

In a small mixing bowl stir together 2 slightly beaten *egg yolks* and 2 teaspoons *water.* Divide mixture among 3 or 4 custard cups. To each cup, stir in a few drops *food coloring.* Brush mixture onto pastry before baking. Makes about 2 tablespoons.

PER SERVING
513 CALORIES
6 g PROTEIN
53 g CARBOHYDRATES
32 g TOTAL FAT
17 g SATURATED FAT
220 mg CHOLESTEROL
172 mg SODIUM

Linzer Apple Torte

With its bright red raspberry glaze, this torte is ideal for the holidays. To make it even more festive, use a cookie cutter to cut stars, trees, or holly leaves from the remaining pastry for decorations on top of the torte.

1½ *cups all-purpose flour*
1 *cup ground hazelnuts (filberts)* **or** *almonds (about 5 ounces)*
⅓ *cup sugar*
¼ *teaspoon ground cinnamon*
½ *cup margarine* **or** *butter*
1 *beaten egg*
¼ *cup margarine* **or** *butter*
2 *pounds apple* **or** *pears, peeled, cored, and sliced (6 cups)*
1 *tablespoon lemon juice*
⅓ *cup sugar*
2 *tablespoons all-purpose flour*
⅛ *teaspoon ground nutmeg*
 Sugar (optional)
½ *cup red raspberry preserves*

For pastry, in a large mixing bowl stir together the 1½ cups flour, hazelnuts or almonds, ⅓ cup sugar, and cinnamon. Cut in the ½ cup margarine or butter till pieces are the size of small peas. Stir egg into flour mixture. Form *one-fourth* of the dough into a ball; set aside. Press the remaining dough onto the bottom and 1¼ inches up the sides of a 9-inch springform pan. Set the springform pan aside.

In a large saucepan melt the ¼ cup margarine or butter. Add apples or pears and lemon juice. Cook and gently stir for 3 to 5 minutes or till apples are just tender. Remove from heat.

In a small mixing bowl stir together ⅓ cup sugar, 2 tablespoons flour, and nutmeg. Then stir sugar mixture into the apple mixture. Spread mixture evenly in the pastry-lined springform pan.

Bake in a 375° oven for 35 to 40 minutes or till the pastry is brown. Cool in the pan on a wire rack.

Meanwhile, on a lightly floured surface, roll the remaining pastry to ⅛-inch thickness. Using 1½-inch hors d'oeuvres or cookie cutters, cut dough into desired shapes. Place cutouts on an ungreased baking sheet. If desired, sprinkle with the additional sugar. Bake in a 375° oven for 5 to 6 minutes or till lightly browned. Remove cutouts and cool on a wire rack.

Before serving, remove sides of the springform pan. In a small saucepan heat raspberry preserves over low heat till melted. Spread melted preserves on top of torte. Then top with pastry cutouts. Let stand till preserves set. Makes 8 to 10 servings.

PER SERVING
522 CALORIES
7 g PROTEIN
66 g CARBOHYDRATES
28 g TOTAL FAT
4 g SATURATED FAT
27 mg CHOLESTEROL
212 mg SODIUM

Honey-Pistachio Tart

½ *cup sugar*
¼ *cup honey*
¼ *cup water*
1½ *cups chopped pistachio nuts* or *pecans, toasted*
½ *cup mixed dried fruit bits* or *raisins*
½ *cup milk*
2 *tablespoons margarine* or *butter*
  Rich Pastry for Double-Crust Tart
1 *beaten egg yolk*

For filling, in a medium saucepan stir together sugar, honey, and water. Bring to boiling, gently stirring till sugar is dissolved. Reduce heat to medium-low. Gently boil about 15 minutes or till mixture turns a light caramel color, stirring occasionally.

Stir toasted nuts, fruit bits or raisins, milk, and margarine or butter into honey mixture. Return to boiling. Gently boil over low heat about 5 minutes more or till slightly thickened, stirring occasionally. Set filling aside to cool to room temperature.

Meanwhile, on a lightly floured surface, use your hands to slightly flatten *one* ball of Rich Pastry for Double-Crust Tart. Roll dough from center to edges, forming a 12-inch circle. Wrap pastry around the rolling pin.

Then unroll pastry onto a 9-inch tart pan with a removable bottom, quiche dish, or cake pan. Ease pastry into pan, pressing pastry into the fluted sides of tart pan or quiche dish. Let pastry hang over edges. Spread filling evenly in the pastry-lined pan or dish.

For top pastry, roll out the remaining ball of pastry dough. Using the tines of a fork, prick pastry. Place the top pastry on filling. Trim both pastries to ½ inch beyond edge of pan. Fold edges over toward the center of the tart, pressing to seal well. Brush egg yolk over pastry.

Bake in 375° oven for 40 to 45 minutes or till pastry is golden. Cool in pan on a wire rack. Remove from pan. Serves 8 to 12.

Rich Pastry for Double-Crust Tart

In a large mixing bowl cut ⅔ cup *margarine* or *butter* into 2 cups *all-purpose flour* till pieces are the size of small peas. In a small mixing bowl beat together 1 *egg* and ¼ cup *cold water*. Add egg mixture to flour mixture. Using a fork, toss till moistened. Divide dough in half. Form *each* half into a ball.

SPECIAL TOUCH
▼ ▼ ▼
If you like, fashion a geometric pattern on top of this nutty, double-crust tart. Using a fork, score lines in the top crust before brushing it with the egg yolk. Simply score crisscross lines. Or, if you're more daring, score swirls.

PER SERVING
543 CALORIES
9 g PROTEIN
57 g CARBOHYDRATES
33 g TOTAL FAT
5 g SATURATED FAT
55 mg CHOLESTEROL
231 mg SODIUM

Peach-Almond Tart

1 *recipe for Nut Sweet-Tart Pastry (using almonds or pecans) (see page 206)*
½ *teaspoon ground nutmeg*
¾ *cup sugar*
¼ *cup cornstarch or ½ cup all-purpose flour*
3 *cups milk*
4 *beaten egg yolks*
1 *tablespoon margarine or butter*
¼ *teaspoon almond extract or 1 teaspoon vanilla*
⅓ *cup peach preserves*
2 *cups thinly sliced, peeled fresh peaches or frozen peach slices*
¼ *cup sliced almonds or chopped pecans, toasted*

Prepare Nut Sweet-Tart Pastry as directed, *except* stir nutmeg in with the flour.

On a lightly floured surface, use your hands to slightly flatten pastry dough. Roll dough from center to edges, forming a 12-inch circle. Wrap pastry around the rolling pin. Then unroll pastry onto a 10-inch tart pan with a removable bottom. Ease pastry into the tart pan, being careful not to stretch it. Press pastry into the fluted sides of the tart pan and trim edges. Using the tines of a fork, prick bottom and sides of pastry generously.

Line pastry shell with a double thickness of foil. Bake in a 375° oven for 10 minutes. Remove foil. Bake for 8 to 10 minutes more or till golden. Completely cool pastry shell in pan on a wire rack.

Meanwhile, for filling, in a heavy medium saucepan stir together sugar and cornstarch or flour. Gradually stir in milk. Cook and stir over medium heat till the mixture is thickened and bubbly. Cook and stir for 2 minutes more. Remove from heat.

Gradually stir about *1 cup* of the hot mixture into egg yolks. Return all of the egg yolk mixture to the saucepan. Bring to a gentle boil, then reduce heat. Cook and stir for 2 minutes more. Remove from heat. Stir in margarine or butter and almond extract or vanilla. Cover surface with plastic wrap. Cool to room temperature. *(Do not stir.)*

Spread peach preserves in the bottom of the cooled pastry shell. Then spread filling on top of preserves. Cover with plastic wrap and chill in the refrigerator for 4 to 24 hours before serving.

If using frozen peaches, thaw, drain, and thinly slice peaches. Just before serving, remove tart from pan. Arrange peach slices on top of the filling. Sprinkle with toasted almonds or pecans. Makes 8 servings.

Melon and Papaya Tart

½ of an 11-ounce package piecrust mix
  (1⅓ cups)
1 8-ounce carton dairy sour cream
1 egg
1 cup ground almonds
½ cup light corn syrup
  Several drops almond extract
½ of an 8-ounce container soft-style cream
  cheese with pineapple (½ cup)
½ to ¾ pound honeydew melon and/or
  cantaloupe, seeded, peeled, and
  thinly sliced
½ of a medium papaya or mango, peeled,
  seeded, and thinly sliced
¼ cup apple jelly

Grease a 10-inch round or 11x8-inch rectangular tart pan with a removeable bottom. Set pan aside.

For crust, in a small mixing bowl combine piecrust mix and ¼ cup of the sour cream. Stir till all of the dough is moistened. Turn dough out onto a lightly floured surface. Using your fingers, knead dough about 12 times or till firm enough to handle easily.

Press the dough evenly onto the bottom and sides of the prepared tart pan; set aside.

For filling, in a medium mixing bowl use a wire whisk or fork to lightly beat the egg. Stir in ground almonds, corn syrup, and almond extract. Pour the filling into the tart shell, spreading evenly.

Bake in a 375° oven for 25 to 30 minutes or till crust is brown and filling is set. Cool tart in pan on a wire rack.

In a small mixing bowl stir together the remaining sour cream and cream cheese. Spread the sour cream mixture on top of the cooled almond filling. Then arrange melon and papaya or mango on top. Cover with plastic wrap and chill in the refrigerator till serving time or for up to 2 hours.

Just before serving, remove tart from pan. In a small saucepan heat and stir apple jelly over low heat till melted. Brush jelly over fruit. Makes 8 servings.

SPECIAL TOUCH
▼ ▼ ▼
A tart that tastes this fresh deserves a spectacular presentation. Place the tart on a pedestal cake plate or a rectangular serving platter. Then surround the tart with lemon leaves.

PER SERVING
372 CALORIES
6 g PROTEIN
40 g CARBOHYDRATES
22 g TOTAL FAT
8 g SATURATED FAT
52 mg CHOLESTEROL
174 mg SODIUM

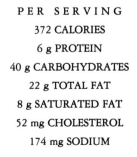

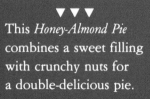

This *Honey-Almond Pie* combines a sweet filling with crunchy nuts for a double-delicious pie.

Honey-Almond Pie

*Flaky Pie Pastry for a single crust
    (see recipe, page 205)*
3   *eggs*
¾   *cup sugar*
¾   *cup honey*
⅓   *cup margarine* or *butter, melted*
1   *tablespoon amaretto* or *¼ teaspoon
    almond extract*
1   *cup sliced almonds, toasted*
2   *cups Flavored Whipped Cream
    (using amaretto* or *almond extract)
    (see recipe, page 210)*

For piecrust, on a lightly floured surface, use your hands to slightly flatten Flaky Pie Pastry. Roll dough from center to edges, forming a 12-inch circle. Wrap pastry around the rolling pin. Then unroll pastry onto a 9-inch pie plate. Ease into pie plate, being careful not to stretch it.

Trim pastry to ½ inch beyond edge of pie plate. Fold under extra pastry. Crimp edge.

Line pastry shell with a double thickness of foil. Bake in a 450° oven for 8 minutes. Remove foil. Bake for 4 to 6 minutes more or till golden.

Meanwhile, for filling, in a medium mixing bowl use a rotary beater or wire whisk to lightly beat eggs *just till mixed.* Stir in sugar, honey, margarine or butter, and amaretto or almond extract. Mix well. Stir in almonds.

Set the pastry shell on the oven rack; pour the almond filling into the pastry shell. To prevent overbrowning, cover edge of pie with foil. Reduce oven temperature to 350° and bake for 35 minutes. Remove foil. Bake for 10 to 15 minutes more or till a knife inserted near the center comes out clean. Cool pie on a wire rack.

Serve pie with Flavored Whipped Cream. Cover and refrigerate to store. Serves 8.

SPECIAL TOUCH
▼ ▼ ▼

Transform your pie from simple to grand with a few, easy pastry decorations. To have enough pastry for cutouts, make the Flaky Pie Pastry for a double crust instead of for a single crust. Attach the cutouts to the edge of the pie with beaten egg white before baking. For the top of the pie, bake the cutouts separately and lay them on top after the the pie is baked.

PER SERVING
628 CALORIES
8 g PROTEIN
65 g CARBOHYDRATES
38 g TOTAL FAT
12 g SATURATED FAT
121 mg CHOLESTEROL
194 mg SODIUM

Gingered Rhubarb Pie

1¼   cups sugar
¼   cup all-purpose flour
5   cups fresh or frozen unsweetened sliced
     rhubarb
1   tablespoon finely chopped crystallized
     ginger
1   teaspoon finely shredded orange peel
¾   cup chopped dried cranberries or
     cherries
     Flaky Pie Pastry for a double crust
     (see recipe, page 205)
     Buttery Orange Sauce or Crème
     Fraîche (see recipe, page 208)

In a large mixing bowl stir together sugar
and flour. Add fresh or frozen rhubarb,
crystallized ginger, and orange peel. Gently
toss till rhubarb is coated. If using frozen
rhubarb, let stand for 15 to 30 minutes or
till *partially* thawed, but still icy.

In a small saucepan add enough *water* to the
dried cranberries or cherries to cover. Bring
to boiling, then remove from heat. Cover
and let stand for 5 minutes. Drain
cranberries or cherries; set aside.

For piecrust, on a lightly floured surface, use
your hands to slightly flatten *one* ball of Flaky
Pie Pastry dough. Roll dough from center to
edges, forming a 12-inch circle. Wrap pastry
around the rolling pin. Then unroll pastry

onto a 9-inch pie plate. Ease pastry into pie
plate, being careful not to stretch it. For top
crust, roll out remaining ball of pastry
dough. Cut dough into ½-inch-wide strips.

Stir cranberries or cherries into rhubarb
mixture, then transfer to pastry-lined pie
plate. Trim bottom pastry to ½ inch beyond
edge of plate. Weave strips on top of filling
to make a lattice. Press ends of strips into
rim of bottom crust, trimming as necessary.
Fold bottom pastry over strips. Seal and
crimp edge.

To prevent overbrowning, cover edge of pie
with foil. Bake in a 375° oven for 25
minutes for fresh rhubarb (50 minutes for
frozen rhubarb). Remove foil. Bake 20 to 25
minutes more for fresh rhubarb (20 to 30
minutes for frozen) or till top is golden.
Cool pie on a wire rack. Serve with Buttery
Orange Sauce or Crème Fraîche. Serves 8.

Buttery Orange Sauce

In a small saucepan combine ½ cup *sugar,*
¼ cup *half-and-half* or *light cream,* and
3 tablespoons *butter.* Cook and stir over
medium heat till mixture boils and sugar
dissolves. Boil for 1 minute. Remove from
heat. Stir in 2 to 3 teaspoons *orange juice,*
orange liqueur, or *brandy.* Serve warm. Makes
about ⅔ cup.

Sour Cream, Raisin, and Pear Pie

¾ cup light raisins

1 recipe Flaky Pie Pastry for a single crust (see page 205)

1 teaspoon ground cinnamon

3 egg yolks

1½ cups dairy sour cream

1 cup sugar

½ cup milk

3 tablespoons all-purpose flour

1 teaspoon ground cinnamon

¼ teaspoon ground nutmeg

¼ teaspoon ground cloves

Milk (optional)

Sugar (optional)

⅔ cup packed brown sugar

2 tablespoons dark corn syrup

1 tablespoon lemon juice

2 small pears, peeled and thinly sliced (about 2 cups)

1 teaspoon cornstarch

In a small saucepan add enough *water* to raisins to cover. Bring to boiling, then remove from heat. Cover and let stand for 5 minutes. Drain raisins; set aside.

For piecrust, prepare Flaky Pie Pastry as directed, *except* stir in 1 teaspoon ground cinnamon with the flour and salt. On a lightly floured surface, use your hands to slightly flatten pastry dough. Roll dough from center to edges, forming a 12-inch circle. Wrap pastry around the rolling pin. Then unroll pastry onto a 9-inch pie plate. Ease pastry into pie plate, being careful not to stretch it. Trim pastry to ½ inch beyond edge of pie plate. Fold under extra pastry. Crimp edge. *Do not prick pastry.*

For filling, in a medium mixing bowl use a rotary beater or wire whisk to lightly beat egg yolks *just till mixed.* Stir in sour cream, 1 cup sugar, milk, flour, 1 teaspoon cinnamon, nutmeg, cloves, and the raisins. Mix well.

Set pastry shell on the oven rack; pour the filling into the pastry shell. If desired, brush pastry edge with the additional milk, then sprinkle with the additional sugar.

To prevent overbrowning, cover edge of pie with foil. Bake in a 375° oven for 20 minutes. Remove foil. Bake for 20 to 25 minutes more or till center appears *nearly* set when shaken. Cool on a rack about 1 hour.

Meanwhile, in a large saucepan bring 1½ cups *water,* brown sugar, corn syrup, and lemon juice to boiling. Add pear slices; reduce heat. Cover and simmer about 5 minutes or till pears are tender. Drain pears, reserving ⅓ *cup* of the poaching liquid. Slightly cool pears.

Transfer the reserved poaching liquid to a small saucepan. Stir together cornstarch and the 1 tablespoon *water,* then stir mixture into poaching liquid. Cook and stir over medium heat till thickened and bubbly. Cook and stir for 2 minutes more. Remove saucepan from heat and cool slightly.

Arrange pear slices on top of the sour cream filling. Brush pears with the thickened poaching liquid. Cool completely before serving. Cover and refrigerate to store. Makes 8 servings.

SPECIAL TOUCH
▼ ▼ ▼
The poached pears make a fine finish for this creamy custard pie. But for added attention and extra flavor, sprinkle the pears with freshly grated nutmeg.

PER SERVING
509 CALORIES
6 g PROTEIN
80 g CARBOHYDRATES
20 g TOTAL FAT
9 g SATURATED FAT
100 mg CHOLESTEROL
112 mg SODIUM

Almond Cake-in-Crust

Sweet-Tart Pastry (see recipe,
   page 206)
¼ cup all-purpose flour
½ teaspoon baking powder
1 8-ounce can almond paste*
½ cup margarine or butter
½ cup sifted powdered sugar
4 eggs
¼ cup milk
2 teaspoons finely shredded lemon peel
1 recipe for Marzipan Treasures (see
   page 104) or 1 pound purchased
   marzipan

Grease the sides of an 8- or 9-inch springform pan; set pan aside.

For crust, divide the ball of Sweet-Tart Pastry in half, then shape each half into a ball. On a lightly floured suface, use your hands to slightly flatten *one* ball of dough. Roll dough from center to edges, forming an 8- or 9-inch circle. Trim edges of dough to make an even circle. Line the bottom of the springform pan with the dough circle.

Roll out the remaining ball of dough to a ⅛-inch-thick rectangle. Cut 2 or 3 strips of dough from the rectangle (for an 8-inch pan, cut strips 2 inches wide; for a 9-inch pan cut strips 1½ inches wide). Arrange strips end-to-end around sides of the springform pan. Press ends of strips together to seal well. Then press bottom edge of the strips to the pastry circle. Chill crust in the refrigerator while preparing the filling.

For filling, in a small mixing bowl stir together flour and baking powder. Set flour mixture aside.

Crumble almond paste in a large mixing bowl. Add margarine or butter. Beat with an electric mixer on medium to high speed about 30 seconds or till well combined. Add powdered sugar. Beat till combined. Then add eggs, one at a time, beating till combined. Alternately add flour mixture and milk, beating on low to medium speed after each addition *just till combined* (batter will appear slightly curdled). Stir in lemon peel.

Spread the batter into the crust-lined springform pan. Bake in a 350° oven for 30 to 40 minutes or till the top is puffed and springs back when lightly touched. Cool cake in pan on a wire rack.

Meanwhile, if using, prepare Marzipan Treasures as directed, *except* do not shape. Tint and roll the homemade or purchased marzipan to an 8- or 9-inch circle as directed for sheets (see page 232).

Loosen crust from sides of pan. Then remove sides of the springform pan. Trim edges of marzipan to make an even circle. Place the marzipan circle on top of the cake, tucking in the edges of the marzipan so it fits inside the side crust. Makes 10 servings.

*Almond paste containing corn syrup or fructose may result in a product more moist than expected.

▼ery Berry Cheesecake

6 tablespoons margarine **or** butter
1½ cups finely crushed vanilla wafers
      (about 40)
1 cup cottage cheese
2 8-ounce packages cream cheese, softened
¾ cup sugar
2 tablespoons all-purpose flour
2 teaspoons vanilla
¼ cup blackberry brandy, cherry brandy,
      or orange juice
3 eggs
1½ cups fresh raspberries, blueberries,
      blackberries, **and/or** chopped pitted
      cherries
      Fresh Berry Topping

For crust, in a small saucepan melt margarine or butter. Stir in crushed vanilla wafers. Spread mixture evenly into an 8-inch springform pan. Press onto bottom and about 1¾ inches up the sides to form a firm, even crust. Set springform pan aside.

For filling, place cottage cheese in a blender container or food processor bowl. Cover and blend or process till smooth.

In a large mixing bowl beat cream cheese, sugar, flour, and vanilla with an electric mixer on medium to high speed till combined. Stir in cottage cheese and brandy or orange juice. Add eggs all at once. Beat on low speed just till combined.

Pour about half of the filling into crust-lined springform pan. Sprinkle 1 cup of the berries on top of the filling in pan. Then top with remaining filling and ½ cup of the berries. Place springform pan on a shallow baking pan on the oven rack. Bake in a 375° oven for 40 to 45 minutes or till center appears nearly set when shaken.

Remove springform pan from baking pan. Cool cheesecake in springform pan on a wire rack for 15 minutes. Loosen crust from sides of pan and cool for 30 minutes more. Remove sides of the springform pan. Cool completely, then chill in the refrigerator for at least 4 hours before serving. Slice and serve with Fresh Berry Topping. Serves 12.

▐resh Berry Topping

In a medium mixing bowl toss together 2 cups fresh raspberries, blueberries, blackberries, and/or chopped pitted cherries; 1 tablespoon sugar; and 1 tablespoon blackberry brandy, cherry brandy, or orange juice. Cover and chill in the refrigerator till serving time. Makes 2 cups.

SPECIAL TOUCH
▼ ▼ ▼
Play up the fruit theme of this luscious cheesecake by choosing plates and table linens with a berry motif. Then serve slices of this luscious cheesecake with raspberry-flavored tea.

PER SERVING
369 CALORIES
8 g PROTEIN
30 g CARBOHYDRATES
23 g TOTAL FAT
10 g SATURATED FAT
105 mg CHOLESTEROL
305 mg SODIUM

The brink of summer coincides with the beginning of berry season. Celebrate the seasonal splendor with *Lemon Butter Shortcakes with Summer Berries*.

Lemon Butter Shortcakes with Summer Berries

1½ *cups sliced strawberries*
1 *cup blueberries*
1 *cup raspberries* **or** *blackberries*
¼ *cup sugar*
1 *cup all-purpose flour*
1 *tablespoon sugar*
1 *teaspoon baking powder*
¼ *cup butter*
1 *beaten egg yolk*
¼ *cup half-and-half, light cream,* **or** *milk*
1½ *teaspoons finely shredded lemon peel*
½ *cup whipping cream*
1 *slightly beaten egg white*
   Coarse-grain **or** *crystal sugar* **or**
      granulated sugar
½ *cup Crème Fraîche (see recipe,*
      page 208)

In a large mixing bowl toss together the strawberries, blueberries, raspberries or blackberries, and ¼ cup sugar. Set berry mixture aside.

Chill a mixing bowl and the beaters of an electric mixer in the refrigerator while preparing the shortcakes.

For shortcakes, in a medium mixing bowl stir together the flour, 1 tablespoon sugar, and baking powder. Cut in the butter till mixture resembles coarse crumbs. Make a well in the center of the dry mixture.

In a small mixing bowl stir together the egg yolk, half-and-half, and lemon peel. Add egg yolk mixture all at once to dry mixture. Using a fork, stir *just till moistened.*

Turn the dough out onto a lightly floured surface. Gently knead the dough for 10 to 12 strokes or till dough is *nearly* smooth. Pat dough into a circle. Cut the dough into quarters. Shape *each* piece into a ball. Then place dough balls on an ungreased baking sheet. Using the palm of your hand, flatten *each* ball to about ¾-inch thickness. Brush tops with beaten egg white, then lightly sprinkle with coarse-grain or crystal sugar or additional granulated sugar. Bake in a 450° oven for 8 to 10 minutes or till golden. Remove from baking sheet and cool slightly on a wire rack.

Meanwhile, for cream mixture, in the chilled mixing bowl stir together the whipping cream and Crème Fraîche. Beat with the chilled beaters of the electric mixer on low speed till soft peaks form.

To serve, if desired, split warm shortcakes in half horizontally. Assemble by spooning the berry mixture and cream mixture between shortcake layers and over the tops. *Or,* do not split shortcakes. Serve the berry mixture and cream mixture to the side of the shortcakes. Makes 4 servings.

SPECIAL TOUCH
▼ ▼ ▼
An old-fashioned dessert turns contemporary with this fun presentation. For triangle-shaped shortcakes, pat the dough to a 6x4-inch rectangle. Using a floured knife, cut the rectangle into six 2-inch squares. Then cut each square diagonally in half; bake and serve as directed at left.

PER SERVING
551 CALORIES
7 g PROTEIN
56 g CARBOHYDRATES
35 g TOTAL FAT
21 g SATURATED FAT
157 mg CHOLESTEROL
249 mg SODIUM

Banana Cake with Toasted Pecan Filling

2   cups all-purpose flour
1½ cups sugar
1½ teaspoons baking powder
¾   teaspoon baking soda
½   teaspoon salt
1   cup mashed ripe banana
½   cup shortening
½   cup buttermilk or sour milk
2   eggs
1   teaspoon vanilla
⅔   cup finely chopped pecans, toasted
¼   cup dairy sour cream
2   cups Pastry Cream (see recipe, page 209)
2   cups Chocolate Glaze (see recipe, page 211)

Grease and lightly flour two 9x1½-inch or
8x1½-inch round baking pans; set aside.

In a large mixing bowl stir together flour,
sugar, baking powder, baking soda, and salt.
Add banana, shortening, buttermilk or sour
milk, eggs, and vanilla. Beat with an electric
mixer on low to medium speed about
30 seconds or till combined. Then beat on
medium to high speed for 3 minutes.

Pour batter into the prepared pans. Bake in a
350° oven for 25 to 30 minutes or till a
wooden toothpick inserted near the centers
of the cakes comes out clean. Cool cakes in
pans on wire racks for 10 minutes. Then
remove cakes from pans and cool completely
on the racks.

For filling, fold the chopped pecans and the
sour cream into the Pastry Cream.

To assemble, cut *each* cake horizontally into
two even layers. Place first layer on a large
serving plate. Spread *one-third* of the filling on
top of the cake layer. Top with a second
layer of cake. Repeat layering filling and
cake 2 more times. Pour Chocolate Glaze
over cake, spreading as necessary to glaze
top and sides completely.

If desired, garnish by pressing the 1 cup
chopped pecans onto the sides of the cake
and the pecan halves onto the top of the
cake. Lightly cover and refrigerate to store.
Makes 16 servings.

PER SERVING
477 CALORIES
8 g PROTEIN
49 g CARBOHYDRATES
29 g TOTAL FAT
12 g SATURATED FAT
276 mg CHOLESTEROL
214 mg SODIUM

Mango Buttercream Cake

2½ cups all-purpose flour
2 cups sugar
1 teaspoon baking powder
½ teaspoon baking soda
⅛ teaspoon salt
1⅓ cups buttermilk or sour milk
½ cup margarine or butter, softened
1 teaspoon vanilla
4 egg whites
3 to 4 ripe mangos, peeled, seeded, and
   cut up
1 cup sugar
6 beaten egg yolks
3 tablespoons orange liqueur or brandy
2 cups unsalted butter, softened

Grease and lightly flour two 9x1½-inch or 8x1½-inch round baking pans. Set aside.

In a large mixing bowl stir together flour, 2 cups sugar, baking powder, baking soda, and salt. Then add buttermilk or sour milk, ½ cup margarine or butter, and vanilla. Beat with an electric mixer on low to medium speed about 30 seconds or till combined. Then beat on medium to high speed for 2 minutes, scraping sides of the bowl occasionally. Add the egg whites and beat for 2 minutes more.

Pour batter into the prepared pans. Bake in a 350° oven for 30 to 35 minutes or till a wooden toothpick inserted near the centers of the cakes comes out clean. Cool cakes in pans on wire racks for 10 minutes. Then remove cakes from pans and cool completely on the racks.

For mango buttercream, place about *one-third* of the mangos in a blender container or food processor bowl. Cover and blend or process till smooth. Repeat 2 more times with remaining mangos. (You should have *1½ cups* purée.) In a large heavy saucepan gently simmer mango purée over medium-low heat till reduced to *1 cup,* stirring frequently to prevent scorching. Remove from heat.

Stir 1 cup sugar into the mango purée in saucepan. Cook and stir over medium heat till bubbly. Remove from heat. Gradually stir about *1 cup* of the hot mixture into the beaten egg yolks. Return all of the egg yolk mixture to the saucepan. Bring to a gentle boil; reduce heat. Cook and stir for *2* minutes more. Remove from heat. Stir in the liqueur. Cool to room temperature.

In a large mixing bowl beat the 2 cups butter with an electric mixer on medium to high speed till fluffy. Add cooled mango mixture into the beaten butter. Beat till combined. Set aside ¾ *cup* of the buttercream.

To assemble, cut *each* cake horizontally into *two* even layers. Place first cake layer on a large serving plate. Spread about ½ cup of the buttercream on top of the cake layer. Top with a second layer of cake. Repeat layering buttercream and cake 2 more times. Spread remaining buttercream on sides and top of cake. Spoon the ¾ cup reserved buttercream into a decorating bag fitted with a large star tip (about ½-inch opening). Pipe stars on top of the cake. Lightly cover and refrigerate to store. Makes 12 servings.

SPECIAL TOUCH
▼ ▼ ▼

Wrap this towering cake in cookies and bows. Lightly press pirouette cookies into the buttercream around the sides of the cake so that one end of each cookie is even with the bottom of the cake. The tops will extend above the cake. Then tie a long, fancy ribbon around the cookies and cake.

PER SERVING
702 CALORIES
7 g PROTEIN
78 g CARBOHYDRATES
42 g TOTAL FAT
21 g SATURATED FAT
191 mg CHOLESTEROL
229 mg SODIUM

Walnut Torte with Buttercream

1⅓ cups broken walnuts
¾ cup crushed zwieback
6 egg yolks
⅓ cup sugar
1 teaspoon finely shredded lemon peel
6 egg whites
¼ cup sugar
1 recipe for 2 cups Buttercream (see page 211)
1 teaspoon finely shredded lemon peel
⅓ cup apricot preserves

Grease the bottoms only of two 9x1½-inch or 8x1½-inch round baking pans. Line the bottoms with waxed paper. Grease the paper, then lightly flour the pans. Set pans aside.

In a blender container or food processor bowl place the walnuts. Cover and blend or process till very fine but dry (not oily). In a small mixing bowl stir together ground walnuts and zwieback; set aside.

In a medium mixing bowl beat egg yolks and ⅓ cup sugar with an electric mixer on high speed about 6 minutes or till yolks are thick and lemon-colored. Stir in 1 teaspoon finely shredded lemon peel; set aside.

Thoroughly wash beaters. In a large mixing bowl beat egg whites on medium to high speed till soft peaks form (tips curl).

Gradually add ¼ cup sugar, about *1 tablespoon* at a time, beating on high speed till stiff peaks form (tips stand straight).

Fold *about 1 cup* of the egg white mixture into the the egg yolk mixture. Then fold all of the yolk mixture into the remaining egg white mixture.

Sprinkle about *one-third* of the walnut mixture over batter, then gently fold in. Repeat sprinkling nuts and folding in one-third of the walnuts at a time. Pour batter into prepared pans. Bake in a 350° oven about 25 minutes or till a wooden toothpick inserted near the centers of the cakes comes out clean. Invert cakes in pans on wire racks; cool cakes in pans for 10 minutes. (Cakes may fall slightly.) Remove pans and peel off waxed paper. Then cool cakes completely.

Meanwhile, prepare Buttercream as directed *except* substitute 1 teaspoon finely shredded lemon peel for the liqueur or vanilla.

In a small saucepan heat apricot preserves till melted. To assemble, place first cake layer on a large serving plate. Spread melted preserves on top of the cake layer. Top with remaining cake layer. Frost the sides and top of the cake with Buttercream. Lightly cover and refrigerate to store. Makes 12 servings.

PER SERVING
415 CALORIES
7 g PROTEIN
35 g CARBOHYDRATES
29 g TOTAL FAT
12 g SATURATED FAT
221 mg CHOLESTEROL
54 mg SODIUM

Pecan Cake with Tangerine Cream Filling

2½ cups broken pecans, toasted
3 tablespoons all-purpose flour
4 teaspoons baking powder
6 eggs
1 cup sugar
1 8-ounce package cream cheese, softened
¼ cup margarine or butter
½ cup packed brown sugar
1 teaspoon finely shredded tangerine or
   orange peel
1 teaspoon vanilla
   Tangerine Cream Frosting

Grease and lightly flour two 8x1½-inch round baking pans. Set pans aside. Place *half* of the pecans in a blender container or food processor bowl. Cover and blend or process till coarsely ground. Transfer pecans to a medium mixing bowl. Repeat blending or processing the remaining pecans. Stir flour and baking powder into the ground pecans. Set nut mixture aside.

In the blender container or food processor bowl place eggs and sugar. Cover and blend or process till smooth. Add nut mixture. Then cover and blend or process till smooth. (When necessary, stop, stir, and scrape sides; batter may be foamy).

Spread batter into the prepared pans. Bake in a 350° oven for 25 to 30 minutes or till lightly browned and top springs back when lightly touched (center may dip slightly). Cool cakes in pans on wire racks for 10 minutes. Then remove cakes from pans and cool completely on the racks.

For tangerine filling, in a small mixing bowl beat cream cheese and margarine or butter with an electric mixer on medium to high speed till fluffy. Gradually add brown sugar, beating for 3 to 4 minutes or till smooth. Stir in tangerine or orange peel and vanilla.

To assemble, cut *each* cake layer into *two* even layers. Place first cake layer on a large serving plate. Spread *one-third* of the tangerine filling on top of the cake layer. Top with a second layer of cake. Repeat layering the filling and cake 2 more times. Frost sides and top of cake with Tangerine Cream Frosting. Lightly cover and refrigerate to store. Makes 12 servings.

Tangerine Cream Frosting

Chill a mixing bowl and the beaters of an electric mixer in the refrigerator. In the chilled bowl combine 1½ cups *whipping cream,* 2 tablespoons *sugar,* and ¾ teaspoon finely shredded *tangerine* or *orange peel.* Beat with the chilled beaters of the electric mixer on low speed till soft peaks form. Makes 3 cups.

SPECIAL TOUCH
▼ ▼ ▼
With a refreshing citrus-flavored cream cheese filling and a whipped-cream frosting, this cake is perfect for afternoon tea. Celebrate by setting the table with your finest china. You'll need to use large dessert plates to hold these extra-tall cake slices.

PER SERVING
507 CALORIES
7 g PROTEIN
35 g CARBOHYDRATES
40 g TOTAL FAT
14 g SATURATED FAT
168 mg CHOLESTEROL
256 mg SODIUM

▼ ▼ ▼
Nut lovers will go nuts over this incredible *Cream-Filled Caramel Cake Roll.* Three nuts— hazelnuts, almonds, and pecans—in creamy, sweet caramel create the sinfully delicious filling.

Cream-Filled Caramel Cake Roll

½ cup all-purpose flour
1 teaspoon baking powder
4 egg yolks
½ teaspoon vanilla
⅓ cup sugar
4 egg whites
½ cup sugar
  Powdered sugar
1 egg
⅔ cup sugar
1 5-ounce can (⅔ cup) evaporated milk
¼ cup margarine or butter
½ cup chopped toasted hazelnuts (filberts)
½ cup chopped toasted almonds
½ cup chopped toasted pecans
2 cups Sweetened Whipped-Cream Frosting (see recipe, page 210)

Grease and lightly flour a 15x10x1-inch baking pan. In a small mixing bowl stir together flour and baking powder. Set the baking pan and flour mixture aside.

In a medium bowl beat egg yolks and vanilla with an electric mixer on high speed for 5 minutes or till thick and lemon-colored. Gradually add the ⅓ cup sugar, beating on high speed till sugar is *almost* dissolved.

Thoroughly wash the beaters. In a large mixing bowl beat the egg whites on medium to high speed till soft peaks form (tips curl). Gradually add the ½ cup sugar, *2 tablespoons at a time*, beating on medium to high speed till stiff peaks form (tips stand straight).

Fold *about 1 cup* of the egg white mixture into egg yolk mixture. Then fold all of the egg yolk mixture into remaining egg white mixture. Sprinkle flour mixture over egg mixture. Gently fold in just till combined.

Spread batter evenly into the prepared pan. Bake in a 375° oven for 12 to 15 minutes or till top springs back when lightly touched. *Immediately* loosen cake from pan. Invert cake onto a towel sprinkled with powdered sugar. Trim ⅛ inch from cake edges. Roll up warm cake and towel, jelly-roll style, starting from one of the short sides. Cool completely.

Meanwhile, for the nut filling, in a small saucepan beat the whole egg just till mixed. Then stir in ⅔ cup sugar, evaporated milk, and margarine or butter. Cook and stir over medium heat about 6 minutes or till thickened and bubbly. Stir in hazelnuts, almonds, and pecans. Cool thoroughly.

Gently unroll the cake. Spread nut filling on cake to within ½ inch of the edges. Then spread *1 cup* of the Sweetened Whipped-Cream Frosting on top of the nut filling to within 1 inch of the edges of the cake. Roll up cake, *without* towel, jelly-roll style, starting from one of the short sides. Transfer cake to a large serving plate or platter.

Spoon the remaining Sweetened Whipped-Cream Frosting into a decorating bag fitted with a medium round tip (about ¼-inch opening). Pipe frosting on top of the cake roll in a decorative pattern. Serves 10.

SPECIAL TOUCH
▼ ▼ ▼
Highlight the nuts featured in this wonderful cake by simply sprinkling chopped nuts on top and adding nut-decorated skewers. For the skewers, make a hole in each nut with the pointed end of a bamboo skewer. Then stick the skewers into the cake and place the nuts onto the ends of the skewers.

PER SERVING
402 CALORIES
8 g PROTEIN
33 g CARBOHYDRATES
28 g TOTAL FAT
9 g SATURATED FAT
144 mg CHOLESTEROL
145 mg SODIUM

Praline Cookies

SPECIAL TOUCH
▼ ▼ ▼

SPECIAL TOUCH
▼ ▼ ▼

Sweet, crunchy, and huge—
these cookies make tasty
gifts for co-workers,
teachers, and anyone else
on your gift list. Place each
cookie in a small plastic
bag. Twist the opening of
the bag close and fasten
with a satin bow.

Margarine or *butter*
⅓ *cup sugar*
2 *tablespoons water*
1 *cup chopped toasted hazelnuts (filberts)*
    or *pecans*
1 *cup margarine* or *butter*
2½ *cups all-purpose flour*
1 *cup packed brown sugar*
½ *cup sugar*
2 *eggs*
1 *teaspoon vanilla*
½ *teaspoon baking soda*
2 *ounces semisweet* or *bittersweet*
    chocolate, chopped (optional)
2 *tablespoons finely chopped hazelnuts*
    (filberts) or *pecans (optional)*

Grease a large baking sheet with the
margarine or butter. Set baking sheet aside.

For praline, in a heavy medium saucepan stir
together ⅓ cup sugar and water. Cook and
stir over medium-high heat till boiling. Then
cook for 2½ to 3½ minutes more or till
syrup is a deep golden brown. Remove from
heat. Stir in 1 cup nuts. *Immediately* pour onto
the prepared baking sheet. Cool completely
on a wire rack till firm.

When firm, transfer the praline to a heavy
plastic bag. Using a rolling pin, crush the
praline into small pieces; set aside.

For cookies, in a large mixing bowl beat the
1 cup margarine or butter with an electric
mixer on medium to high speed about 30
seconds or till softened.

Add about *half* of the flour, all of the brown
sugar, ½ cup sugar, eggs, vanilla, and baking
soda. Beat till thoroughly combined, scraping
sides of bowl occasionally. Then beat or stir
in remaining flour. Stir in crushed praline.

Drop ¼ *cup* of dough at a time 4 inches
apart on an ungreased cookie sheet. Flatten
to 1-inch thickness. Bake in a 350° oven for
13 to 15 minutes or till edges are lightly
browned. Cool cookies on cookie sheets for
1 minute. Then remove cookies and cool on
a wire rack.

If desired, melt chocolate according to the
directions on page 225; cool. Drizzle the
melted chocolate over cookies and, if
desired, sprinkle with the 2 tablespoons
chopped nuts. Makes about 18.

PER COOKIE
279 CALORIES
3 g PROTEIN
34 g CARBOHYDRATES
15 g TOTAL FAT
2 g SATURATED FAT
24 mg CHOLESTEROL
156 mg SODIUM

F*ig Bars*

6 ounces Calimyrna (light) dried figs,
 finely chopped (about 1 cup)
½ cup coarsely chopped light raisins
½ cup chopped candied red cherries
½ teaspoon finely shredded orange peel
¼ cup orange juice
2 tablespoons honey
½ teaspoon ground cinnamon
⅛ teaspoon ground allspice
 Rich Tart Pastry (see recipe, page 206)
1 tablespoon milk
 Orange Icing

In a large mixing bowl stir together figs,
raisins, cherries, orange peel, orange juice,
honey, cinnamon, and allspice. Set aside.

For crust, divide Rich Tart Pastry dough in
half. Then form *each* half into a small ball.
On a lightly floured surface, use your hands
to slightly flatten *one* ball of dough. Roll
dough to form a 10-inch square. Wrap pastry
around the rolling pin. Then unroll pastry
onto an ungreased 8x8x2-inch baking pan.

Ease the pastry into the baking pan, allowing
dough to extend 1 inch up the sides of the
baking pan.

For top crust, roll out remaining ball of
dough to form an 8-inch square. Cut slits in
crust. Evenly spread fig mixture in pastry-
lined pan. Place top crust on filling. Press
together edges of bottom and top crust to
seal. Brush top crust with milk.

Bake in a 375° oven for 35 to 40 minutes or
till golden. Cool in baking pan on wire rack.
Drizzle with Orange Icing. Cut into squares.
Makes 12.

O*range Icing*

In a small mixing bowl combine ½ cup sifted
powdered sugar and ½ teaspoon finely
shredded *orange peel.* Stir in 1 to 2 teaspoons
orange juice till icing is of drizzling
consistency. Makes about ¼ cup.

SPECIAL TOUCH
▼ ▼ ▼
Dress up these pie-like bars
by using hors d'oeuvres or
small cookie cutters to cut
decorative shapes in the top
crust instead of cutting slits.

PER BAR
247 CALORIES
3 g PROTEIN
42 g CARBOHYDRATES
9 g TOTAL FAT
5 g SATURATED FAT
56 mg CHOLESTEROL
83 mg SODIUM

Mascarpone Cheese and Fruit Torte

3 *egg whites*
1 *teaspoon vanilla*
¼ *teaspoon cream of tartar*
  Dash salt
1 *cup sugar*
12 *ounces mascarpone cheese* or soft-style cream cheese*
5 *cups desired fresh fruit (such as sliced, peeled kiwi fruits; halved strawberries; sliced, peeled peaches; cubed, peeled pineapple; and/or halved grapes)*
2 *cups Sweetened Whipped Cream (see recipe, page 210)*

(see recipe, page 210)

Naturally sweet fresh fruit is hard to beat for topping off this billowy creation. Create a decorative border with your choicest berries, kiwi fruits, peaches, pineapple, and grapes.

In a large mixing bowl let egg whites stand at room temperature for 30 minutes. Meanwhile, line a baking sheet with parchment paper or plain brown paper. Draw a 9-inch circle on the paper. Set baking sheet aside.

Add vanilla, cream of tartar, and salt to the egg whites. Beat with an electric mixer on medium to high speed till soft peaks form (tips curl). Gradually add sugar, *1 tablespoon* at a time, beating on high speed about 7 minutes or till very stiff peaks form (tips stand straight) and sugar is *almost* dissolved.

Using a spoon or a spatula, spread meringue mixture over the circle on the prepared baking sheet, building the sides up to form a shell. *Or,* spoon meringue mixture into a decorating bag fitted with a medium round or star tip (about ¼-inch opening). Pipe shell on the prepared baking sheet, building up the sides.

Bake in a 300° oven for 45 minutes. Turn off oven. Then let the meringue shell dry in the oven with the door closed for 1 hour. *(Do not open oven.)*

Peel meringue shell from paper. Spread the mascarpone or cream cheese in the bottom of the meringue shell. Cover and chill in the refrigerator for 4 to 24 hours.

To serve, arrange desired fruit on top of cheese in shell. Then top with Sweetened Whipped Cream. Makes 8 servings.

*Mascarpone cheese looks and tastes like extra-rich cream cheese. Look for it at supermarkets, cheese shops, and Italian specialty shops.

PER SERVING
411 CALORIES
4 g PROTEIN
38 g CARBOHYDRATES
28 g TOTAL FAT
7 g SATURATED FAT
41 mg CHOLESTEROL
49 mg SODIUM

Orange Soufflé with Strawberries

Margarine *or* butter
Sugar
¼ *cup margarine* **or** *butter*
⅓ *cup all-purpose flour*
1 *cup milk*
2 *teaspoons finely shredded orange peel*
3 *tablespoons orange liqueur* **or** *orange*
   juice
6 *beaten egg yolks*
6 *egg whites*
1 *teaspoon vanilla*
⅓ *cup sugar*
1 *cup Crème Anglaise (using orange*
   liqueur, if desired) (see recipe,
   page 212)
1 *cup sliced strawberries*

Grease the sides of a 2-quart soufflé dish
with margarine or butter. For a collar on the
soufflé dish, measure enough foil to wrap
around the top of the soufflé dish and add 3
inches. Fold the foil in thirds lengthwise.
Lightly grease 1 side with margarine or
butter; sprinkle with sugar. Attach the foil,
sugar side in, around the outside of the dish
so that the foil extends about 2 inches above

the dish. Tape ends of foil together. Sprinkle
sides of dish with sugar. Set dish aside.

In a small saucepan melt ¼ cup margarine or
butter. Stir in flour. Add milk. Cook and stir
over medium heat till thickened and bubbly.
Remove from heat. Stir in orange peel and
orange liqueur or orange juice. Gradually
stir the mixture into the beaten egg yolks.
Then set egg yolk mixture aside.

If necessary, thoroughly wash beaters of the
electric mixer. In a large mixing bowl beat
egg whites and vanilla on medium speed till
soft peaks form (tips curl). Gradually add the
⅓ cup sugar, about *1 tablespoon* at a time,
beating on medium to high speed till stiff
peaks form (tips stand straight).

Gently fold the egg yolk mixture into the
egg white mixture. Spoon mixture into the
prepared soufflé dish. Bake in a 350° oven
for 40 to 45 minutes or till a knife inserted
near center comes out clean. Serve at once
with Crème Anglaise and strawberries.
Makes 8 servings.

SPECIAL TOUCH
▼ ▼ ▼

While this soufflé bakes,
arrange the sliced
strawberries on individual
dessert plates. Then drizzle
the Crème Anglaise in
zigzags over the
strawberries. Serve the
soufflé over the berries
and sauce.

PER SERVING
308 CALORIES
7 g PROTEIN
27 g CARBOHYDRATES
19 g TOTAL FAT
7g SATURATED FAT
216 mg CHOLESTEROL
142 mg SODIUM

Poached Pears with Almonds is a sophisticated alternative to the simple idea of poached pears.

Poached Pears with Almonds

⅓ cup packed brown sugar
¼ cup orange juice
½ teaspoon ground nutmeg
1 tablespoon amaretto **or** ½ teaspoon
    almond extract
3 ripe medium pears
2 cups warm Crème Anglaise (see recipe,
    page 212)
⅓ cup sliced almonds, toasted
    Ground nutmeg

In a large skillet stir together brown sugar, orange juice, and ½ teaspoon nutmeg. Cook and stir over low heat till brown sugar is melted. Then stir in amaretto or almond extract. Set caramel-orange mixture aside.

Cut pears in half lengthwise, leaving stems intact on a half of each pear. Remove core and peel the pear halves. Place pear halves on a cutting board, flat sides down. Make about *seven* lengthwise cuts in *each* pear half, starting about ½ inch from stem end and cutting to the bottom.

Transfer the pear halves, flat sides down, to the skillet with caramel-orange mixture. Spoon caramel-orange mixture over pears. Then bring to boiling. Reduce heat. Cover and simmer for 10 to 15 minutes or till tender, occasionally spooning caramel-orange mixture over pears.

Remove pears from skillet and transfer to individual serving dishes. Gently boil caramel-orange liquid for 3 to 4 minutes or till reduced to *half.*

To serve, pour warm Crème Anglaise around pears in dishes. Then drizzle the caramel-orange mixture on top of the Crème Anglaise. Sprinkle with almonds and additional ground nutmeg. Makes 6 servings.

SPECIAL TOUCH
▼ ▼ ▼

For a pretty-as-a-picture presentation, spoon some of the Crème Anglaise around each pear or each dessert plate. Next drizzle the warm pear-cooking liquid over the Crème Anglaise in large zigzags or swirls. As a final note, sprinkle with almonds and nutmeg.

PER SERVING
434 CALORIES
4 g PROTEIN
51 g CARBOHYDRATES
25 g TOTAL FAT
13 g SATURATED FAT
143 mg CHOLESTEROL
27 mg SODIUM

Mocha Caramel-and-Chocolate Apples

6 *large apples (about 3½ pounds)*
6 *wooden sticks*
3 *cups chopped toasted hazelnuts (filberts), almonds,* **or** *pecans*
2 *tablespoons* hot *water*
½ *teaspoon instant coffee crystals*
21 *ounces chocolate* **or** *vanilla caramels (about 72)*
1 *tablespoon coffee liqueur* **or** *water*
12 *ounces semisweet* **or** *bittersweet chocolate* **or** *chocolate-flavored candy coating, chopped*
2 *tablespoons shortening*

Wash and dry apples. Remove stems. Insert a wooden stick into the stem end of each apple. Set apples aside. Place the chopped nuts in a pie plate; set aside.

In a small mixing bowl stir together the hot water and coffee crystals. Stir till dissolved. Set coffee mixture aside.

In a heavy medium saucepan combine *unwrapped* caramels, coffee liqueur or water, and coffee mixture. Heat and stir over medium-low heat just till caramels are melted. Remove from heat.

Dip each apple into the hot caramel mixture, spooning the caramel mixture evenly over the apple. Allow excess caramel mixture to drip off. (If caramel mixture becomes too stiff, return to low heat and stir till soft again.) *Immediately* roll apples in nuts. Place apples, bottom sides down, on waxed paper. Let stand about 25 minutes or till firm.

Melt semisweet or bittersweet chocolate or candy coating with shortening according to the directions on page 225. Cool for 5 minutes. Spoon melted chocolate mixture to a decorating bag fitted with a small round tip (about ⅛-inch opening). Pipe the melted chocolate over the caramel-and-nut coated apples. Allow chocolate to drip down the apples. Then let stand till dry.

If desired, after chocolate is dry, wrap the apples in plastic wrap or place them in a covered container. Store in the refrigerator for up to 1 week. Makes 6.

Tropical Trifle

3 eggs
1¼ cups milk
¼ cup sugar
1 teaspoon vanilla
1 layer Hot Milk Sponge Cake (see recipe,
     page 208)
3 tablespoons rum, orange juice,
     pineapple juice, or mango juice
2 ripe mangos or papayas, peeled, seeded,
     and cubed
2 ripe kiwi fruits, peeled and sliced
2 cups Sweetened Whipped Cream
     (see recipe, page 210)

For custard, in a heavy medium saucepan use a rotary beater or wire whisk to lightly beat eggs *just till mixed.* Then stir in milk and sugar. Cook and stir over medium heat. Continue cooking egg mixture about 7 minutes or till mixture *just coats* a metal spoon. Remove from heat. Stir in vanilla.

Quickly cool the custard by placing the saucepan in a sink or bowl of *ice water* for 1 to 2 minutes, stirring constantly. Pour custard in a medium mixing bowl. Cover surface with plastic wrap and set aside.

Cut the Hot Milk Sponge Cake into 1-inch cubes. In a 2-quart clear glass serving bowl with straight sides or soufflé dish, place *half* of the cake cubes. Sprinkle with *half* of the rum or juice. Top with *half* of the mango or papaya and *all* of the kiwi fruit. Then pour *half* of the custard over fruit. Repeat layering cake, rum or orange juice, mango or papaya, and custard.

Cover and chill in the refrigerator for 4 to 6 hours before serving. Just before serving, spread Sweetened Whipped Cream over top. Makes 8 servings.

PER SERVING
335 CALORIES
6 g PROTEIN
40 g CARBOHYDRATES
16 g TOTAL FAT
8 g SATURATED FAT
151 mg CHOLESTEROL
121 mg SODIUM

The marvelous flavors of fresh peaches and tart cherries with a hint of ginger will entice you to try this *Gingered Fruit en Papillote*.

Gingered Fruit en Papillote

½ cup dried cherries, dried blueberries, raisins, *or* currants

¼ cup orange liqueur *or* orange juice
Parchment paper

2 tablespoons margarine *or* butter, melted

4 cups thinly sliced, peeled peaches, nectarines, *or* apples

¼ cup packed brown sugar

2 tablespoons finely chopped crystallized ginger

½ teaspoon finely shredded orange peel

4 tablespoons margarine *or* butter

½ cup Crème Fraîche (see recipe, page 208) (optional)
Candied Citrus Peel (using oranges) (see recipe, page 217) (optional)

In a small saucepan combine dried fruit and orange liqueur or orange juice; heat just to boiling. Remove from heat and let stand for 5 minutes. Drain fruit and discard liquid. Set the fruit aside.

To assemble bundles, cut four 20x10-inch rectangles from Parchment paper. Brush both sides of the 4 paper rectangles with the 2 tablespoons melted margarine or butter.

Mound peach, nectarine, or apple slices on the right half of the rectangles, leaving about 2 inches of parchment paper showing around edges. Top with the drained, dried fruit.

In a small mixing bowl stir together brown sugar, ginger, and orange peel. Sprinkle brown sugar mixture over fruit. Place *1 tablespoon* margarine or butter on *each* mound of fruit. Then fold the left half of the paper rectangles over the fruit, matching edges. To seal each package, starting at 1 side of the rectangle, fold the edges together in a triple fold. Fold only 1 side at a time to ensure a tight seal. Then twist the 4 corners to close the package.

Place bundles on an ungreased 15x10x1-inch baking pan. Bake in a 400° oven for 18 to 20 minutes or till paper puffs up and fruit is tender (*carefully* open paper to check doneness).

To serve, cut bundles open by slashing a large X on top of each, then pull back the paper. Transfer bundles to dessert plates. If desired, serve with Crème Fraîche and garnish with Candied Citrus Peel. Serves 4.

Gingered Fruit en Casserole

Omit the 2 tablespoons melted margarine or butter. Place sliced fruit in an 8x8x2-inch baking dish or 9-inch quiche dish. Top with the drained, dried fruit. Sprinkle with brown sugar mixture. Dot with the 4 tablespoons margarine or butter. Cover with foil. Bake in a 375° oven for 30 to 35 minutes or till fruit is tender. Stir before serving. To serve, spoon fruit mixture into dessert dishes and, if desired, serve with Crème Fraîche.
Per Serving: Same as main recipe, except 336 calories, 12 g total fat, 2 g saturated fat, and 137 mg sodium.

PER SERVING
387 CALORIES
2 g PROTEIN
54 g CARBOHYDRATES
17 g TOTAL FAT
3 g SATURATED FAT
0 mg CHOLESTEROL
203 mg SODIUM

Pineapple-Orange Brown Betty

SPECIAL TOUCH
▼ ▼ ▼
To garnish this sweet and tangy dessert, save several leaves from the top of the pineapple and cut spears from the remaining fresh pineapple. At serving time, tuck a pineapple leaf and a spear into each serving.

4   slices raisin bread, cut into ½-inch cubes (about 3 cups)
3   medium oranges
1   cup packed brown sugar
2   tablespoons orange liqueur or orange juice
1   tablespoon cornstarch
1   teaspoon ground cinnamon
2   cups cubed, peeled fresh pineapple or one 20-ounce can pineapple chunks (juice pack), drained
½   cup broken pecans
⅓   cup margarine or butter, melted
1   cup Citrus Sauce (using orange peel and juice) (see recipe, page 214)

Arrange the bread cubes in a single layer in a shallow baking pan. Bake in a 375° oven for 10 to 15 minutes or till golden, stirring once or twice. Set bread aside.

Meanwhile, finely shred 1 teaspoon orange peel from the oranges. Then peel and section the oranges.

For filling, in a large mixing bowl stir together the orange peel, brown sugar, orange liqueur or juice, cornstarch, and cinnamon. Add orange sections and pineapple. Then gently toss till coated with brown sugar mixture. Set filling aside.

In a medium mixing bowl toss together bread cubes, pecans, and the melted margarine or butter.

In a 1½-quart casserole place half of the filling. Top with half of the bread cube mixture. Repeat layering filling and bread. Bake in a 375° oven for 35 to 40 minutes or till filling is bubbly, covering with foil after 25 minutes to prevent overbrowning. Serve warm with Citrus Sauce. Makes 6 servings.

PER SERVING
490 CALORIES
3 g PROTEIN
79 g CARBOHYDRATES
19 g TOTAL FAT
3 g SATURATED FAT
0 mg CHOLESTEROL
215 mg SODIUM

Gingered Apple-Cranberry Crisp

¾ cup rolled oats
¼ cup packed brown sugar
2 tablespoons all-purpose flour
⅓ cup margarine or butter
1 egg yolk
¾ cup coarsely crushed gingersnaps
½ cup chopped almonds or pecans
6 medium cooking apples, peeled, cored,
    and sliced (about 5½ cups)
1 cup cranberries, chopped
⅓ cup sugar
1 cup Caramel Sauce (see recipe,
    page 213) (optional)

For topping, in a medium mixing bowl stir together the oats, brown sugar, and flour.

Cut in the margarine or butter till mixture resembles coarse crumbs. Add the egg yolk; stir till combined. Stir in the gingersnaps and almonds or pecans. Set topping aside.

For filling, in a large mixing bowl combine the apples, cranberries, and sugar. Toss till combined. Transfer the filling to an ungreased 12x7½x2-inch baking dish.

Sprinkle the topping on the filling. Bake in a 375° oven for 30 to 35 minutes or till apples are tender (if necessary, cover with foil the last 10 minutes to prevent overbrowning). Serve warm. If desired, serve with Caramel Sauce. Makes 6 servings.

SPECIAL TOUCH
▼ ▼ ▼
Add a scoop of cinnamon or vanilla ice cream and a splash of Caramel Sauce to top off this fall fruit duo.

PER SERVING
433 CALORIES
5 g PROTEIN
64 g CARBOHYDRATES
19 g TOTAL FAT
4 g SATURATED FAT
36 mg CHOLESTEROL
199 mg SODIUM

Plum-Blackberry Cobbler

1 cup all-purpose flour
1½ teaspoons baking powder
1 teaspoon sugar
¼ cup margarine or butter
¾ cup sugar
3 tablespoons cornstarch
3 cups sliced, peeled plums or sliced, peeled fresh or frozen peaches
3 cups fresh or frozen blackberries or black raspberries
¼ cup water
2 tablespoons crème de cassis (optional)
⅓ cup milk
1 teaspoon sugar (optional)
⅛ teaspoon ground cinnamon (optional)
   Half-and-half, light cream, or ice cream (optional)

SPECIAL TOUCH
▼ ▼ ▼

Making a homestyle dessert, such as this juicy cobbler, is one way to express warm, loving feelings. To enhance your message, top the cobbler with hearts by using a heart-shaped cutter to cut out the dough. Then add a design to each biscuit by pressing a smaller heart-shaped cutter into each cutout, about halfway through the dough (do not cut all the way through).

For biscuit topping, in a medium mixing bowl stir together flour, baking powder, and 1 teaspoon sugar. Cut in margarine or butter till mixture resembles coarse crumbs. Make a well in the center of the dry mixture. Then set dry mixture aside.

For filling, in a large saucepan stir together ¾ cup sugar and cornstarch. Add plums or peaches, berries, and water. Cook and stir over medium heat till slightly thickened and bubbly. If desired, stir in the crème de cassis. Keep mixture hot.

Add milk all at once to the dry topping mixture. Using a fork, stir *just till moistened.* Turn dough out onto a lightly floured surface. Gently knead dough for 10 to 12 strokes or till dough is *nearly* smooth. Roll dough to ½-inch thickness. Using a floured 2¾-inch cookie cutter and dipping the cutter into flour between cuts, cut the dough into 6 desired shapes.

Transfer the *hot* filling to an ungreased 10x6x2-inch baking dish or a 1½-quart casserole. *Immediately* place the dough cutouts on top of the hot filling. If desired, stir together the 1 teaspoon sugar and cinnamon; sprinkle over cutouts.

Bake in a 400° oven about 20 minutes or till a wooden toothpick inserted into the center of a biscuit comes out clean. Serve warm and, if desired, with half-and-half, light cream, or ice cream. Makes 6 servings.

PER SERVING
311 CALORIES
3 g PROTEIN
58 g CARBOHYDRATES
9 g TOTAL FAT
1 g SATURATED FAT
1 mg CHOLESTEROL
179 mg SODIUM

Petite Temptations

Grand treats sometimes come in petite packages. Each exquisite dessert morsel in this chapter is a perfect treat for occasions that call for the nibbling of sweets and a scrumptious bite to just pop in your mouth! Within the next few pages you'll uncover recipes for tiny desserts such as Lemon Tea Cakes, Coconut Tassies, Double-Dipped Fruits, and Orange-Walnut Madeleines.

▼ ▼ ▼

Honey-Pecan Ravioli Pastries

½ cup finely chopped pecans, toasted
2 tablespoons sugar
¼ teaspoon ground cinnamon
2 tablespoons honey
½ teaspoon lemon juice
    Ravioli Pastry
1 slightly beaten egg white
1 tablespoon coarse-grain or crystal sugar, or cinnamon sugar
1 cup Caramel Sauce, Bittersweet Chocolate Sauce, or Citrus Sauce (using orange peel and juice) (see recipes, pages 212–214)

For filling, in a small mixing bowl stir together pecans, 2 tablespoons sugar, and cinnamon. Add honey and lemon juice, then stir till combined. Set filling aside.

On a lightly floured surface, use your hands to slightly flatten Ravioli Pastry dough. Roll dough to form a 12-inch square. Using a fluted pastry wheel, cut six 2-inch-wide strips.

To assemble, spoon about 1 teaspoon of the filling at 1½-inch intervals on 1 strip. Brush egg white on dough strip around mounds of filling. Then lay another strip on top, matching edges. Use the side of your hand to press down around each mound to seal the 2 strips of dough. Repeat with remaining filling, dough strips, and egg white.

To separate the ravioli, use the fluted pastry wheel to cut halfway between the mounds of filling. If necessary, press the edges together to seal.

Place ravioli 2 inches apart on an ungreased baking sheet. Brush tops of ravioli with water, then sprinkle with the 1 tablespoon coarse-grain or granulated sugar or cinnamon sugar. Bake in a 375° oven about 20 minutes or till golden and crisp. Remove ravioli and cool on a wire rack. Serve the Caramel Sauce, Bittersweet Chocolate Sauce, or Citrus Sauce as a dipping sauce for the ravioli. Makes 24.

Ravioli Pastry

In a medium mixing bowl stir together 1½ cups all-purpose flour and ¼ teaspoon salt. Cut in ½ cup margarine or butter till pieces are the size of small peas. Sprinkle 1 tablespoon cold water over flour mixture, then gently toss with a fork. Repeat till all is moistened, using a total of 4 to 5 tablespoons cold water. Form dough into a ball.

Berries-and-Cream Tartlets

1 *tablespoon margarine* **or** *butter*
⅔ *cup finely crumbled soft coconut macaroons (about 4 cookies)*
⅓ *cup toasted pecans, ground*
2 *3-ounce packages cream cheese, softened*
¼ *cup sugar*
1½ *teaspoons dark rum* **or** *½ teaspoon rum flavoring*
½ *teaspoon vanilla*
⅓ *cup whipping cream, whipped*
1½ *cups desired fresh fruits (such as blueberries; raspberries; Champagne grapes; nectarine slices; and/or small strawberries, fanned)*

Line twelve 2½-inch muffin cups with foil bake cups; set aside. In a small saucepan melt margarine or butter. Stir in crumbled macaroons and ground pecans. Press *about 1 tablespoon* of the crumb mixture into the bottom of *each* cup to form a firm, even crust. Bake in a 375° oven for 7 to 8 minutes or till edges are lightly browned. Completely cool crusts in muffin cups on a wire rack. Remove crusts from foil bake cups and set aside.

Meanwhile, for filling, in a medium mixing bowl beat cream cheese and sugar with an electric mixer on medium speed about 1 minute or till fluffy. Add rum or rum flavoring and vanilla. Beat till thoroughly combined. Stir in whipped cream.

Spoon filling into a decorating bag fitted with a large star or round tip (about ½-inch opening). Pipe the mixture onto each cookie crust. *Or,* dollop the mixture onto each crust. Transfer to a plastic container. Cover and chill in the refrigerator till serving time or for up to 6 hours.

Before serving, top each cream tartlet with desired fruit, then let stand at room temperature for 10 minutes. Makes 12.

SPECIAL TOUCH
▼ ▼ ▼
These colorful tarts are so pretty they can stand on their own without garnishing. Just serve them on dessert plates lined with colored doilies.

PER TARTLET
157 CALORIES
2 g PROTEIN
12 g CARBOHYDRATES
12 g TOTAL FAT
5 g SATURATED FAT
25 mg CHOLESTEROL
59 mg SODIUM

Chocolate Truffle Tartlets

Sweet-Tart Pastry (see recipe, page 206)
4 ounces semisweet or bittersweet chocolate, chopped
¼ cup whipping cream
3 tablespoons butter
1 beaten egg yolk
2 tablespoons desired liqueur (such as amaretto, or coffee, praline, hazelnut, orange, raspberry, or cherry liqueur) or whipping cream

For pastry shells, shape Sweet-Tart Pastry dough into thirty-six ¾-inch balls. Then press the balls into ungreased 1¾-inch muffin cups, pressing an even layer onto the bottom and up the sides of each cup. Bake in a 450° oven for 6 to 8 minutes or till edges are lightly browned. Completely cool pastry shells in muffin cups on a wire rack. Remove pastry shells from muffin cups and set aside.

Meanwhile, for filling, in a heavy medium saucepan heat and stir chocolate, the ¼ cup whipping cream, and butter over low heat just till chocolate is melted. Gradually stir about half of the chocolate mixture into the beaten egg yolk. Then return all of the egg yolk mixture to the saucepan. Cook and stir just till mixture begins to bubble, then remove from heat.

Stir desired liqueur or 2 tablespoons whipping cream into chocolate mixture. Transfer chocolate mixture to a medium mixing bowl. Refrigerate for 1½ to 2 hours or till mixture is completely cooled and smooth, stirring occasionally. (Butter may separate out but will blend in when stirred.)

Beat the chilled chocolate mixture with an electric mixer on medium speed about 2 minutes or till light and fluffy. Then spoon the chocolate mixture into a decorating bag fitted with a large star tip (about ½-inch opening). Pipe mixture into the pastry shells. Or, spoon mixture into the shells. Lightly cover and chill in the refrigerator till serving time or for up to 24 hours. Before serving, let stand at room temperature for 15 to 20 minutes. Makes 36.

PER TARTLET
79 CALORIES
1 g PROTEIN
7 g CARBOHYDRATES
6 g TOTAL FAT
3 g SATURATED FAT
29 mg CHOLESTEROL
37 mg SODIUM

Coconut Tassies

4 ounces sweet baking chocolate, *chopped*
⅓ cup margarine *or* butter
1 3-ounce package cream cheese
1 tablespoon water
1 cup all-purpose flour
1 slightly beaten egg
½ cup sweetened condensed *milk*
1⅓ cups coconut, *chopped*
½ cup chopped pecans
1 teaspoon shortening

Melt *half* of the chocolate according to the directions on page 225; cool.

For pastry dough, in a medium mixing bowl beat melted chocolate, margarine or butter, cream cheese, and water with an electric mixer on medium to high speed about 30 seconds or till combined. Add flour, then beat or stir in till combined. Cover and chill in the refrigerator for at least 1 hour or till easy to handle.

Meanwhile, for filling, in another medium mixing bowl stir together the egg and sweetened condensed milk. Then stir in coconut and pecans.

Shape pastry dough into *thirty* 1-inch balls. Then press the balls into ungreased 1¾-inch muffin cups, pressing an even layer onto the bottom and up the sides of each cup. Spoon a *scant 1 tablespoon* of filling into *each* unbaked pastry shell.

Bake tassies in a 325° oven for 20 to 25 minutes or till coconut is lightly browned. Cool tassies in muffin cups on a wire rack. Remove tassies from muffin cups. Melt remaining chocolate with shortening according to the directions on page 225; drizzle on top of tassies. Makes 30.

SPECIAL TOUCH
▼ ▼ ▼
A homemade food gift is as much fun to give as it is to receive. To create your gift, arrange these bite-size sweets in a decorative tin lined with tissue or wrapping paper.

PER TASSIE
113 CALORIES
2 g PROTEIN
10 g CARBOHYDRATES
8 g TOTAL FAT
1 g SATURATED FAT
12 mg CHOLESTEROL
49 mg SODIUM

▼ ▼ ▼
Entertain with the
delightful custom of
afternoon tea. Include
these *Lemon Tea Cakes*
with a variety of cookies,
pastries, biscuits, and
finger sandwiches in
your teatime fare.

Lemon Tea Cakes

1 *recipe for 2 layers Génoise (see page 207)*
1 *tablespoon finely shredded lemon peel (set aside)*
1 *tablespoon lemon juice*
   Lemon Satin Icing

Grease a 13x9x2-inch baking pan. Line the bottom of the baking pan with waxed paper, parchment paper, or plain brown paper; grease paper. Set baking pan aside.

Prepare the batter for two 8- or 9-inch layers of Génoise as directed, *except* stir in lemon juice with the vanilla and fold in lemon peel with the melted butter. Spread batter in the prepared baking pan. Bake in a 350° oven for 20 to 25 minutes or till a wooden toothpick inserted near the center of the cake comes out clean. Cool cake in pan on a wire rack for 10 minutes. Remove cake from pan; peel off paper. Cool completely on the rack.

Trim sides and top of cake to make the edges smooth and straight. Cut cake into 1½-inch squares, diamonds, hearts, and/or circles. Brush off crumbs. Place the cake pieces on wire racks with waxed paper underneath the wire racks.

Insert a 2- or 3-prong long-handled fork into the side of 1 cake piece. Holding the cake over the saucepan of Lemon Satin Icing, spoon on enough icing to cover sides and top. Place frosted cake piece back on the wire rack, making sure other cake pieces do not touch it. Repeat with remaining cake pieces. Let cakes dry 15 minutes.

Repeat with a second layer of icing, *except* set cake pieces *on top* of the fork prongs (do not spear them). Then repeat with a third layer of icing. If necessary, reuse the icing that has dripped onto the waxed paper, straining it to remove crumbs. Makes 35 to 40.

Lemon Satin Icing

In a 3-quart saucepan combine 4½ cups *sugar,* 2¼ cups *hot water,* and ¼ teaspoon *cream of tartar.* Bring mixture to boiling over medium-high heat, stirring constantly for 5 to 9 minutes or till the sugar dissolves.

Reduce heat to medium-low. Clip a candy thermometer to the side of the saucepan. Cook till thermometer registers 226°, stirring only when necessary to prevent sticking. Mixture should boil at a moderate, steady rate over the entire surface (this should take about 15 minutes). Remove saucepan from heat. Cool sugar mixture at room temperature, *without stirring,* to 110° (this should take about 1 hour).

Stir 1 tablespoon *lemon juice* or ¼ teaspoon *almond extract* and 1½ teaspoons *clear vanilla* into sugar mixture. Then stir in 6 to 6¾ cups sifted *powdered sugar* till icing is of drizzling consistency. If necessary, beat the icing with a rotary beater or wire whisk to remove any lumps. If desired, stir in enough *food coloring* to make desired color. (If icing gets too thick to drizzle, beat in an additional few drops *hot water.*) Makes about 5 cups.

SPECIAL TOUCH
▼ ▼ ▼
Gussy up these tiny cakes with candied violets, edible flowers, and/or small silver decorative candies (do not eat the silver candies). Or, place any of the remaining icing or some melted chocolate in a decorating bag fitted with a small round tip and decoratively pipe the icing or chocolate on top of the cakes.

PER CAKE
230 CALORIES
1 g PROTEIN
50 g CARBOHYDRATES
4 g TOTAL FAT
2 g SATURATED FAT
44 mg CHOLESTEROL
12 mg SODIUM

Grand Marnier Roulades

¾ cup egg whites (5 to 6)
¾ cup sifted powdered sugar
½ cup sifted cake flour
¾ teaspoon cream of tartar
½ teaspoon vanilla
½ cup sugar
1 teaspoon finely shredded orange peel
  Powdered sugar
2 tablespoons Grand Marnier
1 cup Citrus Curd (using orange peel
  and *juice*) (see page 215)

In a very large mixing bowl, let egg whites stand at room temperature for 30 minutes. Meanwhile, grease and lightly flour a 15x10x1-inch baking pan. Sift the ¾ cup powdered sugar and cake flour together 3 times. Set pan and flour mixture aside.

Add cream of tartar and vanilla to the egg whites. Beat with an electric mixer on medium to high speed till soft peaks form (tips curl). Gradually add the sugar, about *2 tablespoons* at a time, beating till stiff peaks form (tips stand straight).

Sift about *one-fourth* of the flour mixture over the egg white mixture, then gently fold in.

(If bowl is too full, transfer mixture to a larger bowl.) Repeat sifting and folding in one-fourth of the flour mixture at a time. Fold in orange peel.

Spread batter into the prepared pan. Bake in a 350° oven for 12 to 15 minutes or till top springs back when lightly touched. *Immediately* loosen cake from pan. Invert cake onto a towel sprinkled with powdered sugar. Cut cake in half lengthwise. Quickly separate cake halves on towel to about 6 inches apart. Roll up each half of warm cake and towel, jelly-roll style, starting each half from one of its *long* sides and rolling toward the center. Cool completely on a wire rack.

To assemble roulades, gently unroll each cake roll. Sprinkle with Grand Marnier. Then spread curd on top of each cake to within ½ inch of edges. Roll up each cake *without* towel, jelly-roll style, starting from one of its long sides.

Trim ends of cake rolls. Then cut *each* cake roll diagonally into *eight* pieces. If desired, sift additional powdered sugar over the tops of the roulades. Makes 16.

Orange-Walnut Madeleines

½ cup sugar
2 egg yolks
½ cup butter, melted and cooled
1 teaspoon finely shredded orange peel
1 tablespoon orange juice
½ teaspoon vanilla
½ cup all-purpose flour
½ teaspoon baking powder
¼ teaspoon ground cardamom
⅛ teaspoon baking soda
⅛ teaspoon salt
¼ cup finely chopped walnuts, toasted
2 slightly beaten egg whites
  Powdered sugar

Grease and flour twenty-four 3-inch madeleine molds. Set molds aside.

In a medium mixing bowl beat sugar and egg yolks with electric mixer on medium to high speed about 30 seconds or till thoroughly mixed. Add melted butter, orange peel, orange juice, and vanilla. Beat on low speed till combined.

Sift together flour, baking powder, cardamom, baking soda, and salt. Sift or sprinkle about *one-fourth* of the flour mixture over the egg yolk mixture. Gently fold in the mixture. Repeat sifting and folding in one-fourth of the flour mixture at a time. Fold in nuts. Gently stir in egg whites.

Spoon batter into the prepared molds, filling each mold about half full. Bake in a 375° oven for 10 to 12 minutes or till edges are golden and tops spring back when lightly touched. Cool cakes in molds for 1 minute. Using the point of a knife, loosen cakes from molds. Then invert cakes onto a wire rack. Remove molds and cool cakes completely on the rack. Tightly cover and store at room temperature till serving time or for up to 3 days. Just before serving, sift powdered sugar over tops. Makes 24.

SPECIAL TOUCH
▼ ▼ ▼

For a simple serving suggestion, sift powdered sugar over the tops of these luscious cakelike cookies and shingle them in a V-fashion on a serving platter.

PER COOKIE
78 CALORIES
1 g PROTEIN
6 g CARBOHYDRATES
6 g TOTAL FAT
3 g SATURATED FAT
28 mg CHOLESTEROL
67 mg SODIUM

Black-and-White Romanesque Crisps

SPECIAL TOUCH

▼ ▼ ▼

Plain or filled—these crispy
rolled cookies are delicious
both ways. If you opt to fill
them, use a butter frosting
flavored with chocolate,
liqueur, orange flavoring,
or other desired flavoring.

PER COOKIE

56 CALORIES

1 g PROTEIN

7 g CARBOHYDRATES

3 g TOTAL FAT

0 g SATURATED FAT

0 mg CHOLESTEROL

32 mg SODIUM

2   egg whites
¼   cup margarine or butter
½   teaspoon orange flavoring or vanilla
½   cup sugar
½   cup all-purpose flour
1   tablespoon unsweetened cocoa powder
2   teaspoons milk
     Desired frosting (optional)

In a medium mixing bowl, let egg whites
stand at room temperature for 30 minutes.
Meanwile, generously grease a cookie sheet.
(Repeat greasing cookie sheet for each
batch.) Set cookie sheet aside.

In a small saucepan heat margarine or butter
over low heat just till melted. Stir in orange
flavoring or vanilla. Set margarine mixture
aside to cool.

Beat egg whites with an electric mixer on
medium to high speed till soft peaks form
(tips curl). Gradually add sugar, *1 tablespoon*
at a time, beating till stiff peaks form (tips
stand straight). Fold in about *half* of the
flour. Then gently stir in the margarine
mixture. Fold in the remaining flour till
thoroughly combined.

Remove *¼ cup* of the batter and stir cocoa
powder into it. Then stir milk into the
chocolate batter. Spoon the chocolate batter
into a decorating bag fitted with a small
round tip (about ⅛-inch opening). Set
decorating bag aside.

Drop plain batter from a *slightly rounded
teaspoon* at least 3 inches apart on the
prepared cookie sheet. Spread batter into
2x1-inch rectangles or 2-inch circles. (Bake
only 4 cookies at a time.) Then pipe
chocolate batter in a fine zigzag pattern or in
dots on the cookies. Bake in a 375° oven for
5 to 6 minutes or·till edges of the cookies
are lightly browned.

Immediately remove cookies from cookie
sheet, one at a time. Place cookies upside
down on a table or countertop. For
rectangle-shaped cookies, quickly roll each
around a greased handle of a wooden spoon
or dowel, starting from a long side. For
round cookies, quickly roll each around a
greased cone. Slide the cookie off spoon,
dowel, or cone and cool on a wire rack.
Repeat with remaining warm cookies. (If
cookies harden before you can shape them,
reheat them in the oven about 1 minute.)

If desired, just before serving, spoon desired
frosting into a decorating bag fitted with a
medium star tip (about ¼-inch opening).
Pipe some frosting into each of the cookies.
Makes about 20.

Tinted Romanesque Crisps

Prepare Black-and-White Romanesque Crisps
as directed above, *except* omit cocoa powder
and milk. Stir ½ teaspoon *pink, green, red,* or
orange powdered food coloring into the ¼ cup of
reserved dough. Continue as directed above.
Per Cookie: Same as main recipe, except 55 calories.

Hazelnut-Blackberry Cookies

½ *cup blanched hazelnuts (filberts)* **or** *blanched whole almonds, toasted (about 3 ounces)*
1 *cup all-purpose flour*
¼ *cup sugar*
½ *cup* **cold** *butter*
⅓ *cup blackberry, apricot,* **or** *red raspberry preserves*

Place the nuts in blender container or food processor bowl. Cover and blend or process till very fine but dry (not oily).

In a medium mixing bowl stir together the ground hazelnuts or almonds, flour, and sugar. Cut in the butter till mixture resembles fine crumbs. Form the mixture into a ball and knead till smooth.

On a lightly floured surface, roll dough to ⅛-inch thickness. Using a 1½-inch fluted round cutter, cut dough. Place 1 inch apart on an ungreased cookie sheet.

Bake in a 375° oven for 6 to 8 minutes or till edges are just golden. Cool on cookie sheet for 3 minutes. Then remove cookies and cool on a wire rack.

Tightly cover and store cookies at room temperature till serving time or for up to 3 days.

Before serving, to assemble cookie sandwiches, spread the bottoms of *half* of the cookies with *¼ to ½ teaspoon* preserves each. Then top with remaining cookies, bottom sides down. Makes about 40.

SPECIAL TOUCH
▼ ▼ ▼
Add your personal signature to each sandwich cookie by stenciling a small motif on top. Use plain powdered sugar or powdered sugar mixed with a small amount of powdered food coloring or unsweetened cocoa powder.

PER COOKIE
52 CALORIES
1 g PROTEIN
6 g CARBOHYDRATES
3 g TOTAL FAT
2 g SATURATED FAT
6 mg CHOLESTEROL
24 mg SODIUM

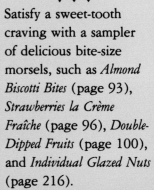

▼ ▼ ▼
Satisfy a sweet-tooth
craving with a sampler
of delicious bite-size
morsels, such as *Almond
Biscotti Bites* (page 93),
*Strawberries la Crème
Fraîche* (page 96), *Double-
Dipped Fruits* (page 100),
and *Individual Glazed Nuts*
(page 216).

Almond Biscotti Bites

⅓ cup margarine or butter
2 cups all-purpose flour
⅔ cup sugar
2 eggs
2 teaspoons baking powder
1 teaspoon vanilla
2 teaspoons finely shredded orange or
    lemon peel
1½ cups slivered almonds or hazelnuts
    (filberts), very finely chopped
1 beaten egg yolk (optional)
1 tablespoon milk (optional)
6 ounces semisweet or bittersweet
    chocolate, chopped (optional)
1 tablespoon shortening (optional)
    Ground almonds or hazelnuts (filberts)
    (optional)

Lightly grease a cookie sheet. Set cookie
sheet aside.

In a medium mixing bowl beat margarine or
butter with an electric mixer on medium to
high speed about 30 seconds or till softened.

Add about *half* of the flour and all of the
sugar, whole eggs, baking powder, and
vanilla to the margarine. Beat till thoroughly
combined, scraping the sides of the bowl
occasionally. Then beat or stir in the
remaining flour and orange or lemon peel.
Stir in the 1½ cups chopped nuts.

Shape dough into *three* 14-inch rolls. Place
rolls about 3 inches apart on the prepared
cookie sheet. Slightly flatten to ¾-inch
thickness. If desired, brush with mixture of
egg yolk and milk. Bake in a 375° oven for
15 to 20 minutes or till lightly browned.
Cool on cookie sheet about 1 hour.

Cut each cookie roll into ¼-inch-thick slices.
Lay slices, cut sides down, on an ungreased
cookie sheet. Bake in a 325° oven for 5
minutes. Turn slices over; bake for 5 to 10
minutes more or till dry and crisp. Remove
cookies; cool on a wire rack.

If desired, quick-temper chocolate with
shortening according to the directions on
page 226. Dip half of each cookie in the
chocolate. Allow excess chocolate to drip off,
then roll in ground nuts. Place cookies on
waxed paper and let stand till dry. Makes
about 120.

SPECIAL TOUCH
▼ ▼ ▼
For an elegant old-time
presentation, place the
candies and cookies in
decorative cups on an
antique-looking doily. To
antique a gold-paper doily,
dip a cotton swab into
acetone (fingernail polish
remover). Then rub the
cotton swab over some of
the embossed areas on
the doily for a silver-and-
gold look.

PER COOKIE
27 CALORIES
1 g PROTEIN
3 g CARBOHYDRATES
1 g TOTAL FAT
0 g SATURATED FAT
4 mg CHOLESTEROL
13 mg SODIUM

Almond Macaroons

6 *ounces almond paste (¾ cup)**
½ *cup sugar*
1 *egg white*
1 *tablespoon water*
2 *ounces semisweet* **or** *bittersweet chocolate, chopped*

SPECIAL TOUCH
▼ ▼ ▼

Celebrate May Day or the first day of spring with a splash of pastel color on these dainty cookies. Instead of drizzling with melted chocolate, drizzle melted pink, yellow, or green vanilla-flavored candy coating over the tops.

Line a cookie sheet with parchment paper, plain brown paper, or foil. Grease the paper or foil. Set cookie sheet aside.

Crumble almond paste in a large mixing bowl. Add sugar, egg white, and water. Beat with an electric mixer on medium speed till throughly combined, scraping the sides of the mixing bowl occasionally.

Spoon almond mixture into a decorating bag fitted with a large round or star tip (about ½-inch opening). Pipe 1¼-inch-wide mounds 2 inches apart onto the prepared cookie sheet. Bake in a 325° oven for 10 to 15 minutes or till edges are lightly browned. Completely cool cookies on cookie sheet; then peel the cookies from paper or foil.

Melt chocolate according to the directions on page 225. Drizzle melted chocolate over cookies. Let cookies stand till chocolate is dry. Makes about 40 to 50.

*Almond paste containing corn syrup or fructose may result in a product softer than expected.

PER COOKIE
36 CALORIES
1 g PROTEIN
5 g CARBOHYDRATES
2 g TOTAL FAT
0 g SATURATED FAT
0 mg CHOLESTEROL
2 mg SODIUM

Meringue Gems and Kisses

½ cup *margarine* or *butter*

1¼ cups *all-purpose flour*

½ cup *sugar*

1 tablespoon *milk*

½ teaspoon *vanilla*

2 *egg whites*

½ teaspoon *vanilla*

¼ teaspoon *cream of tartar*

½ cup *sugar*

⅓ cup *desired preserves (such as apricot, cherry, peach, pineapple, red raspberry, or strawberry) or jelly (such as crab apple, currant, mint-flavored apple, or plum)*

12 *pastel cream mint kisses* or *chocolate kisses*
Desired colored sugars or *powdered sugar mixed with desired powdered food coloring (see page 221)*

For cookie dough, in a medium mixing bowl beat margarine or butter with an electric mixer on medium to high speed about 30 seconds or till softened.

Add about *half* of the flour, the ½ cup sugar, milk, and ½ teaspoon vanilla. Beat till thoroughly combined, scraping sides of bowl occasionally. Then beat or stir in the remaining flour. Shape dough into an 8-inch roll. Wrap in waxed paper or plastic wrap. Then chill in the refrigerator for 4 to 48 hours or in the freezer for 1 to 4 hours or till firm enough to slice.

For meringue, in a small mixing bowl beat egg whites, ½ teaspoon vanilla, and cream of tartar with an electric mixer on medium to high speed till soft peaks form (tips curl). Gradually add ½ cup sugar, *1 tablespoon* at a

time, beating on high speed about 7 minutes or till very stiff peaks form (tips stand straight) and sugar is *almost* dissolved. Spoon meringue mixture into a decorating bag fitted with a medium star tip (about ¼-inch opening).

For Meringue Gems, cut cookie dough into ¼-inch-thick slices. Place 1 inch apart on an ungreased cookie sheet. Pipe some of the meringue in stars or in a line around the outside edge of each cookie to form a border. Spoon about *½ teaspoon* of preserves or jelly into the center of *each* cookie. Bake in a 325° oven for 20 to 22 minutes or till meringue just starts to brown. Cool on cookie sheet for 1 minute. Then remove cookies and cool on a wire rack.
Per Cookie: 74 calories, 1 g protein, 11 g carbohydrate, 3 g total fat, 0 g saturated, 0 mg cholesterol, and 38 mg sodium.

For Meringue Kisses, meanwhile, lightly grease a cookie sheet. On the prepared cookie sheet, pipe *some* of the remaining meringue into 12 rounds, each about 1¼ inches in diameter and ½ inch thick. Lightly press a mint or chocolate kiss into each meringue round. Then pipe meringue around each candy in concentric circles, starting at the base and working toward the top, till the candy is completely covered. Sprinkle with colored sugar or tinted powdered sugar. Bake in the 325° oven for 20 to 25 minutes or till edges are lightly browned. *Immediately,* remove meringue kisses and cool on a wire rack. Makes 30 gems and 12 kisses.
Per Cookie: 43 calories, 1 g protein, 8 g carbohydrate, 1 g total fat, 0 g saturated fat, 1 mg cholesterol, and 9 mg sodium.

SPECIAL TOUCH
▼ ▼ ▼
With one recipe, you can make two cookies—kisses and gems. Look for the pastel cream mint kisses at department store candy counters and candy or food gift shops.

Strawberries la Crème Fraîche

18 *large* **or** *24 medium strawberries* **or** *24 large Medjool dates*
1 *8-ounce package cream cheese, softened*
¼ *cup sifted powdered sugar*
½ *cup Crème Fraîche (see recipe, page 208)*
1 *tablespoon finely crushed Glazed Nuts (see recipe, page 216)* **or** *finely chopped toasted almonds*

If using strawberries, gently wash the berries and remove the hulls. Then pat completely dry with paper towels. Place strawberries stem ends down. Cut each from the top to, *but not through,* the stem end. Repeat to cut each strawberry into 4 wedges. Slightly spread wedges apart. Set strawberries aside. If using dates, cut a lengthwise slit in each date. Remove pits. Slightly spread each date apart. Set dates aside.

For filling, in a small mixing bowl beat cream cheese and powdered sugar with an electric mixer on medium to high speed till combined. Fold in ¼ *cup* of the Crème Fraîche. (Store the remaining Crème Fraîche, covered, in the refrigerator for up to 1 week; serve over fresh fruit.)

Spoon the filling into a decorating bag fitted with a medium star or round tip (about ¼-inch opening). Pipe filling into each strawberry or date. Sprinkle tops with crushed Glazed Nuts or finely chopped almonds. Chill in the refrigerator till serving time or for up to 2 hours. Makes 18 or 24.

SPECIAL TOUCH
▼ ▼ ▼

Small and luscious, these dessert berries make a tasty and pretty complement to any dessert sampler tray. Or, if you would like to serve the berries on their own, stencil a design on each small dessert plate before adding the berries. To create the design, sift cocoa powder or powdered sugar mixed with red powdered food coloring through a doily.

Pictured on page 92

PER FRUIT
65 CALORIES
1 g PROTEIN
3 g CARBOHYDRATES
6 g TOTAL FAT
3 g SATURATED FAT
17 mg CHOLESTEROL
40 mg SODIUM

Chocolate-Framboise Cups

1 *recipe for 4 Praline Baskets* (**see page 216**)
1 *recipe for 2 cups Chocolate Buttercream (see page 211)*
1 *tablespoon Framboise Liqueur, raspberry liqueur,* **or** *½ teaspoon raspberry flavoring*
1 *cup Sweetened Whipped Cream (see recipe, page 210)*
   Fresh raspberries
   Raspberry Sauce **or** *Bittersweet Chocolate Sauce (see recipes, pages 213* **and** *212) (optional)*

For small Praline Baskets, line a large cookie sheet with parchment paper or *heavy* foil. *(Do not use plain brown paper.)* If using foil, grease it.* Grease the outside bases of 3 inverted juice glasses, using glasses that are about 1½ inches in diameter at base. Set baking sheet and glasses aside.

Prepare batter for 4 Praline Baskets as directed. For *each* cookie basket, drop *2 teaspoons* of batter 3 inches apart on the prepared cookie sheet. Spread batter to 1-inch circles. (Bake only 3 cookies at a time.) Bake in a 350° oven about 8 minutes or till cookies are deep golden brown. Cool on cookie sheet about 1 minute or just till cookies are firm enough to hold their shape. Quickly remove cookies from cookie sheet, one at a time. Shape the cookies over the prepared inverted glasses using the handle of a wooden spoon to form ruffles or pleats. (If cookies harden before you can shape them, reheat them in the oven about 1 minute or till softened.) Cool cookie baskets on the inverted glasses. Then remove cookie baskets from glasses and set aside.

For filling, prepare the Chocolate Buttercream as directed, *except* use the Framboise Liqueur or raspberry flavoring as the desired liqueur. *Do not chill* the Chocolate Buttercream.

Fold in *½ cup* of the Sweetened Whipped Cream into *1 cup* of the Chocolate Buttercream. (Store remaining Chocolate Buttercream, covered, in the refrigerator for up to 1 week; use as a filling or frosting on your favorite cake or cutout cookies.) Spoon chocolate filling into a decorating bag fitted with a large round tip (about ½-inch opening). Pipe or spoon the filling into the small Praline Baskets.

Spoon remaining Sweetened Whipped Cream into another decorating bag fitted with a large star tip (about ½-inch opening). Pipe or dollop cream on top of each dessert. Garnish with fresh raspberries. If desired, serve with Raspberry Sauce or Bittersweet Chocolate Sauce. Makes 12 servings.

*Cookies will spread more on the greased *heavy* foil than on the parchment paper.

SPECIAL TOUCH
▼ ▼ ▼

Make a final impression with your dinner guests by serving a spectacular-looking dessert. Spoon a small amount of Raspberry Sauce or Bittersweet Chocolate Sauce onto each dessert plate. Then place a Chocolate-Framboise Cup on top of the sauce. Also, if you like, spoon some of the sauce into a squeeze bottle and squirt the sauce over each dessert in a decorative pattern.

PER SERVING
294 CALORIES
2 g PROTEIN
13 g CARBOHYDRATES
27 g TOTAL FAT
14 g SATURATED FAT
131 mg CHOLESTEROL
10 mg SODIUM

So light and delicate, these *Caramel-Apple Cheesecake Tartlets* are the perfect finale for a light summer meal or a late night get-together.

Caramel-Apple Cheesecake Tartlets

Nut Sweet-Tart Pastry
    (see recipe, page 206)
1 *8-ounce package cream cheese, softened*
1/3 *cup sugar*
2 *teaspoons all-purpose flour*
1 *teaspoon vanilla*
1 *egg*
1 *tablespoon apple brandy, apple*
    schnapps, **or** *apple juice*
1/2 *cup water*
2 *tablespoons sugar*
2 *small apples, cored and very thinly*
    sliced (2 cups)
1 *cup Caramel Sauce (see recipe,*
    page 213)
6 *large Caramel Filigree Garnishes (see*
    recipe, page 217) (optional)

For pastry shells, on a lightly floured surface, use your hands to slightly flatten the Nut Sweet-Tart Pastry dough. Roll dough from center to edges to slightly less than ¼-inch thickness. Cut dough into six 5-inch circles. Carefully line 2½-inch muffin cups or 3-inch fluted tartlet pans. Trim pastry to edges of muffin cups or tartlet pans. Using the tines of a fork, prick bottoms of pastry. If using tartlet pans, place pans on a baking sheet. Bake in a 375° oven for 8 to 12 minutes or just till pastry begins to brown.

Meanwhile, for filling, in a medium mixing bowl beat cream cheese, ⅓ cup sugar, flour, and vanilla with an electric mixer on medium to high speed till combined. Add egg. Beat on low speed *just till combined*. Stir in apple brandy, schnapps, or juice.

Spoon filling into the pastry-lined muffin cups or tartlet pans. Bake in a 375° oven for 20 to 25 minutes or till the centers appear *nearly* set when shaken.

Remove tartlet pans from baking sheet. Cool cheesecakes in muffin cups or tartlet pans on a wire rack for 15 minutes. Carefully, remove cheesecakes from muffin cups or tartlet pans and cool completely. Then chill cheesecakes in the refrigerator for at least 2 hours before serving.

Before serving, in a medium saucepan combine water, 2 tablespoons sugar, and apple slices. Heat to boiling, then reduce heat. Cover and simmer about 5 minutes or till apples are tender. Drain well.

To serve, spoon about *1 tablespoon* Caramel Sauce on top of *each* cheesecake. (Store remaining Caramel Sauce, covered, in the refrigerator for up to 2 weeks; serve over ice cream or pound cake.) Arrange apple slices in an overlapping, spiral pattern on top of each cheesecake working from the outside edge towards the center and curving the outer edges of apple slices to resemble the petals of a rose. If desired, place a caramel filigree on each dessert plate, then place a cheesecake tartlet on top. Makes 6.

SPECIAL TOUCH
▼ ▼ ▼
The thin, poached apple slices are artfully arranged to create pretty, flowerlike garnishes. To make these tiny tarts even sweeter looking, add an edible apple blossom to the center of each apple flower.

PER TARTLET
840 CALORIES
10 g PROTEIN
95 g CARBOHYDRATES
48 g TOTAL FAT
26 g SATURATED FAT
226 mg CHOLESTEROL
325 mg SODIUM

Double-Dipped Fruits

SPECIAL TOUCH
▼ ▼ ▼
So simple to make, yet so
exquisite to serve. Arrange
the Double-Dipped Fruits
in a chocolate lace dish and
accompany with cabernet
sauvignon.

Pictured on page 92

2 *to 3 cups medium strawberries,
maraschino cherries with stems, dried
apricots,* **or** *candied pineapple
wedges*
4 *ounces white baking bar, chopped*
1 *tablespoon shortening*
4 *ounces semisweet* **or** *bittersweet
chocolate, chopped*
1 *tablespoon shortening*

If using strawberries, gently wash the berries
and leave stems and hulls attached. Then pat
completely dry with paper towels. If using
maraschino cherries, drain and pat the
cherries completely dry with paper towels.
Set the fruit aside.

Melt the white baking bar with 1 tablespoon
shortening according to directions on page
225. If necessary, to dip fruit, place 1 piece
of fruit on the end of a wooden skewer. Dip
half of each piece of fruit diagonally into the
melted white baking bar. Allow excess to
drip off, then place fruit on waxed paper. Let
stand till dry.

Meanwhile, quick-temper the chocolate with
1 tablespoon shortening according to the
directions on page 226. Dip half of each
piece of fruit diagonally into the melted
chocolate. Allow the excess chocolate to drip
off, then place the fruit on waxed paper. Let
stand till dry. Serve the fruit the same day it
is dipped. Makes about 1½ pounds
or 24 servings.

PER SERVING
61 CALORIES
1 g PROTEIN
7 g CARBOHYDRATES
4 g TOTAL FAT
1 g SATURATED FAT
0 mg CHOLESTEROL
4 mg SODIUM

Almond Mints

4 ounces (⅔ cup) semisweet mint-flavored
   chocolate pieces
4 ounces semisweet or bittersweet
   chocolate, chopped
5 teaspoons shortening
8 ounces (1¼ cups) blanched whole
   almonds or hazelnuts (filberts),
   toasted
¼ cup unsweetened cocoa powder or
   ¼ cup sifted powdered sugar plus
   2 teaspoons unsweetened cocoa
   powder

Combine mint-flavored chocolate pieces and semisweet or bittersweet chocolate. Quick-temper chocolate with shortening according to the directions on page 226.

To dip nuts, drop several almonds or hazelnuts at a time into the chocolate mixture. Using a fork, lift individual nuts out of the chocolate mixture. Allow excess chocolate mixture to drip off, then place nuts on waxed paper. Let stand till dry.

Toss the chocolate-covered nuts in the cocoa powder or in a mixture of powdered sugar and cocoa powder till coated. Makes about 1 pound or 20 servings.

SPECIAL TOUCH
▼ ▼ ▼
You need to follow only one rule for clever, extra-special presentations—let your imagination go! Place these chocolate-covered almonds in a shallow brass candy dish. Then sprinkle edible flower petals on top.

PER SERVING
268 CALORIES
6 g PROTEIN
20 g CARBOHYDRATES
21 g TOTAL FAT
2 g SATURATED FAT
0 mg CHOLESTEROL
3 mg SODIUM

Raspberry Creams

SPECIAL TOUCH

▼ ▼ ▼

Celebrate Easter with tiny raspberry-filled eggs. After covering a raspberry with the candy mixture, shape the candy into an oval. You may need to use slightly more than a teaspoon of candy mixture for each berry. Then dip the candy into pastel vanilla-flavored candy coating melted with the shortening. After the candy is dry, pipe dots or zigzags on each with a contrasting color of melted vanilla-flavored candy coating.

2 *tablespoons margarine* or *butter, melted*
2 *tablespoons light corn syrup*
1⅓ *cups sifted powdered sugar*
20 *to 30 firm raspberries*
6 *ounces semisweet* or *bittersweet chocolate* or *white baking bar, chopped**
1 *tablespoon shortening*

For candy centers, in a small mixing bowl stir together melted margarine or butter and corn syrup; stir in powdered sugar till smooth. If necessary, cover and chill candy mixture in the refrigerator about 20 minutes or till easy to handle.

Shape candy mixture into balls, using about *1 teaspoon* for each ball. Then flatten each ball to about 2 inches in diameter and shape the candy around a raspberry.

If using semisweet or bittersweet chocolate, quick-temper the chocolate with shortening according to the directions on page 226. If using the white baking bar, melt the white baking bar with shortening according to the directions on page 225.

Dip candy centers into the melted mixture. Allow excess to drip off, then place candy on waxed paper. Let stand till dry. Tightly cover the candy and store in a cool, dry place for up to 5 days. Makes about 20 pieces.

*For a marbledlike coating on candy, quick-temper 6 ounces chopped *semisweet* or *bittersweet chocolate* with 2 tablespoons *shortening* according to directions on page 226. In another container melt 6 ounces chopped *white baking bar* with 2 tablespoons *shortening* according to the directions on page 225.

If desired, to dip candy centers, wear tight-fitting disposable gloves. Use one hand to dip a candy center into the white baking bar mixture. With a small amount of the chocolate mixture on the fingers of your *other* hand, transfer the coated ball to that hand. Then roll the ball off your hand onto waxed paper. (You will get a marbled effect from transferring the candy from one hand to the other hand.) Repeat with remaining candy centers. Let stand till dry. Store as above.

Per Candy: Same as main recipe, except 151 calories, 19 g carbohydrate, 9 g total fat, 2 g saturated fat, and 23 mg sodium.

PER CANDY
89 CALORIES
1 g PROTEIN
13 g CARBOHYDRATES
4 g TOTAL FAT
0 g SATURATED FAT
0 mg CHOLESTEROL
15 mg SODIUM

Honey-Macadamia Nut Fudge

Margarine or butter
1½ cups sugar
1 cup packed brown sugar
⅓ cup half-and-half or light cream
⅓ cup milk
2 tablespoons honey
2 tablespoons margarine or butter
1 teaspoon vanilla
½ cup macadamia nuts, hazelnuts
    (filberts), or pecans, toasted and
    chopped
36 chocolate-dipped macadamia nuts,
    hazelnuts (filberts), or pecans
    (optional)

Line an 8x8x2-inch baking pan with foil, extending foil over edges of the pan. Grease foil with margarine or butter; set aside.

Grease the sides of a heavy 2-quart saucepan with margarine or butter. In the saucepan combine the sugar, brown sugar, half-and-half or light cream, milk, and honey. Cook over medium-high heat to boiling, stirring constantly with a wooden spoon to dissolve sugars. This should take about 5 minutes. Avoid splashing mixture on sides of the pan. Carefully clip a candy thermometer to the side of the saucepan.

Cook over medium-low heat, stirring frequently, till thermometer registers 236°, soft-ball stage. Mixture should boil at a moderate, steady rate over the entire surface. Reaching soft-ball stage should take 15 to 20 minutes. Remove saucepan from heat. Add the 2 tablespoons margarine or butter and vanilla, but *do not stir.* Cool, without stirring, to lukewarm (110°). This should take about 50 minutes.

Remove candy thermometer from saucepan. Beat vigorously with the wooden spoon till fudge is *just beginning to thicken.* Add chopped nuts. Continue beating till very thick and just starts to lose its gloss. This should take about 10 minutes total.

Quickly turn mixture into the prepared pan. While fudge is warm, score it into 1¼-inch squares. If desired, press a chocolate-dipped nut into each square. When candy is firm, use foil to lift it out of the pan; cut it into squares. Tightly cover the fudge and store in a cool, dry place. Makes about 1½ pounds or 36 pieces.

SPECIAL TOUCH
▼ ▼ ▼

Good things come in small packages. For a fun candy gift, wrap each piece of fudge in a square of colored foil. Then tie a fine ribbon on each so the piece of candy looks like a little package.

PER CANDY
80 CALORIES
0 g PROTEIN
15 g CARBOHYDRATES
2 g TOTAL FAT
1 g SATURATED FAT
1 mg CHOLESTEROL
13 mg SODIUM

Marzipan Treasures

1 *8-ounce can almond paste**
¼ *cup butter, softened*
1 *cup sifted powdered sugar*
1 *tablespoon amaretto, rum, orange liqueur,* or *orange juice*
2 *teaspoons light corn syrup*
2¼ *to 3 cups sifted powdered sugar*
  Food coloring (optional)**
  Sugar (optional)

For marzipan, crumble almond paste in a medium mixing bowl. Add butter. Beat with an electric mixer on medium speed till combined. Then add the 1 cup powdered sugar, liqueur or orange juice, and corn syrup. Beat till thoroughly combined. Shape mixture into a ball. Knead in the 2¼ to 3 cups powdered sugar till mixture is firm enough to hold its shape.

If desired, to tint marzipan, divide marzipan into smaller portions. (Use 1 portion for each color.) Add enough food coloring to each portion to make desired color. Shape marzipan into desired shapes. *Or,* wrap each portion of marzipan separately in plastic wrap or foil and refrigerate till ready to shape or for up to 1 week.

For heart shapes, chill pink and/or plain marzipan for at least 1 hour before shaping. To shape, press the marzipan into heart-shaped candy molds. (If desired, knead pink and plain marzipan together to form a marbled effect.) To remove marzipan from molds, tap edge of mold against a hard surface. If needed, use a toothpick to gently pry hearts from molds. *Or,* to omit the chilling step, roll pieces of marzipan in sugar, then mold. (The sugar will help keep the marzipan from sticking to the mold.)

For strawberry shapes, roll red marzipan into strawberry shapes (ovals with one end tapering to a point). With a toothpick, prick holes all over each berry to resemble seeds. For strawberry tops, flatten a small amount of green marzipan to about ¼-inch thickness. Using a small knife cut out strawberry tops. Attach a top to the wide end of each strawberry.

For apricot shapes, roll orange marzipan into balls. Press ends to slightly flatten for top and bottom of apricots. With the blunt edge of a knife make a vertical dent, from top to bottom, on rounded side of each ball. Use green marzipan to make stems. Attach a stem to the top of each ball, pressing gently to make it stick.

Cover and refrigerate marzipan for up to 7 days to store. Makes about 70 pieces.

*Almond paste containing corn syrup or fructose may result in a product softer than expected.

** For marzipan richer in color, use food coloring in paste form instead of the liquid form to tint the marzipan.

Sweet Occasions

Strike up the band for these celebration-made desserts.
You'll find all kinds of desserts that are special enough
to turn even an ordinary day into a festive occasion.
Look for sure pleasers to serve for holiday affairs,
afternoon teas, birthday parties, and romantic dinners.
So, whenever you're in need of fancy fare, turn the
page and select from specialties such as Ribbon-of-
Cranberry Cheesecake, Brown Butter Tart with
Raspberries, or Sherry-Almond Sponge Cake.

▼ ▼ ▼

Brown Butter Tart with Raspberries

Sweet-Tart Pastry (see recipe,
    page 206)
   3 *eggs*
1¼ *cups sugar*
   ½ *cup all-purpose flour*
   1 *vanilla bean, split lengthwise* **or**
       1 teaspoon vanilla
   ¾ *cup butter*
   2 *cups raspberries* **or** *blackberries**
   2 *tablespoons currant jelly*

For pastry shell, on a lightly floured surface, use your hands to slightly flatten the Sweet-Tart Pastry dough. Roll dough from center to edges, forming a 12-inch circle. Wrap pastry around the rolling pin. Then unroll pastry onto a 10-inch tart pan with a removable bottom. Ease pastry into tart pan, being careful not to stretch it. Press pastry into the fluted sides of tart pan and trim edges. Set unbaked pastry shell aside.

In a large mixing bowl use a rotary beater or a wire whisk to lightly beat eggs *just till mixed.* Then stir in sugar, flour and, if using, liquid vanilla. Set egg mixture aside.

In a heavy medium saucepan combine the butter and, if using, vanilla bean. Cook over medium-high heat till the butter turns the color of light brown sugar. Remove from heat. Remove and discard the vanilla bean. Slowly add the browned butter to the egg mixture, stirring till mixed. Pour into the unbaked pastry shell.

Bake in a 350° oven about 35 minutes or till the top is crisp and golden brown. Cool completely in pan on a wire rack.

To serve, remove sides of the tart pan. Arrange fruit on top of the tart. In a small saucepan heat currant jelly till melted. Brush melted jelly over the fruit. Makes 8 servings.

*To substitute nectarines or plums for the berries, pit and thinly slice 2 medium *nectarines* or 4 medium *plums*. Place fruit slices in an 8-inch skillet; add enough *water* just to cover and 2 tablespoons *sugar*. Bring mixture to boiling. Reduce heat and simmer, covered, about 4 minutes or just till fruit is tender. Using a slotted spoon, remove fruit and place on paper towels. Arrange the drained fruit in a decorative pattern on top of tart. Then brush with melted jelly.

SPECIAL TOUCH
▼ ▼ ▼
Spruce up this mouth-watering-good tart with some frosted raspberries or blackberries and a fresh mint leaf or two placed alongside each piece. To frost the berries, lightly mist them with water. Then, sprinkle the berries with sugar.

PER SERVING
553 CALORIES
6 g PROTEIN
62 g CARBOHYDRATES
32 g TOTAL FAT
19 g SATURATED FAT
211 mg CHOLESTEROL
320 mg SODIUM

Crème Brûlée Tart

1¼ cups all-purpose flour
½ teaspoon ground ginger
¼ teaspoon salt
¼ teaspoon ground cinnamon
⅛ teaspoon ground nutmeg
⅓ cup shortening
3 to 4 tablespoons water
3 eggs
⅓ cup sugar
1 teaspoon vanilla
1¼ cups half-and-half, light cream, or milk
¼ cup packed brown sugar

For pastry, in a medium mixing bowl stir together the flour, ginger, salt, cinnamon, and nutmeg. Cut in shortening till pieces are the size of small peas.

Sprinkle *1 tablespoon* of the water over part of the mixture, then gently toss with a fork. Push moistened dough to the side of the bowl. Repeat, using 1 tablespoon of water at a time, till all of the dough is moistened. Form dough into a ball.

On a lightly floured surface, use your hands to slightly flatten dough. Roll dough from center to edges, forming an 11-inch circle.

Wrap pastry around the rolling pin. Then unroll onto a 9-inch tart pan. Ease pastry into tart pan, being careful not to stretch it. Press pastry into the fluted sides of tart pan and trim edges. *Do not prick pastry.* Line pastry shell in tart pan with a double thickness of foil. Bake in a 450° oven for 10 minutes.

Meanwhile, for filling, in a large mixing bowl use a rotary beater or wire whisk to lightly beat eggs *just till mixed.* Stir in sugar and vanilla. Gradually stir in the half-and-half, light cream, or milk.

Remove foil from pastry shell. With the partially baked pastry shell on the oven rack, pour the filling into the pastry shell. Reduce oven temperature to 350°. Bake for 25 to 35 minutes or till a knife inserted near the center comes out clean. Cool completely in pan on a wire rack. Cover and chill in the refrigerator for 2 to 24 hours before serving.

Just before serving, press brown sugar through a sieve evenly over the custard filling. Broil 4 to 5 inches from the heat for 1 to 2 minutes or till brown sugar melts and forms a bubbly crust. Serves 8 to 12.

PER SERVING
278 CALORIES
5 g PROTEIN
31 g CARBOHYDRATES
15 g TOTAL FAT
5 g SATURATED FAT
94 mg CHOLESTEROL
108 mg SODIUM

Coconut-Rum Christmas Pie

Flaky Pie Pastry For a Single Crust
(see recipe, page 205)
1 *recipe for ½ cup Chocolate Glaze (see*
page 211)
1½ *teaspoons rum*
2 *tablespoons cold water*
1 *teaspoon unflavored gelatin*
1 *cup whipping cream*
8 *egg yolks*
½ *cup sugar*
2 *tablespoons rum*
1 *cup whipping cream*
¾ *cup coconut*
2 *cups Sweetened Whipped Cream*
(see recipe, page 210)
¼ *cup coconut, toasted*

Chill a small mixing bowl and the beaters of
an electric mixer in the refrigerator.

Meanwhile, for pastry shell, on a lightly
floured surface, use your hands to slightly
flatten Flaky Pie Pastry dough. Roll dough
from center to edges, forming a 12-inch
circle. Wrap pastry around the rolling pin.
Then unroll pastry onto a 9-inch pie plate.
Ease pastry into pie plate, being careful not
to stretch it.

Trim pastry to ½ inch beyond edge of pie
plate. Fold under extra pastry. Crimp edge.
Using the tines of a fork, prick bottom and
sides of pastry generously. Line pastry shell
with a double thickness of foil. Bake in a
450° oven for 8 minutes. Remove foil. Bake
for 5 to 6 minutes more or till golden. Cool
pastry on a wire rack.

Prepare Chocolate Glaze as directed, *except*
stir the 1½ teaspoons rum into the hot glaze.
Spread the glaze over the bottom of the
baked pastry shell; set aside.

In a custard cup or a 1-cup glass measuring
cup, stir together the cold water and gelatin
till mixed. Let stand for 5 minutes. Place the
custard cup or measuring cup in a saucepan
or skillet with 1 inch of *boiling water*. Cook
and stir about 1 minute or till the gelatin is
completely dissolved. Set aside.

For filling, in a medium saucepan heat 1 cup
whipping cream over medium heat till cream
starts to simmer. Remove from heat. In a
medium mixing bowl beat egg yolks and
sugar till well mixed. Gradually stir warm
cream into egg yolk mixture. Return all of
the mixture to the saucepan. Cook and stir
over low heat just till mixture begins to boil.
Remove from heat. Stir in gelatin mixture
and the 2 tablespoons rum. Transfer to a
medium bowl. Chill in the refrigerator about
30 minutes or till partially set (consistency of
corn syrup), stirring occasionally.

In the chilled bowl beat the 1 cup whipping
cream with chilled beaters on low speed till
soft peaks form. Fold the whipped cream and
¾ cup coconut into the custard mixture.
Pour filling over the chocolate in the baked
pastry shell. Cover and chill in the
refrigerator for 2 to 24 hours or till set.

Before serving, spread Sweetened Whipped
Cream evenly over the coconut filling.
Sprinkle with the toasted coconut. Serves 8.

Brandy Cream Napoleons

1 *portion Quick-Method Puff Pastry (see recipe, page 204) or ½ of a 17¼-ounce package (1 sheet) frozen puff pastry, thawed*
1 *recipe for 1 cup Pastry Cream (see page 209)*
1 *tablespoon brandy*
¼ *cup whipping cream*
  Brown Butter Icing

Line 2 baking sheets with parchment paper or plain brown paper; set aside.

If using Quick-Method Puff Pastry, cut the portion of dough in half *crosswise.* (Cover and return 1 piece of dough to the refrigerator and reserve for another use.) On a lightly floured surface, roll the remaining piece of dough into a 10-inch square. Using a sharp knife, trim off about ½ inch from all 4 sides to make a 9-inch square. *Or,* if using purchased puff pastry, unfold sheet and trim to a 9-inch square.

Cut pastry into nine 3-inch squares. Transfer pastry squares to the prepared baking sheets. Using the tines of a fork, prick pastry.

Bake in a 425° oven for 18 to 23 minutes or till golden. (*Or,* if using purchased puff pastry, bake according to package directions.) Carefully remove pastries from baking sheet and cool on a wire rack.

Meanwhile, prepare Pastry Cream as directed, *except* stir the brandy into the hot Pastry Cream. Cover surface with plastic wrap, then cool just till warm without stirring. In a small mixing bowl beat the whipping cream till soft peaks form. Fold the whipped cream into the warm Pastry Cream. Cover and chill in the refrigerator.

To assemble, using the tines of a fork, separate *each* pastry square horizontally into *three* layers. Spread about *1½ tablespoons* filling on *each* bottom layer. Top with middle pastry layers. Spread another *1½ tablespoons* of the filling on *each* middle pastry layer. Finally top with remaining pastry layers. Spread Brown Butter Icing on tops of pastries. Chill in the refrigerator till serving time or for up to 1 hour. Makes 9 servings.

Brown Butter Icing

In a small saucepan heat 2 tablespoons unsalted *butter* (not margarine) over medium heat about 3 minutes or till butter turns the color of light brown sugar. Remove from heat. Stir in 1 cup sifted *powdered sugar.* Then stir in 2 to 4 teaspoons *boiling water* till icing is smooth and of drizzling consistency. Makes about ⅓ cup.

SPECIAL TOUCH
▼ ▼ ▼
Dress up these splendid pastries by drizzling melted chocolate in a decorative pattern on top of the icing. Then serve them on paper-doily-lined dessert plates.

PER SERVING
443 CALORIES
5 g PROTEIN
39 g CARBOHYDRATES
30 g TOTAL FAT
18 g SATURATED FAT
128 mg CHOLESTEROL
374 mg SODIUM

▼ ▼ ▼
Buttery puff pastry, ultra-rich caramel sauce, fluffy whipped cream, and crushed toffee team to create *Caramel-and-Cream-Filled Puff Pastry,* a fabulous finale.

Caramel-and-Cream-Filled Puff Pastry

1 *recipe for 1 cup Pastry Cream (see page 209)*

1 *cup Caramel Sauce (see recipe, page 213)* **or** *½ cup caramel ice-cream topping*

1 *portion Quick-Method Puff Pastry (see recipe, page 204)* **or** *½ of a 17¼-ounce package (1 sheet) frozen puff pastry, thawed and unfolded*

1 *slightly beaten egg white*

2 *cups Sweetened Whipped-Cream Frosting (see recipe, page 210)*

1 *1.4-ounce bar chocolate-covered English toffee, crushed*

Line a baking sheet with parchment paper or plain brown paper; set aside. For filling, prepare Pastry Cream as directed, *except* fold in *2 tablespoons* of the Caramel Sauce or ice-cream topping. Then cover with plastic wrap and chill in the refrigerator.

If using Quick-Method Puff Pastry, cut the portion in half *crosswise.* (Cover and return 1 piece of dough to the refrigerator and reserve for another use.) On a lightly floured surface, roll remaining piece of dough or purchased puff pastry into a 10½-inch square. Then trim to a 10-inch square. Cut four 1-inch strips off 1 side, making a 10x6-inch rectangle. Set strips aside. Transfer pastry rectangle to the prepared baking sheet. Using the tines of a fork, prick pastry rectangle at 1-inch intervals, making definite holes in the pastry so you can see the baking sheet through the holes. Brush a 1-inch band of egg white around edges of rectangle.

Trim *two* of the reserved pastry strips to 6-inch lengths. Gently twist all strips several times. Place them within ¼ inch of the edges of the pastry rectangle to form a rim around the edges. Gently press to adhere to pastry rectangle. Moisten ends with egg white, then press together to seal.

Bake pastry shell in a 375° oven for 30 to 35 minutes or till golden. (*Or,* if using purchased pastry, bake in the 375° oven for 20 to 25 minutes or till golden.) If pastry is puffed in center, gently press to deflate. Carefully remove pastry from baking sheet and cool on a wire rack.

To assemble, transfer pastry shell to a serving plate. Spread the Pastry Cream mixture into the center of the pastry rectangle. Spoon Sweetened Whipped-Cream Frosting into a decorating bag fitted with a large star tip (about ½-inch opening). Pipe the cream frosting in a lattice pattern on top of the filling. Sprinkle with crushed English toffee. Chill in the refrigerator till serving time or for up to 4 hours.

To serve, drizzle *⅓ cup* of the Caramel Sauce or the remaining caramel topping over the top. (Store the remaining sauce, covered, in the refrigerator for up to 1 week; serve over ice cream.) Makes 6 to 8 servings.

PER SERVING
927 CALORIES
9 g PROTEIN
79 g CARBOHYDRATES
65 g TOTAL FAT
39 g SATURATED FAT
263 mg CHOLESTEROL
628 mg SODIUM

Peanut Butter Éclairs

SPECIAL TOUCH

▼ ▼ ▼

For a little pizzazz, drizzle the Peanut Butter Icing in zigzags or figure eights over the tops of the éclairs.

Cream-Puff Pastry (see recipe, page 205)
1 cup creamy peanut butter
2 3-ounce packages cream cheese
¼ cup whipping cream
1 cup sugar
1 teaspoon vanilla
¾ cup whipping cream
1 cup Chocolate Glaze (see recipe, page 211)
   Peanut Butter Icing

Chill a small mixing bowl of an electric mixer in the refrigerator. Meanwhile, grease a large baking sheet. Set baking sheet aside.

For éclairs, spoon the Cream-Puff Pastry dough into a decorating bag fitted with a large plain round tip (about ½-inch opening). Slowly pipe strips of dough 3 inches apart on the prepared baking sheet, making 12 éclairs, each about 4 inches long, 1¼ inch wide, and about ¾ inch high. Bake in a 400° oven for 30 to 35 minutes or till golden brown and puffy. Remove the éclairs and cool on a wire rack.

For filling, in a large mixing bowl beat peanut butter, cream cheese, sugar, ¼ cup whipping cream, and vanilla with an electric mixer on medium to high speed till combined. In the chilled bowl beat the ¾ cup whipping cream on low speed till soft peaks form. Fold about one-fourth of the whipped cream into the peanut butter mixture. Then fold in the remaining whipped cream. Set filling aside.

To assemble, horizontally cut off the tops of the éclairs. Remove any soft dough from the insides. Spoon about ⅓ cup of the filling into each éclair. Replace tops. Spoon the Chocolate Glaze over the top of éclairs. Drizzle with Peanut Butter Icing. Chill in the refrigerator till serving time or for up to 4 hours. Makes 12 servings.

Peanut Butter Icing

In a small saucepan melt 2 tablespoons creamy peanut butter and 1 tablespoon margarine or butter. Stir in ½ cup sifted powdered sugar. Then stir in 3 to 5 teaspoons milk till the icing is of drizzling consistency. Makes ⅓ cup.

PER SERVING
573 CALORIES
11 g PROTEIN
41 g CARBOHYDRATES
43 g FAT
15 g SATURATED FAT
133 mg CHOLESTEROL
336 mg SODIUM

White Bavarian Cream Cake

¼ *cup sugar*
1 *envelope unflavored gelatin*
1¼ *cups milk*
4 *ounces white baking bar or white vanilla-flavored candy coating, chopped*
4 *slightly beaten egg yolks*
⅓ *cup white crème de cacao*
1 *cup whipping cream*
2 *9-inch layers Génoise (see recipe, page 207)*
3 *cups Sweetened Whipped-Cream Frosting (see recipe, page 210)*
¼ *cup sliced almonds, toasted*

Chill a small mixing bowl and the beaters of an electric mixer in the refrigerator.

For filling, in heavy medium saucepan combine the sugar and gelatin. Stir in the milk. Cook and stir over medium heat till gelatin is dissolved. Add the baking bar or candy coating. Cook and stir till melted.

In a medium mixing bowl use a rotary beater or wire whisk to beat the egg yolks *just till mixed.* Gradually stir some of the gelatin mixture into the egg yolks. Then return all of the mixture to the saucepan. Cook and stir for 2 minutes more or till thickened and bubbly. Stir in crème de cacao. Chill in the refrigerator for 1½ to 2 hours or till mixture is partially set (consistency of corn syrup), stirring occasionally.

In the chilled bowl beat whipping cream with chilled beaters on low speed till soft peaks form. Fold the whipped cream into the partially set gelatin mixture. Then chill the gelatin mixture in the refrigerator till mixture mounds when spooned.

To assemble, place 1 Génoise layer in a 9-inch springform pan. Spread with gelatin mixture. Top with the remaining Génoise layer. Cover and chill in the refrigerator for 4 to 24 hours before serving.

Just before serving, use a thin metal spatula or knife to loosen cake from sides of pan. Remove sides of the springform pan. Spread sides and top of cake with Sweetened Whipped-Cream Frosting. Then sprinkle with toasted almonds. Cover and refrigerate to store. Makes 12 servings.

SPECIAL TOUCH
▼ ▼ ▼
If you'd like to add more color to this luscious cake, serve it with a variety of fresh berries.

PER SERVING
534 CALORIES
9 g PROTEIN
43 g CARBOHYDRATES
35 g TOTAL FAT
20 g SATURATED FAT
268 mg CHOLESTEROL
77 mg SODIUM

Cranberry and White Cake

2½ cups all-purpose flour
2 cups sugar
2 teaspoons baking powder
¼ teaspoon salt
1⅓ cups milk
½ cup margarine **or** butter, softened
1 teaspoon grated orange peel
4 egg whites
  Cranberry Filling
4 cups Sweetened Whipped-Cream Frosting (see recipe, page 210)

Grease and lightly flour two 8x1½-inch or 9x1½-inch round baking pans; set aside.

In a large mixing bowl stir together flour, sugar, baking powder, and salt. Add milk, margarine or butter, and grated orange peel. Beat with an electric mixer on low to medium speed about 30 seconds or till combined. Then beat on medium to high speed for 2 minutes, scraping sides of bowl occasionally. Add egg whites and beat for 2 minutes more, scraping bowl.

Pour batter into the prepared pans. Bake in a 350° oven for 30 to 35 minutes or till a wooden toothpick inserted near centers of the cakes comes out clean. Cool cakes in pans on wire racks for 10 minutes. Then remove cakes; cool completely on the racks.

To assemble, cut *each* cake horizontally into *two* even layers. Place first cake layer on a large serving plate. Spread with *half* of the Cranberry Filling. Top with second cake layer, then spread with ½ cup of the Sweetened Whipped-Cream Frosting. Top with third cake layer, then spread with remaining Cranberry Filling. Finally, top with the remaining cake layer and spread sides and top of the cake with remaining Sweetened Whipped-Cream Frosting. Cover and refrigerate to store. Makes 12 servings.

Cranberry Filling

In a medium saucepan combine 1 cup *sugar* and ½ cup *orange juice.* Bring to boiling, stirring to dissolve sugar. Boil rapidly for 5 minutes. Add 2 cups *cranberries.* Return to boiling; reduce heat. Boil gently over medium-high heat for 3 to 4 minutes or till cranberries pop, stirring occasionally. Remove from heat.

Place cranberry mixture in a blender container or food processor bowl. Cover and blend or process till nearly smooth. Stir in ¾ cup chopped *pecans* or *walnuts.* Cover surface with plastic wrap. Refrigerate till thoroughly chilled. Makes about 2 cups.

Orange-Laced Carrot Cake

2 cups all-purpose flour

2 cups sugar

1 teaspoon baking powder

1 teaspoon baking soda

1 teaspoon ground cinnamon

3 cups finely shredded carrot

1 cup cooking oil

4 eggs

2 teaspoons finely shredded orange peel
Orange Cream Cheese Frosting

⅓ cup orange marmalade

Grease and lightly flour two 9x1½-inch round baking pans. Set pans aside.

In a large mixing bowl stir together the flour, sugar, baking powder, baking soda, and cinnamon. Add carrot, oil, eggs, and orange peel. Beat with an electric mixer on low to medium speed about 30 seconds or till combined.

Spread batter in the prepared pans. Bake in a 350° oven for 30 to 35 minutes or till a wooden toothpick inserted near the centers of the cakes comes out clean. Cool cakes in pans on wire racks for 10 minutes. Then remove cakes; cool completely on the racks.

To assemble, place first cake layer on a large serving plate. Spread with some of the Orange Cream Cheese Frosting. Top with the remaining cake layer. Spread orange marmalade over top. Frost the sides of the cake with some more of the frosting. Spoon the remaining frosting into a decorating bag fitted with a small star tip (about ¼-inch opening). Pipe a lattice design on top of the cake. Then pipe a shell border around the upper edge. Makes 12 servings.

Orange Cream Cheese Frosting

In a large mixing bowl beat one 8-ounce package *cream cheese,* ½ cup *margarine* or *butter,* and 2 teaspoons finely shredded *orange peel* with an electric mixer on medium to high speed till light and fluffy. Gradually add 2½ cups sifted *powdered sugar,* beating well. Gradually beat in 2¼ to 2½ cups additional sifted *powdered sugar* to make the frosting of a spreading consistency. Makes about 3 cups.

SPECIAL TOUCH
▼ ▼ ▼

A cake you can make just as fancy as you like. Leave it plain or press chopped pecans into the frosting on the sides of the cake. Then pipe an elegant lattice pattern on top.

PER SERVING
704 CALORIES
6 g PROTEIN
97 g CARBOHYDRATES
35 g TOTAL FAT
8 g SATURATED FAT
92 mg CHOLESTEROL
274 mg SODIUM

▼ ▼ ▼

Sherry-Almond Sponge Cake is a sweet sensation your guests will long remember. Raspberry preserves nestle between nutty cake layers and sherry-flavored whipped cream encases the entire creation.

Sherry-Almond Sponge Cake

4 egg yolks

⅓ cup dry or cream sherry

⅔ cup sugar

⅔ cup all-purpose flour

¼ cup ground toasted almonds

4 egg whites

½ teaspoon cream of tartar

⅓ cup sugar

3 tablespoons red raspberry or
   strawberry preserves

1 cup whipping cream

1 tablespoon sugar

1 tablespoon dry or cream sherry

1 recipe for Marzipan Treasures (see page
   104) or 1 pound purchased
   marzipan
   Assortment of edible flowers or
      bouquet of flowers (see Special Touch
      at right)

Chill a small mixing bowl in the refrigerator. Meanwhile, in a medium mixing bowl beat egg yolks with an electric mixer on high speed about 6 minutes or till yolks are thick and lemon-colored. Add ⅓ cup sherry. Then beat on low speed till combined. Gradually add ⅔ cup sugar, beating on medium speed about 5 minutes or till sugar is *almost* dissolved and mixture has almost doubled in volume. Fold flour into egg yolk mixture about *half* at a time. Then, fold in the ground almonds.

Thoroughly wash beaters. In a large mixing bowl beat egg whites and cream of tartar on medium to high speed till soft peaks form (tips curl). Gradually add ⅓ cup sugar, about *1 tablespoon* at a time, beating on medium to high speed till stiff peaks form (tips stand straight).

Fold about *1 cup* of the egg white mixture into the egg yolk mixture. Then fold all of the egg yolk mixture into the remaining egg white mixture. Pour batter into 2 ungreased 8x1½-inch round baking pans. Bake in a 325° oven about 25 minutes or till the cake tops spring back when lightly touched in the center.

Immediately invert cakes in pans on wire racks. Cool cakes in pans for 5 minutes. Loosen sides of cakes from pans; remove cakes from pans. Cool cakes completely on wire racks.

Meanwhile, if using, prepare Marzipan Treasures as directed, *except* do not tint or shape. Roll homemade or purchased marzipan to an 8-inch circle as directed for sheets (see page 232). Trim marzipan to make an even circle; set aside.

To assemble, place first cake layer on a large serving plate. Spread with the raspberry or strawberry preserves. Top with the remaining cake layer.

In the chilled bowl combine whipping cream, 1 tablespoon sugar, and 1 tablespoon sherry. Beat on low speed till soft peaks form. Frost the sides of the cake with some of the cream mixture. Then spread a very thin layer of the cream mixture on top of cake; place marzipan circle on top. Garnish top with flowers. Spoon remaining cream mixture into a decorating bag fitted with a medium round tip (about ¼-inch opening). Pipe a border around bottom edge of cake. Cover and refrigerate to store. Makes 12 servings.

SPECIAL TOUCH
▼ ▼ ▼
Fresh flowers top this showy, sherry-spiked layer cake. For an easy floral top, have the florist arrange a bouquet of flowers. Then just before serving, place a piece of plastic wrap on top of the cake before placing on the flowers. Because flowers from a florist are chemically treated, you will need the plastic wrap to keep the flowers from touching the cake.

PER SERVING
459 CALORIES
6 g PROTEIN
64 g CARBOHYDRATES
19 g TOTAL FAT
8 g SATURATED FAT
109 mg CHOLESTEROL
72 mg SODIUM

Italian Crème Cake

1¾ cups all-purpose flour
1½ teaspoons baking powder
¼   teaspoon baking soda
½   cup margarine or butter
⅓   cup shortening
1¾ cups sugar
1   teaspoon vanilla
4   egg yolks
¾   cup buttermilk
1   3½-ounce can flaked coconut
1   cup chopped pecans
4   egg whites
    Cream Cheese-Pecan Frosting

Grease and lightly flour three 8x1½-inch round baking pans. In a small mixing bowl stir together the flour, baking powder, and baking soda. Set the baking pans and flour mixture aside.

In a large mixing bowl beat margarine or butter and shortening with an electric mixer on medium to high speed about 30 seconds or till softened.

Add sugar and vanilla and beat till fluffy. Then add egg yolks, one at a time, beating till combined. Alternately add flour mixture and buttermilk, beating on low to medium speed after each addition *just till combined*. Stir in coconut and chopped pecans.

Thoroughly wash beaters. In a medium mixing bowl beat egg whites on medium to high speed till stiff peaks form (tips stand straight). Stir about a *one-third* of the egg whites into the batter. Then fold in the remaining egg whites.

Spread batter into the prepared pans. Bake in a 350° oven for 25 to 30 minutes or till a wooden toothpick inserted near the centers of the cakes comes out clean. Cool cakes in pans on wire racks for 10 minutes. Then remove cakes; cool completely on the racks.

To assemble, place first cake layer on a large serving plate. Spread with some of the Cream Cheese-Pecan Frosting. Top with second cake layer, then spread with some more of the frosting. Finally, top with the remaining cake layer and spread sides and top of the cake with remaining frosting. Cover and refrigerate to store. Serves 14.

Cream Cheese-Pecan Frosting

In a small mixing bowl beat 12 ounces *cream cheese,* 6 tablespoons *margarine* or *butter,* and 1½ teaspoons *vanilla* with an electric mixer on medium to high speed till light and fluffy. Gradually add 6 cups sifted *powdered sugar,* beating till smooth. Stir in ½ cup chopped *pecans.* Makes 4 cups.

PER SERVING
690 CALORIES
7 g PROTEIN
85 g CARBOHYDRATES
38 g TOTAL FAT
10 g SATURATED FAT
88 mg CHOLESTEROL
305 mg SODIUM

*C*hocolate-Mint Candy Torte

1 *recipe for 2 layers Génoise or Chocolate Génoise (see page 207)*
1 *tablespoon white crème de menthe (optional)*
4 *cups Sweetened Whipped-Cream Frosting (see recipe, page 210)*
½ *cup chopped layered chocolate-mint candies (about 16 candies)*
1 *tablespoon white crème de menthe*

Grease a 15x10x1-inch baking pan. Line the baking pan with parchment paper or plain brown paper; grease paper. Set pan aside.

Prepare batter for two 8- or 9-inch layers of Génoise or Chocolate Génoise as directed, *except* spread batter into the prepared 15x10x1-inch pan. Bake in 350° oven for 12 to 15 minutes or till a wooden toothpick inserted near the center of the cake comes out clean. Cool cake in pan on a wire rack for 10 minutes. Then remove cake from pan and peel off paper. Cool completely on the rack.

If desired, sprinkle cake with 1 tablespoon crème de menthe. Cut the cake crosswise into three 10x5-inch rectangles. Divide the Sweetened Whipped-Cream Frosting in half. Fold the chopped chocolate-mint candies into 1 portion of the frosting. Fold 1 tablespoon crème de menthe into the remaining portion of cream frosting.

To assemble, place first cake layer on a large serving plate. Spread with *half* of the chocolate-mint frosting. Top with second cake layer, then spread on the remaining chocolate-mint frosting. Finally, top with the remaining cake layer. Spread sides and top of cake with the crème-de-menthe-flavored frosting. Lightly cover and chill in the refrigerator till serving time or for up to 24 hours. Makes 12 servings.

SPECIAL TOUCH
▼ ▼ ▼
As if the billows of Sweetened Whipped-Cream Frosting aren't enough of a splurge, pile on chocolate-mint curls to make this torte the ultimate in dessert fantasies. Make small curls from additional layered chocolate-mint candies or long curls from chocolate-mint candy bars.

PER SERVING
381 CALORIES
5 g PROTEIN
33 g CARBOHYDRATES
26 g TOTAL FAT
15 g SATURATED FAT
182 mg CHOLESTEROL
49 mg SODIUM

Tunnel-of-Orange Angel Cake

1½ *cups egg whites (10 to 12 large)*
1½ *cups sifted powdered sugar*
  1 *cup sifted cake flour*
1½ *teaspoons cream of tartar*
  1 *teaspoon vanilla*
  1 *cup sugar*
  ¾ *cup sugar*
  1 *envelope unflavored gelatin*
  2 *teaspoons finely shredded orange peel*
  ⅓ *cup orange juice*
  7 *drops yellow food coloring (optional)*
  1 *drop red food coloring (optional)*
  1 *cup whipping cream*
  1 *recipe for 4 cups Sweetened Whipped-Cream Frosting (see page 210)*

SPECIAL TOUCH
▼ ▼ ▼

Place twisted orange slices and lemon leaves on top of this cake to make it shine with springtime.

In a very large mixing bowl, let egg whites stand at room temperature for 30 minutes. Meanwhile, sift powdered sugar and flour together 3 times. Set flour mixture aside.

Add cream of tartar and vanilla to the egg whites. Beat with an electric mixer on medium to high speed till soft peaks form (tips curl). Gradually add 1 cup sugar, about *2 tablespoons* at a time, beating till stiff peaks form (tips stand straight).

Sift about *one-fourth* of the flour mixture over the egg white mixture, then gently fold in. (If bowl is too full, transfer mixture to a larger bowl.) Repeat sifting and folding in one-fourth of the flour mixture at a time.

Pour batter into an *ungreased* 10-inch tube pan. Gently cut through batter with a knife or narrow metal spatula. Bake on the lowest rack in a 350° oven for 40 to 45 minutes or till top springs back when lightly touched.

Immediately invert cake in pan and cool completely. Loosen sides of cake from pan, then remove cake from pan.

Meanwhile, for orange filling, in a saucepan stir together the ¾ cup sugar, unflavored gelatin, and dash *salt.* Stir in ⅔ cup *cold water, 1 teaspoon* of the orange peel, and orange juice. Cook and stir just till the gelatin dissolves. If desired, stir in food colorings. Cool the gelatin mixture to room temperature. In a medium bowl beat the whipping cream with an electric mixer on low speed till soft peaks form. Fold *one-fourth* of the whipped cream into the gelatin mixture. Then fold all of the gelatin mixture into the remaining whipped cream. Chill the mixture by placing the bowl in a sink of *ice water* till the mixture mounds when spooned, stirring occasionally.

To assemble cake, using a serrated or very sharp knife, cut off the top 1 inch of the cake; set aside. With the knife held parallel to the side of the cake, cut around the hole in the center of the cake, leaving about a 1-inch thickness of cake around the hole. Then cut around inside the outer edge of the cake, leaving the outer cake wall about 1 inch thick. Using a spoon, remove center of cake, leaving about a 1-inch-thick base. Place the hollowed-out cake on a serving plate. Spoon the orange filling into the hollowed-out section. Replace the top of the cake.

Prepare Sweetened Whipped-Cream Frosting as directed, *except* fold in the remaining orange peel. Spread sides and top of cake with frosting. Cover; chill in the refrigerator for 4 to 24 hours before serving. Serves 12.

PER SERVING
428 CALORIES
6 g PROTEIN
55 g CARBOHYDRATES
22 g TOTAL FAT
14 g SATURATED FAT
82 mg CHOLESTEROL
81 mg SODIUM

Minty Meringue Shells

2 egg whites
¼ teaspoon cream of tartar
   Dash salt
⅔ cup sugar
1 cup whipping cream
½ of a 7-ounce jar marshmallow creme
2 tablespoons green crème de menthe **or**
   ½ teaspoon peppermint extract **plus**
   2 drops green food coloring
2 ounces semisweet **or** bittersweet
   chocolate, chopped

Chill a small mixing bowl of an electric mixer in the refrigerator.

For meringue shells, in a medium mixing bowl let egg whites stand at room temperature for 30 minutes. Meanwhile, line a baking sheet with parchment paper or plain brown paper. Draw eight 3-inch circles on the paper. Set baking sheet aside.

Add cream of tartar and salt to the egg whites. Beat with an electric mixer on medium to high speed till soft peaks form (tips curl). Gradually add sugar, *1 tablespoon* at a time, beating on high speed about 7 minutes or till very stiff peaks form (tips stand straight) and sugar is *almost* dissolved.

Using a spoon or spatula, spread meringue mixture over the circles on the prepared baking sheet, building the sides up to form shells. *Or,* spoon the meringue into a decorating bag fitted with a medium round or star tip (about ¼-inch opening). Pipe shells on the prepared sheet.

Bake in a 300° oven for 30 minutes. Turn off oven. Then let meringue shells dry in oven with door closed for 1 hour. *(Do not open oven.)*

For filling, in a medium mixing bowl combine marshmallow creme and crème de menthe or peppermint extract plus green food coloring. Beat with an electric mixer on low speed till smooth. In the chilled bowl beat whipping cream on low speed till soft peaks form. Fold the whipped cream into the marshmallow mixture.

Melt the chocolate according to the directions on page 225. Peel meringue shells from paper. Drizzle shells with melted chocolate. Then spoon filling into meringue shells. Lightly cover and refrigerate for 2 to 24 hours before serving. Makes 8 servings.

PER SERVING
254 CALORIES
2 g PROTEIN
33 g CARBOHYDRATES
13 g TOTAL FAT
7 g SATURATED FAT
41 mg CHOLESTEROL
47 mg SODIUM

▼ ▼ ▼
Festive, fun, and
flavorful! These giant
Holiday Cutout Cookies are
sure to be the star
attraction at your next
get-together.

Holiday Cutout Cookies

⅓ cup *margarine* or *butter*
⅓ cup *shortening*
2 cups *all-purpose flour*
¾ cup *sugar*
1 *egg*
1 *tablespoon milk*
1 *teaspoon baking powder*
1 *teaspoon finely shredded orange peel*
1 *teaspoon vanilla*
¼ *teaspoon ground nutmeg* or *ginger*
   Dash salt
   Royal Icing or *2 to 3 cups desired*
      butter frosting
   Desired colored sugars (optional)

In a large mixing bowl beat margarine or butter and shortening with an electric mixer on medium to high speed about 30 seconds or till softened.

Add about *half* of the flour and all of the sugar, egg, milk, baking powder, orange peel, vanilla, nutmeg or ginger, and salt. Beat till thoroughly combined, scraping sides of bowl occasionally. Then beat or stir in the remaining flour. Divide dough in half. Cover and chill in the refrigerator about 3 hours or till easy to handle.

If a 5-inch cookie cutter is unavailable, draw a simple 5-inch shape (such as a star, heart, Easter egg, or Christmas tree) on a piece of cardboard. Cut shape out to use it as a pattern; set aside.

On a lightly floured surface, roll *each* half of dough to ⅛-inch thickness. Using the 5-inch cutter or cardboard cutout, cut dough into desired shapes. (Flour cutter or cardboard as necessary.) Place cookies 2 inches apart on ungreased cookie sheets.

Bake in a 375° oven for 8 to 10 minutes or till edges are firm and bottoms are lightly browned. Cool on cookie sheet for 1 minute. Then remove cookies; cool on a wire rack.

To decorate, frost and/or pipe Royal Icing or desired butter frosting on cookies. If desired, sprinkle with colored sugars. Let cookies stand till icing is dry before serving. Makes about 20.

Royal Icing

In a large mixing bowl combine 3 *egg whites* (see tip, page 175); one 16-ounce package *powdered sugar,* sifted (about 4¾ cups); 1 teaspoon *vanilla;* and ½ teaspoon *cream of tartar.* Beat with an electric mixer on high speed for 7 to 10 minutes or till very stiff. If desired, divide icing into smaller portions and tint with *food coloring.* Use at once, covering icing in bowl(s) with damp paper towels to prevent drying. Makes 3 cups.

SPECIAL TOUCH
▼ ▼ ▼

Try a host of decorating ideas for these cookies. Frost and sprinkle them with colored sugars as shown in the photograph, drizzle or dip them in melted chocolate, or paint them using food coloring diluted with water.

PER COOKIE
222 CALORIES
2 g PROTEIN
39 g CARBOHYDRATES
7 g TOTAL FAT
1 g SATURATED FAT
11 mg CHOLESTEROL
71 mg SODIUM

Lemon-Glazed Ginger Cookies

½ cup *margarine* or *butter*
2 cups *all-purpose flour*
½ cup *sugar*
⅓ cup *molasses*
1 *egg*
1 *teaspoon baking soda*
1 *teapoon grated gingerroot*
½ *teaspoon ground nutmeg*
¼ *teaspoon ground cloves*
  Lemon Icing

In a large mixing bowl beat margarine or butter with an electric mixer on medium to high speed about 30 seconds or till softened.

Add about *half* of the flour and all of the sugar, molasses, egg, baking soda, gingerroot, nutmeg, and cloves. Beat till thoroughly combined, scraping sides of bowl occasionally. Then beat or stir in the remaining flour.

Drop a *scant ¼ cup* of dough at a time 4 inches apart onto an ungreased cookie sheet. Bake in a 350° oven for 12 to 14 minutes or till edges are firm. Cool on cookie sheet for 1 minute. Then remove cookies and cool on a wire rack. Spoon Lemon Icing over warm cookies to glaze tops. Makes 12.

Lemon Icing

In a small mixing bowl combine 1 cup sifted *powdered sugar*, 1 tablespoon softened *margarine* or *butter*, and ½ teaspoon finely shredded *lemon peel*. Stir in 1 tablespoon *lemon juice*. Stir in 2 to 3 teaspoons *milk* till icing is smooth and of drizzling consistency. Makes about ½ cup.

PER COOKIE
238 CALORIES
3 g PROTEIN
37 g CARBOHYDRATES
9 g TOTAL FAT
2 g SATURATED FAT
18 mg CHOLESTEROL
176 mg SODIUM

Bread Pudding with Bourbon Sauce

4 eggs
2¼ cups half-and-half or light cream
¾ cup sugar
1 tablespoon vanilla
4 cups dry French bread cubes
⅓ cup snipped dried apricots, light raisins, dried cranberries, or dried cherries
⅓ cup chopped pecans or walnuts
Bourbon Sauce

In a large mixing bowl use a rotary beater or wire whisk to lightly beat eggs just till mixed. Then stir in half-and-half or light cream, sugar, and vanilla. Set the egg mixture aside.

In an ungreased 8x8x2-inch baking dish toss together bread cubes; apricots, raisins, dried cranberries, or dried cherries; and pecans or walnuts. Pour the egg mixture evenly over the bread mixture.

Bake in a 350° oven for 40 to 45 minutes or till a knife inserted near the center comes out clean. Serve warm with Bourbon Sauce. Makes 6 servings.

Bourbon Sauce

In a small saucepan melt ¼ cup margarine or butter. Stir in ½ cup sugar, 1 beaten egg yolk, and 2 tablespoons water. Cook and stir over medium-low heat for 4 to 5 minutes or till sugar dissolves and mixture just begins to bubble. Remove from heat. Stir in 2 tablespoons bourbon. Makes about ¾ cup.

SPECIAL TOUCH
▼ ▼ ▼
At last, the bread pudding you've only dreamed about. In just one bite, you'll be convinced this is a superb bread pudding. It features the awesome flavor combination of fruit, nuts, and a bourbon sauce.

To gussy up this grand dessert, serve it in your best dessert bowls along with cups of gourmet coffee.

PER SERVING
556 CALORIES
11 g PROTEIN
66 g CARBOHYDRATES
27 g TOTAL FAT
9 g SATURATED FAT
211 mg CHOLESTEROL
339 mg SODIUM

Gingered Soufflé with Lemon Sauce

SPECIAL TOUCH
▼ ▼ ▼
Sometimes, simplicity fills
the bill when serving a
soufflé. To show off this
light-as-air dessert, just
quickly dust the top with
powdered sugar.

Margarine or *butter*
Sugar
2 *tablespoons margarine* or *butter*
3 *tablespoons all-purpose flour*
¼ *teaspoon ground nutmeg*
1 *cup milk*
2 *tablespoons finely chopped crystallized*
   ginger
4 *beaten egg yolks*
4 *egg whites*
¼ *cup sugar*
1 *cup Citrus Sauce (using lemon peel* **and**
   juice) (see recipe, page 214)

Grease the sides of a 2-quart soufflé dish
with margarine or butter. Sprinkle sides of
dish with sugar. Set the soufflé dish aside.

In a small saucepan melt 2 tablespoons
margarine or butter. Stir in flour and

nutmeg. Add milk. Cook and stir over
medium heat till thickened and bubbly.
Remove from heat. Stir in the finely
chopped crystallized ginger. Then gradually
stir the mixture into the beaten egg yolks.
Set the egg yolk mixture aside.

In a large mixing bowl beat egg whites with
an electric mixer on medium speed till soft
peaks form (tips curl). Gradually add ¼ cup
sugar, about *1 tablespoon* at a time, beating on
medium to high speed till stiff peaks form
(tips stand straight).

Gently fold the egg yolk mixture into the
egg white mixture. Spoon mixture into the
prepared soufflé dish. Bake in a 350° oven
for 35 to 40 minutes or till a knife inserted
near the center comes out clean. Serve at
once with Citrus Sauce. Makes 6 servings.

PER SERVING
225 CALORIES
6 g PROTEIN
28 g CARBOHYDRATES
11 g TOTAL FAT
3 g SATURATED FAT
145 mg CHOLESTEROL
137 mg SODIUM

Cappuccino Soufflé

Margarine or *butter*

Sugar

3 tablespoons margarine or *butter*

¼ cup *all-purpose flour*

¼ cup *sugar*

2 teaspoons *instant coffee crystals*

⅔ cup *milk*

2 tablespoons *coffee liqueur* or *milk*

1½ teaspoons *finely shredded orange peel*

4 beaten egg yolks

4 egg whites

¼ cup *sugar*

1 cup *Flavored Whipped Cream (using coffee liqueur) (see recipe, page 210)*

½ cup *Bittersweet Chocolate Sauce (see recipe, page 212)*

Grease the sides of a 1½-quart soufflé dish with margarine or butter. For a collar on the soufflé dish, measure enough foil to wrap around the top of the soufflé dish and add 3 inches. Fold the foil in thirds lengthwise. Lightly grease 1 side with margarine or butter; sprinkle with sugar. Attach the foil, sugar side in, around the outside of the dish so that the foil extends about 2 inches above the dish. Tape ends of foil together. Sprinkle sides of dish with sugar; set dish aside.

In a small saucepan melt 3 tablespoons margarine or butter. Stir in flour, ¼ cup sugar, and coffee crystals. Add milk. Cook and stir over medium heat till thickened and bubbly. Remove from heat. Stir in coffee liqueur and orange peel. Then gradually stir the mixture into the beaten egg yolks. Set egg yolk mixture aside.

In a large mixing bowl beat egg whites with an electric mixer on medium speed till soft peaks form (tips curl). Gradually add ¼ cup sugar, about *1 tablespoon* at a time, beating on medium to high speed till stiff peaks form (tips stand straight).

Gently fold the egg yolk mixture into the egg white mixture. Spoon the mixture into the prepared soufflé dish. Bake in a 325° oven about 50 minutes or till a knife inserted near the center comes out clean. Serve soufflé at once with Flavored Whipped Cream and Bittersweet Chocolate Sauce. Makes 8 servings.

SPECIAL TOUCH
▼ ▼ ▼

For a unique twist on after-dinner coffee, spoon the Cappuccino Soufflé into china coffee cups and place the cups on saucers.

PER SERVING

311 CALORIES

5 g PROTEIN

30 g CARBOHYDRATES

19 g TOTAL FAT

8 g SATURATED FAT

142 mg CHOLESTEROL

107 mg SODIUM

▼ ▼ ▼
Here's an old-time favorite, *Ricotta-Filled Crepes,* updated as an attractive, dynamite dessert.

Ricotta-Filled Crepes

2 cups ricotta cheese
¼ cup sugar
2 teaspoons vanilla
¼ cup finely chopped pistachio nuts
2 tablespoons finely chopped Candied
   Citrus Peel (using oranges) (see
   recipe, page 217)
1 ounce semisweet **or** bittersweet
   chocolate, grated
1½ cups milk
1 cup all-purpose flour
2 eggs
2 tablespoons sugar
1 tablespoon cooking oil
1 teaspoon finely shredded orange peel
2 cups desired sauce(s) (such as
   Bittersweet Chocolate Sauce,
   Raspberry Sauce, Kiwi Sauce,
   and/or Citrus Sauce) (see recipes,
   pages 212–214)

For filling, in a medium mixing bowl combine ricotta cheese, ¼ cup sugar, and vanilla. Stir till smooth. Fold in chopped pistachio nuts, Candied Citrus Peel, and grated chocolate. Cover and chill in the refrigerator for 1 to 24 hours.

For crepes, in a medium mixing bowl combine milk, flour, eggs, 2 tablespoons sugar, oil, and shredded orange peel. Beat with a rotary beater till well mixed.

Heat a lightly greased 6-inch skillet. Remove from heat. Spoon 2 *tablespoons* of the batter into the skillet; lift and tilt the skillet to spread batter. Return to heat; brown on 1 side only. Invert the skillet over paper towels; remove crepe. Repeat with remaining batter to make 18 crepes, greasing skillet as necessary. *Or,* cook crepes on an inverted crepe maker according to manufacturer's directions.

To assemble crepes, invert crepes so that the browned sides will be out. Spoon about 2 *tablespoons* of the filling on one-fourth of the unbrowned side of *each* crepe. Fold each crepe in half, then fold each crepe in half again. Cover and chill in the refrigerator till serving time or for up to 1 hour. Serve crepes with desired sauce(s). Serves 9.

Note: To free yourself from last-minute cooking hassles, make and freeze the crepes in advance. Stack the crepes with 2 sheets of waxed paper between crepes. Place the stack in a freezer container or in plastic freezer bag. Then, seal, label, and freeze for up to 4 months. To use, thaw at room temperature about 1 hour.

SPECIAL TOUCH
▼ ▼ ▼
Use one sauce or several and create your own signature presentation. In addition, if you want to add a stencil design to the plate, place a stencil on the plate. Then lightly brush melted margarine or butter in the holes or spray with nonstick coating, sprinkle with ground nuts, and remove stencil.

PER SERVING
534 CALORIES
14 g PROTEIN
55 g CARBOHYDRATES
32 g TOTAL FAT
12 g SATURATED FAT
116 mg CHOLESTEROL
117 mg SODIUM

Ribbon-of-Cranberry Cheesecake

6   tablespoons margarine **or** butter
1½ cups finely crushed vanilla wafers
      (about 33)
1   cup sugar
2   tablespoons cornstarch
1½ cups cranberries
1   cup orange juice
1   cup cottage cheese
2   8-ounce packages cream cheese, softened
1   cup sugar
2   tablespoons all-purpose flour
2   teaspoons vanilla
3   eggs
2   teaspoons finely shredded orange peel
1   8-ounce carton vanilla yogurt

For crust, in a small saucepan melt margarine or butter. Stir in crushed vanilla wafers. Spread mixture evenly into a 9-inch springform pan. Press onto bottom and 1 inch up sides of the pan to form a firm, even crust. Set pan aside.

For sauce, in a medium saucepan stir together 1 cup sugar and the cornstarch. Stir in cranberries and orange juice. Cook and stir over medium heat till thickened and bubbly. Cook and stir for 2 minutes more. Remove ¾ cup of the sauce; cool slightly. Meanwhile, cover and chill remaining sauce in the refrigerator till serving time.

Place the ¾ cup sauce in a blender container or food processor bowl. Cover and blend or

process till smooth. Set the puréed sauce aside. Wash the blender container or food processor bowl.

For filling, place cottage cheese in the blender container or food processor bowl. Cover and blend or process till smooth. Transfer cottage cheese to a large mixing bowl. Add cream cheese, 1 cup sugar, flour, and vanilla. Beat with an electric mixer on medium to high speed till combined. Add eggs all at once. Beat on low speed *just till combined.* Stir in orange peel.

Pour *half* of the filling into the crust-lined springform pan. Drizzle puréed sauce over the filling in the pan. Carefully top with the remaining filling, covering sauce as much as possible. Then place on a shallow baking pan on the oven rack. Bake in a 375° oven for 45 to 50 minutes or till center appears *nearly* set when shaken.

Remove springform pan from baking pan. Cool cheesecake in springform pan on a wire rack for 15 minutes. Loosen crust from sides of the pan and cool for 30 minutes more. Remove sides of the springform pan. Cool completely, then chill in the refrigerator for at least 4 hours before serving.

Just before serving, spread cheesecake with vanilla yogurt. Top with some of the chilled cranberry sauce. Pass remaining sauce. Makes 12 to 16 servings.

Maple Praline Cheesecake

1/3 cup margarine or butter
1/4 cup packed brown sugar
1/4 teaspoon vanilla
1 cup all-purpose flour
1/4 cup finely chopped pecans
2 8-ounce packages cream cheese, softened
1 cup sugar
2 tablespoons all-purpose flour
4 eggs
1 cup half-and-half or light cream
1/3 cup maple or maple-flavored syrup
1/3 cup finely chopped pecans
  Individual Glazed Nuts (using pecans)
  (see recipe, page 216) (optional)

For crust, in a small mixing bowl beat margarine or butter with an electric mixer on medium to high speed about 30 seconds or till softened. Add brown sugar and vanilla and beat till fluffy. Then add 1 cup flour and 1/4 cup pecans. Beat on low to medium speed *just till combined.* Pat dough onto bottom and 1 1/2 inches up the sides of a 9-inch springform pan to form a firm, even crust.

Bake the crust in a 375° oven about 10 minutes or till lightly browned. Cool on a wire rack while preparing filling.

For filling, in a large mixing bowl beat cream cheese, sugar, and 2 tablespoons flour with an electric mixer on medium to high speed till combined. Add eggs all at once. Beat on low speed *just till combined.* Stir in half-and-half or light cream, maple syrup, and 1/3 cup pecans.

Pour filling into the crust-lined springform pan. Then place on a shallow baking pan on the oven rack. Bake in a 375° oven for 45 to 50 minutes or till center appears *nearly* set when shaken.

Remove springform pan from baking pan. Cool cheesecake in springform pan on a wire rack for 15 minutes. Loosen crust from sides of pan and cool for 30 minutes more. Remove sides of the springform pan. Cool completely, then cover and chill in the refrigerator for at least 4 hours before serving. If desired, garnish with Individual Glazed Nuts. Makes 12 to 16 servings.

PER SERVING
398 CALORIES
7 g PROTEIN
36 g CARBOHYDRATES
26 g TOTAL FAT
11 g SATURATED FAT
120 mg CHOLESTEROL
207 mg SODIUM

Coffee Cheesecake

¾ cup all-purpose flour
3 tablespoons brown sugar
⅓ cup margarine or butter
1 slightly beaten egg yolk
¼ teaspoon vanilla
¼ cup milk
1 tablespoon instant coffee crystals
3 8-ounce packages cream cheese, softened
½ cup packed brown sugar
½ cup sugar
2 tablespoons all-purpose flour
2 teaspoons vanilla
3 eggs
Coffee Sauce

For crust, in a medium mixing bowl stir together ¾ cup flour and 3 tablespoons brown sugar. Cut in margarine or butter till pieces are the size of small peas. In a small bowl, use a fork to mix egg yolk and ¼ teaspoon vanilla; stir into flour mixture till all the dough is moistened. Remove sides from an 8- or 9-inch springform pan. Press *one-third* of the dough onto the bottom of the pan. Bake the bottom crust in a 400° oven about 5 minutes or till golden. Cool crust on pan bottom or on a wire rack.

Grease the sides of the springform pan; attach the sides to the bottom. Press the remaining dough 1½ inches up the sides of a 9-inch pan or 2 inches up the sides of an 8-inch pan. Set pan aside.

Combine the milk and instant coffee crystals; let stand till coffee crystals dissolve, stirring occasionally.

PER SERVING
407 CALORIES
7 g PROTEIN
34 g CARBOHYDRATES
27 g TOTAL FAT
14 g SATURATED FAT
134 mg CHOLESTEROL
257 mg SODIUM

For filling, in a large mixing bowl beat cream cheese, ½ cup brown sugar, sugar, 2 tablespoons flour, and 2 teaspoons vanilla on medium to high speed till combined. Add eggs all at once. Beat on low speed *just till combined.* Stir in coffee mixture.

Pour filling into the crust-lined springform pan. Then place on a shallow baking pan on the oven rack. Bake in a 375° oven for 40 to 50 minutes or till center appears *nearly* set when shaken.

Remove springform pan from baking pan. Cool cheesecake in springform pan on a wire rack for 15 minutes. Loosen crust from sides of pan and cool for 30 minutes more. Remove sides of the springform pan. Cool completely, then cover and chill in the refrigerator for at least 4 hours before serving. Serve with Coffee Sauce. Makes 12 to 16 servings.

Coffee Sauce

In a small saucepan combine ½ cup *water,* ¼ cup light *corn syrup,* 2 teaspoons *cornstarch,* and 1 teaspoon *instant coffee crystals.* Cook and stir over medium heat till mixture is thickened and bubbly. Cook and stir for 2 minutes more. Remove from heat. Stir in ¼ teaspoon *vanilla.* Then, if desired, stir in 1 teaspoon *coffee liqueur.* Cover and chill the sauce in the refrigerator till serving time. Makes about ¾ cup.

Raisin-and-Rum-Sauced Custard Ring

6 eggs
3 cups milk
½ cup sugar
¼ teaspoon salt
½ cup packed brown sugar
1 tablespoon cornstarch
½ cup water
⅓ cup raisins
1 to 2 tablespoons rum

In a large mixing bowl use a rotary beater or wire whisk to lightly beat eggs *just till mixed.* Then stir in milk, sugar, and salt.

Place an ungreased 4½- or 5-cup ovenproof ring mold (about 8 inches in diameter) in a 13x9x2-inch baking pan. Then set the baking pan on the oven rack. Pour the egg mixture into the mold. Pour *boiling* or *very hot tap water* into the pan around the mold to a depth of 1 inch. Bake in a 325° oven for 35 to 45 minutes or till a knife inserted near the center comes out clean.

Remove ring mold from water in pan. Cool custard in the ring mold on a wire rack. Then cover and chill in the refrigerator for at least 2 hours before serving.

Meanwhile, for sauce, in a heavy small saucepan stir together brown sugar and cornstarch. Stir in water and raisins. Cook and stir over medium heat till thickened and bubbly. Cook and stir for 2 minutes more. Remove from heat. Stir in rum. Cover surface with plastic wrap. Serve warm or cool to room temperature.

To unmold the custard, run a knife around the edges. Then slip the tip of the knife down the side of the mold to let air in. Invert a serving plate over the custard, then turn the mold and the plate over together. Lift off the mold. Serve with sauce. Serves 8.

SPECIAL TOUCH
▼ ▼ ▼
Here's an elegant way to serve this luscious custard. Unmold the custard onto a large flat serving plate. Place a clear glass bowl in the center of the custard ring. Then carefully pour the sauce into the bowl. Use a silver cake server and ladle to serve the dessert.

PER SERVING
224 CALORIES
8 g PROTEIN
36 g CARBOHYDRATES
6 g TOTAL FAT
2 g SATURATED FAT
167 mg CHOLESTEROL
165 mg SODIUM

Rice Pudding with Molasses-Rum Sauce

SPECIAL TOUCH
▼ ▼ ▼
Trim this extra-special
rice pudding with simple
orange-peel curls.

4 *eggs*
2 *cups half-and-half, light cream,* **or** *milk*
½ *cup sugar*
1 *teaspoon vanilla*
¼ *teaspoon salt*
1½ *cups cooked rice, cooled*
½ *to* ¾ *cup raisins*
⅛ *teaspoon ground nutmeg*
⅛ *teaspoon ground cinnamon*
Molasses-Rum Sauce

In an ungreased 2-quart casserole use a rotary beater or wire whisk to lightly beat eggs *just till mixed.* Then stir in milk, half-and-half, or cream; sugar; vanilla; and salt. Stir in rice and raisins.

Place the casserole in a 13x9x2-inch baking pan on an oven rack. Then set pan on the oven rack. Pour *boiling water* or *very hot tap water* into the baking pan around the casserole to a depth of 1 inch. Bake in a 325° oven for 30 minutes. Stir well; sprinkle with nutmeg and cinnamon. Bake for 20 to 30 minutes more or till a knife inserted near the center comes out clean. Remove the casserole from water in baking pan. Serve warm or chilled.

To serve warm, spoon pudding into dessert dishes and drizzle with Molasses-Rum Sauce. *Or,* to serve chilled, cover and refrigerate pudding for up to 3 days. Then spoon into dessert dishes and drizzle with warm Molasses-Rum Sauce. Makes 8 servings.

Molasses-Rum Sauce

In a heavy small saucepan combine ½ cup packed *brown sugar* and 1 tablespoon *cornstarch.* Stir in ⅓ cup *half-and-half, light cream,* or *milk;* ¼ cup *water;* and 1 tablespoon *molasses* or 2 tablespoons dark *corn syrup.* Cook and stir over medium heat till thickened and bubbly (mixture may appear curdled). Cook and stir for 2 minutes more. Remove from heat. Stir in 1 tablespoon *margarine* or *butter* and 1 tablespoon *rum* or 1 teaspoon *rum flavoring.* Serve warm. Makes about 1 cup.

PER SERVING
331 CALORIES
7 g PROTEIN
49 g CARBOHYDRATES
12 g TOTAL FAT
6 g SATURATED FAT
132 mg CHOLESTEROL
150 mg SODIUM

Old-World Classics

The origins of old-world, pastry-shop fancies from
various countries date back hundreds of years. Many of
these desserts were first prepared for kings and queens
or for festive occasions in restaurants. Today, the love
of these famous delights has spread throughout the
world. Here you'll find traditional desserts such as
Sacher Torte, Babas au Rhum, Black Forest Cherry
Cake, Baklava, and Apple Strudel.

▼ ▼ ▼

Sacher Torte

SPECIAL TOUCH
▼ ▼ ▼

For many years, a Viennese court debated the definition of Sacher Torte. The final decision—two chocolate cake layers filled with apricot jam and completely covered with a chocolate glaze. Many pastry chefs still pipe the word "Sacher" on their tortes to show authenticity.

To serve slices of this rich torte, place the pieces on clear or colored glass dessert plates. For an added touch, pipe a stripe of the whipped cream along one side of each slice.

6 egg whites
5 ounces semisweet or bittersweet chocolate, chopped
½ cup unsalted butter
6 egg yolks
1½ teaspoons vanilla
½ cup sugar
¾ cup all-purpose flour
⅔ cup apricot preserves
1 cup Chocolate Glaze (see recipe, page 211)
1 cup Sweetened Whipped Cream (see recipe, page 210) (optional)

In a very large mixing bowl, let egg whites stand at room temperature for 30 minutes. Meanwhile, grease and lightly flour a 9-inch springform pan. Set the pan aside.

In a medium saucepan melt chocolate with butter according to the directions on page 225; cool.

Stir egg yolks and vanilla into the cooled chocolate mixture. Set mixture aside.

Beat egg whites with an electric mixer on medium to high speed till soft peaks form (tips curl). Gradually add the sugar, about 1 tablespoon at a time, beating about 4 minutes or till stiff peaks form (tips stand straight).

Fold about 1 cup of the egg white mixture into the chocolate mixture. Then fold the chocolate mixture into the remaining egg white mixture.

Sift about one-third of the flour over the egg mixture, then gently fold in. (If the bowl is too full, transfer mixture to a larger bowl.) Repeat sifting and folding in one-third of the flour mixture at a time.

Spread the batter into the prepared springform pan. Bake in a 350° oven for 35 to 40 minutes or till a wooden toothpick inserted near the center of the cake comes out clean. Completely cool the cake in the pan on a wire rack.

In a small saucepan, heat the apricot preserves till melted. Then press apricot preserves through a sieve. Cool slightly.

Meanwhile, remove sides of springform pan. Brush crumbs from edges of cake. (Top crust will be slightly flaky.) Remove bottom of springform pan from cake.

To assemble, cut cake horizontally into two even layers. Place the first layer on a large serving plate. Spread the preserves on top of the cake layer. Top with the second cake layer. Pour Chocolate Glaze over torte, spreading as necessary to glaze top and sides completely. Let torte stand at room temperature for at least 1 hour before serving. If desired, serve with Sweetened Whipped Cream. Makes 12 servings.

PER SERVING
368 CALORIES
6 g PROTEIN
40 g CARBOHYDRATES
23 g TOTAL FAT
9 g SATURATED FAT
146 mg CHOLESTEROL
40 mg SODIUM

Salzburger Nockerl

6 *egg whites*
¼ *cup milk*
1½ *teaspoons finely shredded lemon peel (set aside)*
1 *tablespoon lemon juice*
1 *teaspoon vanilla*
¼ *cup sugar*
4 *egg yolks*
1 *tablespoon all-purpose flour*
  Powdered sugar

In a large mixing bowl, let egg whites stand at room temperature for 30 minutes. Meanwhile, grease six 10-ounce soufflé dishes or custard cups or a 12x7½x2-inch baking dish. (If using soufflé dishes or custard cups, place them in a 15x10x1-inch baking pan.) Pour *2 teaspoons* milk into *each* soufflé dish or custard cup or pour all of the milk into the baking dish; set aside.

Add lemon juice and vanilla to the egg whites. Beat with an electric mixer on medium to high speed till soft peaks form (tips curl). Gradually add the sugar, about *1 tablespoon* at a time, beating on high speed about 6 minutes or till very stiff peaks form (tips stand straight) and sugar is *completely* dissolved. Set aside.

Wash beaters. In a medium mixing bowl beat egg yolks on medium to high speed about 5 minutes or till thick and lemon-colored. Fold in flour and lemon peel.

Fold about *1 cup* of the egg white mixture into the egg yolk mixture. Then fold all of the egg yolk mixture into the remaining egg white mixture. Spoon the mixture into the prepared soufflé dishes, custard cups, or baking dish. (If using the baking dish, spoon the mixture into 6 mounds.)

Bake in a 375° oven for 10 to 12 minutes or till golden and a knife inserted near the centers of the desserts comes out clean. Immediately sift powdered sugar over tops. Serve at once. Makes 6 servings.

SPECIAL TOUCH
▼ ▼ ▼

Still a favorite on Austrian tables, these lemony puffs were created in the early 17th century for a dessert-loving Archbishop of Salzburg.

Whether you bake this dessert in individual dishes or a baking dish, keep the garnish simple. Just sprinkle a little finely shredded lemon peel on top.

PER SERVING
103 CALORIES
6 g PROTEIN
12 g CARBOHYDRATES
4 g TOTAL FAT
1 g SATURATED FAT
143 mg CHOLESTEROL
65 mg SODIUM

Punschtorte

SPECIAL TOUCH
▼ ▼ ▼

Translated as punch cake,
this wonderful three-layer
creation features rum-
soaked cake cubes in the
center. To give the torte
just the right touch of
elegance, sprinkle candied
rose petals over the pastel-
frosted cake.

1¼ cups sifted cake flour
    Dash salt
6   egg yolks
⅓   cup sugar
1   teaspoon finely shredded lemon or
    orange peel
6   egg whites
¼   teaspoon cream of tartar
⅓   cup sugar
½   cup water
¼   cup sugar
¼   cup orange juice
3   tablespoons rum
2   tablespoons lemon juice
2   drops red food coloring
½   cup seedless red raspberry preserves
    Fluffy Pink Frosting
    Candied Flowers (using rose petals) (see
    recipe, page 219) (optional)

Grease and lightly flour two 8x1½-inch
round baking pans. In a small mixing bowl
stir together flour and salt. Set pans and flour
mixture aside.

In a medium mixing bowl beat egg yolks
with an electric mixer on high speed about
6 minutes or till egg yolks are thick and
lemon-colored. Gradually add ⅓ cup sugar,
beating on medium speed about 2 minutes
or till sugar is *almost* dissolved. Gradually add
about *one-fourth* of the flour mixture to the

egg yolk mixture, beating on low to medium
speed *just till moistened*. Repeat, beating in
one-fourth of the flour mixture at a time. Stir
in lemon or orange peel.

Thoroughly wash beaters. In a large mixing
bowl beat egg whites and cream of tartar on
medium to high speed till soft peaks form
(tips curl). Gradually add ⅓ cup sugar, about
1 tablespoon at a time, beating on medium to
high speed till stiff peaks form (tips stand
straight).

Fold about *3 cups* of the egg white mixture
into the egg yolk mixture, using about 1 cup
at a time. Then fold all of the egg yolk
mixture into the remaining egg white
mixture.

Spread the batter into the prepared pans.
Bake in a 350° oven for 20 to 25 minutes or
till a wooden toothpick inserted near the
centers of the cakes comes out clean. Cool
cakes in pans on wire racks for 10 minutes.
Then remove cakes and cool completely on
the wire racks.

For the rum syrup, in a small saucepan
combine the water and the ¼ cup sugar.
Bring to boiling; boil for 3 minutes. Remove
from heat. Stir in the orange juice, rum,
lemon juice, and red food coloring. Set the
rum syrup aside.

PER SERVING
252 CALORIES
5 g PROTEIN
50 g CARBOHYDRATES
3 g FAT
1 g SATURATED FAT
107 mg CHOLESTEROL
54 mg SODIUM

In a small saucepan heat the red raspberry preserves over low heat till melted.

To assemble torte, cut *one* cake horizontally into *two* even layers. Place the bottom portion of the cake, cut side up, on a large serving plate. Spread *half* of the melted preserves on the cut side of the bottom cake portion; spread remaining melted preserves on the cut side of the top cake portion. Set the top cake portion aside.

Holding a sharp knife parallel to the side of the remaining whole cake, cut a 5-inch cake circle out of the center. Remove the cake circle. You will have about a 1-inch-wide cake ring remaining. Place the cake ring on top of the cake layer on the serving plate.

Cut the 5-inch cake circle into ½-inch cubes. Soak about *two-thirds* of the cake cubes in the rum syrup about 3 minutes or till the cake cubes are completely moistened, but not falling apart.

Place the soaked and dry cake cubes in the center of the cake ring, arranging the cubes so the dry cubes are surrounded by the soaked cubes. Lightly press the cake cubes to make an even layer. Finally, top with the remaining top portion of the cut cake, preserve-side down. Cover and chill in the refrigerator for 8 to 24 hours before serving.

Before serving, frost sides and top of the cake torte with the Fluffy Pink Frosting. If desired, decorate with Candied Flowers. Makes 12 servings.

Fluffy Pink Frosting

In a medium saucepan combine 1 cup *sugar,* ⅓ cup *water,* and ¼ teaspoon *cream of tartar.* Bring mixture to boiling over medium heat, stirring constantly till sugar dissolves. Remove from heat.

In a small mixing bowl combine 2 *egg whites,* 1 tablespoon *dark rum,* and 1 or 2 drops *red food coloring.* Beat with an electric mixer on medium to high speed till soft peaks form (tips curl). Very slowly add the sugar mixture to egg white mixture, beating constantly with an electric mixer on high speed about 7 minutes or till stiff peaks form (tips stand straight). Makes about 4 cups.

▼ ▼ ▼
After one bite, you'll know why this raspberry-jam-filled *Linzer Torte* ranks as one of the most famous Austrian desserts.

Linzer Torte

⅔ cup *margarine* or *butter*
⅔ cup *sugar*
1 *egg*
2 *hard-cooked egg yolks, sieved*
1 *tablespoon kirsch (cherry brandy)* or
   water
1 *teaspoon finely shredded lemon peel*
½ *teaspoon ground cinnamon*
¼ *teaspoon ground cloves*
1½ *cups all-purpose flour*
1¼ *cups ground almonds* or *hazelnuts*
   (filberts)
1 *12-ounce jar seedless red raspberry jam*
   Powdered sugar

In a medium mixing bowl beat the margarine or butter with an electric mixer on medium to high speed about 30 minutes or till softened.

Add the sugar, whole egg, hard-cooked egg yolks, kirsch or water, lemon peel, cinnamon, and cloves to the margarine. Beat till thoroughly combined, scraping sides of bowl occasionally. Using a wooden spoon, stir in the flour and almonds or hazelnuts.

Form dough into a ball. Wrap dough in plastic wrap and chill in the refrigerator for 1 hour.

On a lightly floured surface, use your hands to slightly flatten *two-thirds* of the dough. (Refrigerate remaining dough till ready to use.) Roll dough from the center to edges, forming an 11-inch circle. Wrap dough around the rolling pin. Then unroll dough onto an ungreased 10x1-inch tart pan with a removable bottom or a 10-inch springform pan. Ease dough into pan, pressing dough about ½ inch up the sides. Spread the raspberry jam over the bottom of the dough in the pan.

Roll the remaining dough to form a 10x6-inch rectangle. Cut six 1-inch-wide strips. Carefully weave strips on top of jam to make a lattice. Press ends of strips into rim of bottom crust, trimming ends as necessary.

Bake in a 325° oven for 35 to 40 minutes or till crust is golden. Cool the pastry torte in the pan on a wire rack. Remove the sides of the tart or springform pan. Before serving, sift powdered sugar over top. Serves 8.

PER SERVING
545 CALORIES
8 g PROTEIN
68 g CARBOHYDRATES
28 g TOTAL FAT
4 g SATURATED FAT
80 mg CHOLESTEROL
194 mg SODIUM

Apple Strudel

Strudel Dough*
½ cup sugar
¾ teaspoon ground cinnamon
½ teaspoon finely shredded lemon peel
3 cups thinly sliced, peeled tart apples
⅓ cup light raisins
¼ cup margarine **or** butter, melted
2 tablespoons margarine **or** butter, melted
Powdered sugar

Prepare Strudel Dough as directed. While the Strudel Dough is resting for the 30 minutes, prepare the apple filling.

For apple filling, in a large mixing bowl stir together sugar, cinnamon, and lemon peel. Add apples and raisins, then gently toss till coated. Set the apple filling aside.

Lightly grease a 15x10x1-inch baking pan. Set the baking pan aside.

To assemble the strudel, stretch dough as directed. Brush the stretched dough with the ¼ cup melted margarine or butter.

Beginning 4 inches from a short side of the dough, spoon the apple filling in a 4-inch-wide band across the dough.

Using the cloth underneath the dough as a guide, gently lift the 4-inch piece of dough and lay it over the filling. Then slowly and evenly lift the cloth and roll up the dough and filling, jelly-roll style, into a tight roll. If necessary, cut excess dough from ends to within 1 inch of apple filling. Fold ends under to seal.

Carefully transfer the strudel roll to the prepared baking pan. Slightly curve the roll to form a crescent shape. Brush the top of the strudel with the 2 tablespoons melted margarine or butter.

Bake in a 350° oven for 35 to 40 minutes or till golden. Carefully remove strudel from baking pan and cool on a wire rack. Before serving, sift powdered sugar over strudel. Makes 12 to 16 servings.

PER SERVING
213 CALORIES
2 g PROTEIN
29 g CARBOHYDRATES
11 g TOTAL FAT
2 g SATURATED FAT
18 mg CHOLESTEROL
157 mg SODIUM

Strudel Dough

In a large mixing bowl stir together 1½ cups *all-purpose flour* and ¼ teaspoon *salt.* Cut in ¼ cup *margarine* or *butter* till pieces are the size of small peas. In a small mixing bowl stir together 1 beaten *egg yolk* and ⅓ cup *warm water* (110° to 115°). Add egg yolk mixture to flour mixture. Stir till combined.

Turn the dough out onto a lightly floured surface. Knead dough for 5 minutes. Cover with plastic wrap, then let dough stand at room temperature for 1 hour.

Cover a large surface (at least 4x3 feet) with a cloth. Lightly flour the cloth. On the cloth roll the dough into a 15-inch square. Brush with 2 tablespoons melted *margarine* or *butter.* Cover dough with plastic wrap. Let dough rest for 30 minutes.

To stretch the dough, use the palms of your hands and work underneath the dough.

Starting from the middle and working toward the edges, gently lift and pull your hands apart. At the same time, pull the dough away from the middle toward yourself. Continue stretching till dough is paper thin, forming a 40x20-inch rectangle. Use scissors to trim thick or uneven edges.

*To substitute frozen *phyllo dough* for the Strudel Dough, thaw *10 to 12 sheets* of phyllo dough. Cover a large surface with a cloth. Lightly flour the cloth. Unfold the sheets of phyllo dough. Stack *2 sheets* of phyllo on the floured cloth. *(Do not brush margarine or butter between sheets.)* Arrange another stack of 2 sheets on the cloth, overlapping the stacks 2 inches. Add 3 or 4 more stacks, forming a rectangle about 40x20 inches (stagger stacks so all seams are not down the middle). If necessary, trim to a 40x20-inch rectangle. Continue as directed for Apple Strudel recipe, *except* brush with ⅓ *cup* melted margarine or butter before filling and shaping.

Dobostorte

SPECIAL TOUCH
▼ ▼ ▼
For the crowning touch, pipe or dollop puffs of Sweetened Whipped Cream between the Caramel Filigree Garnishes. Then place a whole almond in the center of each whipped cream puff.

1¼ cups sifted cake flour
   Dash salt
6 egg yolks
¼ cup sugar
6 egg whites
¼ teaspoon cream of tartar
½ cup sugar
⅓ cup amaretto or coffee liqueur
3 cups Chocolate Buttercream (see recipe, page 211)
⅔ cup chopped or sliced almonds, toasted
   Caramel Filigree Garnishes (see recipe, page 217)
1 cup Sweetened Whipped Cream (see recipe, page 210) (optional)

Grease the bottoms only of three 8x1½-inch round baking pans. Line bottoms of the pans with waxed paper. Grease the paper, then lightly flour the pans. In a small mixing bowl stir together cake flour and salt. Set pans and flour mixture aside.

In a medium mixing bowl beat egg yolks with an electric mixer on high speed about 6 minutes or till egg yolks are thick and lemon-colored. Gradually add the ¼ cup sugar, beating on medium speed about 2 minutes or till sugar is *almost* dissolved.

Thoroughly wash beaters. In a large mixing bowl beat egg whites and cream of tartar on medium to high speed till soft peaks form (tips curl). Gradually add the ½ cup sugar, about 2 tablespoons at a time, beating on medium to high speed till stiff peaks form (tips stand straight).

Fold about *1 cup* of the egg white mixture into the egg yolks. Then fold all of the egg yolk mixture into the remaining egg white mixture. Sprinkle about *one-fourth* of the flour mixture over the egg mixture, then gently fold in *just till moistened.* Repeat folding in the remaining flour mixture by fourths.

Spread the batter into the prepared pans. Bake in a 350° oven about 20 minutes or till the tops of the cakes spring back when lightly touched. Cool cakes in pans on wire racks for 10 minutes. Then remove cakes from pan. Peel off waxed paper and cool cakes completely on the racks.

To assemble, cut *each* cake horizontally into *two* even layers. Use a pastry brush to brush the amaretto or coffee liqueur over the tops of the top cake portions. Place a bottom cake portion on a large serving plate. Spread about ⅓ cup of Chocolate Buttercream on top of the bottom cake portion. Top with a top cake portion and spread with ⅓ cup more buttercream. Continue layering cakes and buttercream 4 more times, ending with a layer of buttercream. Spread remaining buttercream on sides of torte.

Gently press the chopped or sliced almonds into the Chocolate Buttercream on the sides of the torte. Arrange the Caramel Filigree Garnishes in a circle in a standing position on top of the torte. Slightly tilt the filigrees to one side. If desired, garnish with the Sweetened Whipped Cream. Serves 12.

PER SERVING
587 CALORIES
8 g PROTEIN
57 g CARBOHYDRATES
37 g TOTAL FAT
19 g SATURATED FAT
233 mg CHOLESTEROL
53 mg SODIUM

Zuger Kirschtorte

1 *9-inch layer Génoise (see recipe, page 207)*
6 *egg whites*
2½ *cups sifted powdered sugar*
2 *tablespoons cornstarch*
¾ *cup ground toasted almonds* **or** *hazelnuts (filberts)*
¼ *cup water*
2 *tablespoons sugar*
3 *tablespoons kirsch (cherry brandy)*
3 *cups Buttercream (see recipe, page 211) Powdered sugar*
½ *cup sliced almonds, toasted*

Set cake layer aside. In a large mixing bowl let egg whites stand at room temperature for 30 minutes.

Line 2 baking sheets with parchment paper or plain brown paper. Draw one 9-inch circle on each piece of paper; set aside.

Stir together 2½ cups powdered sugar and cornstarch; set aside.

Beat the egg whites with an electric mixer on medium to high speed till soft peaks form (tips curl). Gradually add the powdered sugar mixture, a small amount at a time, beating on high speed about 12 minutes or till very stiff peaks form (tips stand straight). Fold in the ground almonds or hazelnuts.

Using a spoon or a spatula, spread meringue mixture evenly over the circles on the prepared baking sheets. Bake in a 325° oven for 30 minutes. Completely cool meringue layers on baking sheets on wire racks. Then peel meringue layers from paper.

Meanwhile, for syrup, in a small saucepan combine the water and the 2 tablespoons sugar. Bring to boiling, stirring constantly till sugar dissolves. Remove from heat; cool.

Stir the kirsch into the cooled syrup. Spoon the syrup evenly over the Génoise cake layer till all of the syrup is absorbed.

To assemble, place first meringue layer on a large serving plate. Spread about *½ cup* of Buttercream on top of the meringue layer. Top with the Génoise cake layer, then spread with *½ cup* Buttercream. Finally, top with the remaining meringue layer. Spread the remaining Buttercream on sides and top of the torte. Sift additional powdered sugar over the top of the torte. Gently press the sliced almonds into the Buttercream around the top edge of torte. Makes 12 servings.

SPECIAL TOUCH
▼ ▼ ▼
A heavy dusting of powdered sugar is the traditional topping for this torte. Use a doily to help you stencil an elaborate design.

PER SERVING
587 CALORIES
8 g PROTEIN
57 g CARBOHYDRATES
37 g TOTAL FAT
19 g SATURATED FAT
233 mg CHOLESTEROL
53 mg SODIUM

▼ ▼ ▼

When it's time to indulge, have a slice of *Marjolaine.* Extra-rich mocha filling nestled between layers of hazelnut cake bestow ultra satisfaction.

Marjolaine

6 egg whites
2 cups hazelnuts (filberts)
2 tablespoons all-purpose flour
1 cup sugar
Mocha Ganache
2 cups Buttercream (see recipe, page 211)

In a large mixing bowl let egg whites stand at room temperature for 30 minutes. Meanwhile, grease three 8x1½-inch round baking pans. Line the bottoms with waxed paper; grease paper. Set pans aside.

Place *half* of the hazelnuts in a blender container or food processor bowl. Cover and blend or process till very fine but dry (not oily). Repeat blending or processing with remaining nuts. In a medium mixing bowl stir together *2 cups* of the ground hazelnuts and the flour. Set hazelnut-flour mixture aside. Reserve remaining ground hazelnuts for garnishing cake.

Beat egg whites with an electric mixer on medium to high speed till soft peaks form (tips curl). Gradually add sugar, *1 tablespoon* at a time, beating on high speed about 8 minutes or till very stiff peaks form (tips stand straight) and sugar is *almost* dissolved. Fold ground hazelnut-flour mixture into egg white mixture. Spread mixture evenly in the prepared pans.

Bake in a 300° oven for 40 to 45 minutes or till very lightly browned and just set when lightly touched. Cool layers in pans on wire racks for 10 minutes. Carefully loosen sides of cakes from pans. Then remove cakes from pans. Peel off waxed paper and cool cakes completely on the racks.

To assemble, place first cake layer on a large serving plate. Spread *half* of the Mocha Ganache on top of the cake layer to within ¼ inch of the edge. Chill in the freezer for 5 minutes. Then spread ½ *cup* of the Buttercream on top of the Mocha Ganache. Top with second cake layer. Spread with remaining Mocha Ganache. Top with remaining cake layer. Spread remaining Buttercream on sides and top of cake.

To garnish, gently press remaining ground hazelnuts into Buttercream on sides of torte. Lightly cover and refrigerate for 4 to 24 hours. Before serving, let stand at room temperature for 10 minutes. Serves 20.

Mocha Ganache

In a medium saucepan combine 8 ounces coarsely chopped *semisweet* or *bittersweet chocolate,* 1 cup *whipping cream,* 3 tablespoons unsalted *butter,* and 2 teaspoons instant *espresso coffee powder* or *coffee granules.* Heat and stir over low heat till chocolate is melted. Remove from heat. Place the saucepan in a bowl of *ice water.* Using a rubber spatula, stir constantly for 6 to 8 minutes or till mixture thickens to a spreading consistency. Remove the saucepan from the bowl of ice water. Makes about 2 cups.

SPECIAL TOUCH
▼ ▼ ▼

For an elegant pastry-shop look, top this sensational hazelnut torte with chocolate lace garnishes and chocolate-dipped nuts.

PER SERVING
362 CALORIES
5 g PROTEIN
26 g CARBOHYDRATES
29 g TOTAL FAT
11 g SATURATED FAT
89 mg CHOLESTEROL
25 mg SODIUM

Babas au Rhum

2 *cups all-purpose flour*
1 *package active dry yeast*
⅓ *cup milk*
1 *tablespoon sugar*
½ *teaspoon salt*
4 *eggs*
½ *cup margarine* or *butter*
½ *cup light raisins*
1 *teaspoon finely shredded lemon peel*
1½ *cups water*
¾ *cup sugar*
¼ *cup rum* or *1 teaspoon rum flavoring*
1 *cup apricot preserves*
2 *tablespoons water*
4 or *6 red* or *green candied cherries,*
halved (optional)
Sliced almonds, toasted (optional)
2 *cups Sweetened Whipped Cream (see*
recipe, page 210) (optional)

In a large mixing bowl stir together *1½ cups* of the flour and the yeast. Set the flour mixture aside.

In a small saucepan heat and stir milk, the 1 tablespoon sugar, and salt *just till warm* (120° to 130°). Add to the flour mixture. Then add eggs. Beat with an electric mixer on low to medium speed for 30 seconds, scraping sides of bowl. Beat on high speed for 3 minutes. Using a spoon, stir in the remaining flour (batter will be soft and very sticky). Cut margarine into small pieces; place on top of the batter. Cover; let rise in a warm place till double (about 1 hour).

Generously grease twelve ½-cup baba molds, twelve 2½-inch muffin cups, or eight cups of a popover pan. Set molds or cups aside.

Stir margarine or butter, raisins, and lemon peel into the batter. Divide the batter between molds or cups, filling each ½ to ⅔ full. Cover and let rise for 20 to 30 minutes or till batter fills the molds or cups.

Bake in a 350° oven for 15 to 20 minutes or till golden. Remove babas from molds or cups. Cool on a wire rack with waxed paper underneath the racks.

Meanwhile, for the sugar syrup, in a small heavy saucepan stir together the 1½ cups water and the ¾ cup sugar. Cook and stir over medium heat till the sugar is dissolved. Then bring to boiling. Boil, without stirring, for 5 minutes. Remove from heat; cool slightly. Stir in rum or rum flavoring.

Using the tines of a large fork, prick babas all over. Then dip babas, top sides down, in the sugar syrup 2 or 3 times or till babas are moistened with syrup. Return babas to the wire rack. Spoon any remaining sugar syrup over the babas.

If necessary snip any large pieces of apricot in the preserves. In a small saucepan combine the preserves and the 2 tablespoons water. Heat and stir over low heat till preserves are melted. Brush some of the mixture over the babas. If desired, decorate tops with candied cherries and almonds. Then gently brush the remaining preserves over tops. If desired, serve with Sweetened Whipped Cream. Makes 8 or 12.

SPECIAL TOUCH
▼ ▼ ▼
Credit for the origin of these rum-glazed cakes goes to a Polish king who was exiled to France. Finding his yeast cake too dry, he soaked it in rum and named it after his favorite character, Ali Baba.

Give these moist yeast cakes a starring role by using the candied cherries and almonds to make stars on the tops. Just center a cherry half on each cake and then arrange the almonds around the cherry to look like the points of a star.

PER SERVING
482 CALORIES
7 g PROTEIN
78 g CARBOHYDRATES
15 g TOTAL FAT
3 g SATURATED FAT
107 mg CHOLESTEROL
310 mg SODIUM

Paris-Brest

Cream-Puff Pastry (see recipe,
   page 205)
1 slightly beaten egg
2 cups Pastry Cream (see recipe,
   page 209)
3 tablespoons Praline Powder
   Powdered Sugar
1 cup Sweetened Whipped Cream (see
   recipe, page 210) (optional)
   Praline Powder (optional)

Grease and lightly flour a large baking sheet.
Then use your finger to draw a 7-inch circle
in the flour on the baking sheet.

Drop the Cream-Puff Pastry dough into 12
mounds on the circle on the prepared baking
sheet, allowing the sides of the mounds to
just touch each other. Brush dough mounds
with the slightly beaten egg.

Bake in a 400° oven for 35 to 40 minutes or
till golden brown and puffy. Carefully slide
the pastry ring from the baking sheet to a
wire rack. Cool completely on the rack.

Cut off the top third of the pastry ring.
Remove any soft dough from the inside of
the ring. Place the bottom of the ring on a
large serving plate.

Spoon the Pastry Cream into the ring. Then
sprinkle with the 3 tablespoons Praline
Powder. Replace the top. Sift powdered
sugar over top. If desired, serve with
Sweetened Whipped Cream and additional
Praline Powder. Makes 6 to 8 servings.

Praline Powder

Line a large baking sheet with foil. Set
baking sheet aside.

Place ¾ cup ground *hazelnuts (filberts)* or
almonds in a medium skillet. Cook and stir
over medium-low heat for 4 to 5 minutes or
till golden. Remove from heat. Set toasted
ground nuts aside.

In a small heavy saucepan combine 1 cup
sugar and ⅓ cup *water.* Bring to boiling,
stirring occasionally. Cook over medium
heat, without stirring, about 15 minutes or
till the syrup is golden brown. Immediately
stir in ground nuts. Then pour the mixture
onto the prepared baking sheet; cool.

Break the cooled praline into pieces. Place
broken pieces in a blender container or food
processor bowl. Cover and blend or process
till praline is a powder. Place any unused
Praline Powder in a tightly covered
container. Store in a cool, dry place for up to
1 month; serve over ice cream or pudding.
Makes about 2 cups.

SPECIAL TOUCH
▼ ▼ ▼

An enterprising baker, who
owned a pastry shop on the
route of the Paris-Brest
bicycle race, created this
praline-and-cream-filled
pastry in 1891. In honor
of the race, he shaped the
pastry to resemble a
bicycle wheel.

   Crown this ring of
cream-puff pastry with
dollops of whipped cream.
For the finishing touch,
sprinkle the cream with a
light dusting of Praline
Powder

PER SERVING
515 CALORIES
12 g PROTEIN
43 g CARBOHYDRATES
33 g TOTAL FAT
11 g SATURATED FAT
349 mg CHOLESTEROL
447 mg SODIUM

Tarte Tatin

This upside-down apple tart
bears the name of the Tatin
sisters, who first served
it in their restaurant in the
early 1900s.

Frame the caramel-apple
filling with whipped cream.
And for an added touch,
crisscross thin strips of
orange peel on top of the
cream.

⅔ *cup sugar*
½ *cup margarine* **or** *butter*
2 *pounds (about 6) tart apples, peeled,
    cored, and quartered*
2 *cups all-purpose flour*
¼ *cup sugar*
⅔ *cup margarine* **or** *butter*
1 *slightly beaten egg*
1 *cup Sweetened Whipped Cream (see
    recipe, page 210) (optional)*

In a 10-inch *ovenproof* skillet combine the
⅔ cup sugar and the ½ cup margarine or
butter. Cook over medium heat, stirring
occasionally, till boiling. Continue cooking,
without stirring, over medium-low heat for
9 to 10 minutes more or till mixture just
begins to turn brown. (Mixture may appear
separated.) Remove from the heat.

Arrange the apples in a single layer on top
of the sugar mixture with cored sides up and
overlapping, if necessary. Cover and cook
over low heat about 10 minutes or till the
apples are tender.

Meanwhile, in a medium mixing bowl stir
together flour and the ¼ cup sugar. Cut in
the ⅔ cup margarine or butter till pieces are
the size of small peas. Using a fork, stir in
egg till all of the dough is moistened. Form
dough into a ball.

On a lightly floured surface, use your hands
to slightly flatten dough. Roll dough from
center to edges, forming a 10-inch circle. If
necessary, trim pastry to make an even circle.
Cut slits in the pastry. Wrap pastry around
the rolling pin. Then unroll pastry over the
apples in the skillet, being careful not to
stretch the pastry.

Bake in a 375° oven about 30 minutes or till
the pastry is golden. Remove the skillet from
the oven. Cool dessert in the skillet on a
wire rack for 5 minutes. Then invert the
dessert onto a large serving plate. Lift off the
skillet. If desired, garnish with Sweetened
Whipped Cream. Serve warm. Serves 8.

PER PIECE
500 CALORIES
4 g PROTEIN
61 g CARBOHYDRATES
28 g TOTAL FAT
4 g SATURATED FAT
27 mg CHOLESTEROL
319 mg SODIUM

Pots de Crème au Chocolat

▼ FRANCE

2 *cups whipping cream*
6 *ounces semisweet* or *bittersweet chocolate, coarsely chopped*
⅓ *cup sugar*
5 *beaten egg yolks*
1 *teaspoon vanilla*
½ *cup whipping cream*
  Candied Flowers (using violets) (see recipe, page 219) or *purchased candied violets (optional)*

In a heavy medium saucepan combine the 2 cups whipping cream, chocolate, and sugar. Cook and stir over medium heat about 10 minutes or till mixture comes to a full boil and thickens. (If chocolate flecks remain, use a rotary beater or wire whisk to beat mixture till blended.)

Gradually stir all of the *hot* mixture into the beaten egg yolks. Then stir in vanilla. Pour into 6 pot de crème cups, small ramekins, or oriental tea cups. Cover and chill in the refrigerator for 4 to 24 hours before serving.

Before serving, chill a small mixing bowl and the beaters of an electric mixer in the refrigerator.

In the chilled mixing bowl beat the ½ cup whipping cream with the chilled beaters on low speed till soft peaks form. Spoon the whipped cream into a decorating bag fitted with a large star tip (about ½-inch opening). Pipe a star of whipped cream on top of each dessert. *Or,* spoon a dollop of the cream on top of each. If desired, garnish with the candied violets. Makes 6 servings.

SPECIAL TOUCH
▼ ▼ ▼
A single, candied violet or edible flower gives just the right note of elegance to each serving of this silky, smooth chocolate dessert.

PER SERVING
567 CALORIES
6 g PROTEIN
31 g CARBOHYDRATES
50 g TOTAL FAT
24 g SATURATED FAT
313 mg CHOLESTEROL
44 mg SODIUM

▼ ▼ ▼
The crispy *Almond Tile Wafers* (page 154) contrast with the satiny smooth *Spanish Caramel Flan* for a winning dessert combination.

Spanish Caramel Flan

1 *lemon* or *orange*
1½ *cups half-and-half* or *light cream*
3 *inches stick cinnamon*
⅓ *cup sugar*
3 *eggs*
⅓ *cup sugar*

Using a vegetable peeler or a sharp knife, remove *half* of the peel from the lemon or orange. (Reserve remaining lemon or orange for another use.)

In a heavy medium saucepan combine half-and-half or light cream, stick cinnamon, and the lemon or orange peel. Cook over medium heat till mixture simmers. Remove from heat and set aside to cool. Remove and discard stick cinnamon and peel.

To caramelize sugar, in a heavy 8-inch skillet cook ⅓ cup sugar over medium-high heat till the sugar begins to melt, shaking the skillet occasionally to heat the sugar evenly. *(Do not stir.)* Reduce the heat to low and cook about 5 minutes more or till the sugar is melted and golden brown, stirring frequently.

Remove skillet from heat and immediately divide the caramelized sugar among 4 ungreased 6-ounce custard cups or ramekins; tilt the custard cups or ramekins to coat bottoms evenly. Let stand for 10 minutes.

Meanwhile, in a large mixing bowl use a rotary beater or wire whisk to lightly beat eggs *just till mixed.* Then stir in the cooled half-and-half mixture and ⅓ cup sugar.

Place the custard cups or ramekins in an 8x8x2-inch baking pan. Then set the pan on the oven rack. Pour egg mixture evenly into the custard cups or ramekins. Pour *boiling* or *very hot tap water* into the baking pan around the cups to a depth of 1 inch. Bake in a 325° oven for 30 to 40 minutes or till a knife inserted near the centers comes out clean.

Remove cups from water in pan. Cool slightly in the cups on a wire rack before serving. *Or,* cool completely in the custard cups or ramekins. Then cover and chill in the refrigerator till serving time. To unmold chilled flans, run a knife around the edges. Then slip the tip of the knife down the side of each cup to let the air in. Invert a dessert plate over each flan, and turn custard cup or ramekin and plate over together. Lift off the cup. Makes 4 servings.

SPECIAL TOUCH
▼ ▼ ▼

This delicately flavored custard requires a delicate garnish. Accompany each serving with an exquisite edible flower, such as a pansy or a violet, or sprinkle with edible petals.

PER SERVING
294 CALORIES
7 g PROTEIN
36 g CARBOHYDRATES
14 g TOTAL FAT
8 g SATURATED FAT
193 mg CHOLESTEROL
84 mg SODIUM

Almond Tile Wafers

¼ cup margarine or butter
2 egg whites
½ cup sugar
¼ teaspoon almond extract
½ cup all-purpose flour
⅔ cup sliced almonds, toasted

SPECIAL TOUCH
▼ ▼ ▼

These thin, crispy cookies are popular in both Spain and France. In Spain, it's customary to savor the cookies with a glass of sweet wine or sherry.

Pictured on page 152

Generously grease a large cookie sheet. (Repeat greasing the cookie sheet for each batch.) Set cookie sheet aside.

In a small saucepan melt margarine or butter over low heat; cool slightly.

In a small mixing bowl combine egg whites, sugar, and almond extract. Using a wire whisk or fork, beat till frothy. Then gradually stir flour into egg white mixture. Stir in the margarine or butter and almonds.

Drop the dough by *rounded teaspoons* about 3 inches apart onto the prepared cookie sheet. Spread batter into thin flat circles. (Bake only 4 or 5 cookies at a time.) Bake in a 350° oven for 5 to 7 minutes or till edges are lightly browned.

Immediately remove cookies from cookie sheet and drape the cookies, right sides up, over a rolling pin. (If cookies harden before you can shape them, reheat them in the oven for 1 to 2 minutes or till softened.) When cookies are firm, transfer them to a wire rack and cool completely. Makes about 30.

PER COOKIE
55 CALORIES
1 g PROTEIN
5 g CARBOHYDRATES
3 g TOTAL FAT
0 g SATURATED FAT
0 mg CHOLESTEROL
22 mg SODIUM

Baklava

4 cups walnuts, finely chopped (1 pound)

½ cup sugar

1 teaspoon ground cinnamon

1¼ cups margarine **or** butter, melted

1 16-ounce package frozen phyllo dough, thawed

1½ cups sugar

1 cup water

¼ cup honey

½ teaspoon finely shredded lemon peel

2 tablespoons lemon juice

2 inches stick cinnamon

For filling, in a large mixing bowl stir together chopped walnuts, the ½ cup sugar, and ground cinnamon. Set filling aside.

Brush the bottom of a 15x10x1-inch baking pan with some of the melted margarine or butter. Unfold phyllo dough. Layer about *one-fourth* of the phyllo sheets in the pan, generously brushing each sheet with melted margarine or butter and allowing phyllo to extend up the sides of the pan. Sprinkle about *1½ cups* of the filling on top of the phyllo in the pan. Repeat layering phyllo and filling 2 more times.

Layer remaining phyllo sheets in the pan, brushing each sheet with margarine or butter. Drizzle any remaining margarine or butter over the top layer. Trim edges of phyllo to fit the pan. Using a sharp knife, cut through all the layers to make triangle- or diamond-shaped pieces or squares. Bake in a 325° oven for 45 to 50 minutes or till golden. Slightly cool baklava in pan on a wire rack.

Meanwhile, in a medium saucepan stir together the 1½ cups sugar, water, honey, lemon peel, lemon juice, and stick cinnamon. Bring to boiling. Reduce heat. Simmer, uncovered, for 20 minutes. Remove cinnamon. Pour honey mixture over warm baklava in the pan. Cool completely. Makes about 60 pieces.

SPECIAL TOUCH

▼ ▼ ▼

Just a small piece of this sweet, buttery creation satisfies even the biggest sweet tooth. Before serving, drizzle honey over small dessert plates. Then add the triangular or diamond-shaped pieces of Baklava.

PER PIECE

130 CALORIES

3 g PROTEIN

13 g CARBOHYDRATES

8 g TOTAL FAT

1 g SATURATED FAT

0 mg CHOLESTEROL

71 mg SODIUM

Classic Ricotta Cheesecake

▼ ITALY

SPECIAL TOUCH
▼ ▼ ▼
When in Rome (or at home), do as the Romans do. Enjoy this Italian classic with a cup of espresso or cappuccino.

¾ *cup all-purpose flour*
3 *tablespoons sugar*
½ *teaspoon finely shredded lemon peel*
⅓ *cup margarine or butter*
1 *beaten egg yolk*
  Margarine or butter
3 *cups ricotta cheese*
½ *cup sugar*
¼ *cup milk*
2 *tablespoons all-purpose flour*
3 *eggs*
¼ *cup light raisins*
2 *tablespoons chopped Candied Citrus Peel (using oranges) (see recipe, page 217)*
1 *teaspoon finely shredded lemon peel*

For crust, in a medium mixing bowl stir together ¾ cup flour, 3 tablespoons sugar, and ½ teaspoon lemon peel. Cut in ⅓ cup margarine or butter till pieces are the size of small peas. Using a fork, stir in egg yolk till all of the dough is moistened.

Remove the sides from an 8-inch springform pan. Press *one-third* of the dough onto the bottom of the springform pan. Bake in a 350° oven for 7 to 10 minutes or till golden. Cool on a wire rack.

Grease the sides of the springform pan with the additional margarine or butter. Then attach the sides to the bottom. Press remaining dough 1½ inches up the sides of the pan. Set the pan aside.

For filling, in a large mixing bowl beat the ricotta cheese, ½ cup sugar, milk, and 2 tablespoons flour with an electric mixer on medium to high speed till combined. Add whole eggs all at once. Beat on low speed *just till combined.* Stir in raisins, Candied Citrus Peel, and 1 teaspoon lemon peel.

Pour filling into the crust-lined springform pan. Then place the springform pan on a shallow baking pan on the oven rack. Bake in a 350° oven about 45 minutes or till center appears *nearly* set when shaken.

Remove springform pan from baking pan. Cool cheesecake in springform pan on a wire rack for 15 minutes. Loosen crust from sides of pan and cool for 30 minutes more. Remove sides of the springform pan. Cool completely, then chill cheesecake in the refrigerator for at least 4 hours before serving. Makes 8 to 10 servings.

PER SERVING
371 CALORIES
15 g PROTEIN
37 g CARBOHYDRATES
19 g TOTAL FAT
7 g SATURATED FAT
136 mg CHOLESTEROL
243 mg SODIUM

Crostata

2 *cups all-purpose flour*
⅓ *cup sugar*
2 *teaspoons baking powder*
⅔ *cup margarine* **or** *butter*
1 *slightly beaten egg*
¼ *cup milk*
1 *teaspoon vanilla*
4 *cups sliced, peeled tart apples*
⅔ *cup apricot* **or** *peach preserves*
¼ *cup sugar*
   Milk
   Sugar

In a medium mixing bowl stir together flour, ⅓ cup sugar, and baking powder. Cut in margarine or butter till mixture resembles coarse crumbs. Make a well in the center of the dry mixture.

In a small mixing bowl stir together egg, milk, and vanilla. Add egg mixture all at once to dry mixture. Using a fork, stir *just till moistened.*

Turn dough out onto a lightly floured surface. Gently knead the dough for 10 to 12 strokes or till dough is *nearly* smooth.

Chill *one-third* of the dough in the refrigerator. Meanwhile, pat the remaining dough onto the bottom and up sides of a 10-inch tart pan with a removable bottom.

Arrange the apple slices on top of the pastry in the tart pan. Stir together preserves and ¼ cup sugar. Spread the preserve mixture evenly over the apples.

On a lightly floured surface, use your hands to slightly flatten the chilled dough. Roll dough from center to edges, forming a 10-inch circle. Cut circle into ½-inch-wide strips. Weave strips on top of filling to make a lattice. Press ends of strips into rim of bottom crust, trimming as necessary. Brush lattice with milk; sprinkle with sugar.

Bake in a 375° oven for 45 to 50 minutes or till apples are tender (if necessary, loosely cover tart with foil the last 10 to 15 minutes to prevent overbrowning). Cool slightly in pan on a wire rack. Remove from pan and serve warm. Makes 8 to 10 servings.

SPECIAL TOUCH
▼ ▼ ▼

Present slices of this tart in pools of cream. Place the slices in shallow dessert dishes. Then carefully pour some half-and-half or light cream around each slice.

PER SERVING
481 CALORIES
4 g PROTEIN
82 g CARBOHYDRATES
17 g TOTAL FAT
3 g SATURATED FAT
27 mg CHOLESTEROL
268 mg SODIUM

Brandy Snaps, filled with a marvelous brandy-flavored whipped cream, are always considered to be a fabulous first-class cookie.

Brandy Snaps

½ cup packed brown sugar
⅓ cup margarine **or** butter, melted
¼ cup dark corn syrup **or** light molasses
1 tablespoon brandy
¾ cup all-purpose flour
½ teaspoon ground ginger
½ teaspoon ground nutmeg
  Brandy-Cream Filling

Line a cookie sheet with *heavy* foil. Grease the foil. (If necessary, line the cookie sheet with a new piece of *heavy* foil and grease the foil for each batch.) Set cookie sheet aside.

In a medium mixing bowl stir together brown sugar, melted margarine or butter, corn syrup or molasses, and brandy. Stir in flour, ginger, and nutmeg till thoroughly combined.

Drop batter from a *level teaspoon* 3 inches apart on the prepared cookie sheet. (Bake only 4 or 5 cookies at a time.) Bake in a 350° oven for 5 to 6 minutes or till cookies are bubbly and a deep golden brown.

Cool cookies on the cookie sheet about 2 minutes or till set. Quickly remove cookies, one at a time. Place each cookie, upside down, on a heatproof surface. *Immediately* roll each cookie around a metal cone or a greased handle of a wooden spoon. When the cookie is firm, slide the cookie off the cone or wooden spoon and cool completely on a wire rack. (If cookies harden before you can shape them, reheat them in the oven about 1 minute or till softened.)

Just before serving, spoon the Brandy-Cream Filling into a decorating bag fitted with a large star tip (about ½-inch opening). Pipe some of the cream filling into each cookie. Makes about 54.

Brandy-Cream Filling

Chill a large mixing bowl and the beaters of an electric mixer in the refrigerator. In the chilled mixing bowl combine 2 cups *whipping cream,* ¼ cup sifted *powdered sugar,* and 2 tablespoons *brandy.* Beat with the chilled beaters on low speed till stiff peaks form. Makes about 4 cups.

SPECIAL TOUCH
▼ ▼ ▼

A yuletide favorite, these cream-filled lace cookies are flavored with a hint of ginger and nutmeg. For a holiday look, tie a small bow around each cookie.

PER COOKIE
63 CALORIES
0 g PROTEIN
5 g CARBOHYDRATES
4 g TOTAL FAT
2 g SATURATED FAT
12 mg CHOLESTEROL
18 mg SODIUM

English Trifle

1 *layer Hot Milk Sponge Cake (see recipe, page 208)*
2 *tablespoons cream sherry* or *orange juice*
¼ *cup red raspberry* or *strawberry preserves*
¼ *cup sliced almonds, toasted*
2 *cups Crème Anglaise (without liqueur) (see recipe, page 212)*
2 *cups Sweetened Whipped Cream (see recipe, page 210)*
1 *cup raspberries* or *1½ cups small strawberries*

Cut or tear the Hot Milk Sponge Cake into 1-inch pieces.

In a 1½-quart clear glass serving bowl with straight sides, soufflé dish, or serving bowl place *half* of the cake pieces. Sprinkle with *half* of the sherry or orange juice. Then spoon on *half* of the raspberry or strawberry preserves by small teaspoonfuls. Sprinkle with all of the almonds. Then pour *half* of the Crème Anglaise over all. Repeat the layers using the remaining cake pieces, sherry or orange juice, preserves, and Crème Anglaise. Cover and chill in the refrigerator for 3 to 24 hours before serving.

Just before serving, spread about *half* of the Sweetened Whipped Cream over top. Then arrange raspberries or strawberries on top, reserving some berries to garnish.

To garnish, spoon the remaining Sweetened Whipped Cream into a decorating bag fitted with medium star tip (about ¼-inch opening). Pipe stars around the outer edge of the trifle. Place a berry in the center of each star. Makes 6 servings.

PER SERVING
645 CALORIES
6 g PROTEIN
64 g CARBOHYDRATES
42 g TOTAL FAT
23 g SATURATED FAT
234 mg CHOLESTEROL
127 mg SODIUM

Richmond Maids of Honor

Rich Tart Pastry (see recipe, page 206)
4½ *teaspoons red raspberry jam* **or**
     preserves
 ½ *cup whole almonds*
 3 *tablespoons margarine* **or** *butter*
 ½ *cup sugar*
 1 *egg*
 ¼ *teaspoon almond extract*

For tartlet shells, on a lightly floured surface, use your hands to slightly flatten the Rich Tart Pastry dough. Roll dough from center to edges to ⅛-inch thickness. Using a 2¾-inch round cutter, cut out 18 circles. Then line 1¾-inch muffin cups with pastry circles.

Spoon ¼ *teaspoon* of the raspberry jam or preserves into *each* of the tartlet shells.

For filling, place almonds in a blender container or food processor bowl. Cover and blend or process till almonds are very fine and dry (not oily). Set almonds aside.

In a medium mixing bowl beat margarine or butter with an electric mixer on medium to high speed about 30 seconds or till softened.

Add sugar to margarine and beat till combined. Then add egg, beating till combined. Stir in the ground almonds and almond extract. Spoon about *1 tablespoon* filling on top of jam in *each* tartlet shell, filling each to ¼ inch from the top.

Bake in a 375° oven about 25 minutes or till golden. Remove tartlets from pans and cool on a wire rack. Makes 18.

SPECIAL TOUCH
▼ ▼ ▼

These tiny tarts were first served to the court of Henry VIII in the 16th century. Today, they still frequently appear at English teas.

For a display fit for a king, arrange these almond-filled tarts on a silver platter lined with a large paper doily.

PER TARTLET
146 CALORIES
2 g PROTEIN
14 g CARBOHYDRATES
10 g TOTAL FAT
4 g SATURATED FAT
37 mg CHOLESTEROL
79 mg SODIUM

*S*chaumtorte

4 *egg whites*
¼ *teaspoon cream of tartar*
¾ *cup sugar*
2 *cups whipping cream*
¼ *cup sugar*
3 *tablespoons strawberry, raspberry,* **or** *orange liqueur*
2 *cups sliced strawberries* **or** *3 cups raspberries*

In a large mixing bowl let egg whites stand at room temperature for 30 minutes. Meanwhile, line 2 baking sheets with parchment paper or plain brown paper. Draw four 7-inch circles about 3 inches apart on the paper. Set baking sheets aside.

Add cream of tartar to the egg whites. Beat with an electric mixer on medium to high speed till soft peaks form (tips curl). Gradually add ¾ cup sugar, *1 tablespoon* at a time, beating on high speed about 9 minutes or till very stiff peaks form (tips stand straight) and sugar is *almost* dissolved.

Spoon about *one-third* of the meringue mixture into a decorating bag fitted with a large star tip (about ½-inch opening). Pipe a lattice design on the prepared baking sheet over *one* of the circles. Then pipe a border around the lattice.

Spoon another *one-third* of the meringue mixture into the decorating bag. Pipe 2 rings using *two* circles on the paper as guides.

Using a spoon or spatula, spread the remaining meringue mixture over the remaining circle on the paper.

Bake in a 300° oven for 20 minutes. Turn off oven. Then let the meringues dry in the oven with the door closed for 1 hour. *(Do not open the oven.)* Meanwhile, chill a medium mixing bowl and the beaters of an electric mixer in the refrigerator.

For the filling, in the chilled bowl combine whipping cream, ¼ cup sugar, and liqueur. Beat with the chilled beaters on low speed till soft peaks form. Fold in the sliced strawberries or raspberries; set aside.

To assemble, peel meringues from paper. Place the solid meringue circle on a large serving plate. Then stack the 2 meringue rings on top to form a shell. Spoon the filling into the shell. Finally, top with the meringue lattice. Cover and chill in the refrigerator for 4 to 18 hours before serving. Makes 8 to 10 servings.

Black Forest Cherry Cake

▼ **GERMANY**

1 *slightly beaten egg*
⅔ *cup sugar*
½ *cup milk*
4 *ounces unsweetened chocolate, coarsely chopped*
1¾ *cups all-purpose flour*
1 *teaspoon baking soda*
½ *teaspoon salt*
½ *cup shortening*
1 *cup sugar*
1 *teaspoon vanilla*
2 *eggs*
1 *cup milk*
3 *cups Chocolate Buttercream (see recipe, page 211)*
   Tart Cherry Filling
2 *cups Sweetened Whipped-Cream Frosting (see recipe, page 210)*

In a heavy medium saucepan combine the 1 slightly beaten egg, ⅔ cup sugar, ½ cup milk, and chopped chocolate. Bring just to boiling over medium heat, stirring constantly. Remove from heat. If necessary, stir till chocolate is melted. Set aside to cool.

Meanwhile, grease and lightly flour three 9x1½-inch round baking pans. In a small mixing bowl stir together flour, baking soda, and salt. Set pans and flour mixture aside.

In a large mixing bowl beat shortening with an electric mixer on medium to high speed about 30 seconds or till softened. Add 1 cup sugar and vanilla and beat till combined. Then add the 2 eggs, one at a time, beating till combined. Alternately add flour mixture

and 1 cup milk, beating on low to medium speed after each addition *just till combined.* Stir in chocolate mixture.

Pour the batter into the prepared pans. Bake in a 350° oven for 18 to 20 minutes or till a wooden toothpick inserted near the centers of the cakes comes out clean. Cool the cakes in pans on wire racks for 10 minutes. Then remove the cakes; cool completely on racks.

To assemble, place first cake layer on a large serving plate. Using ¾ *cup* of the Chocolate Buttercream, spread a ½-inch-wide and ¾-inch-high border around the top edge. Then spread *half* of the chilled Tart Cherry Filling in the center. Top with the second cake layer. Using ¾ *cup* buttercream, repeat spreading a border on top edge of cake and spread remaining filling in center. Finally, top with remaining cake. Frost sides with remaining buttercream; frost top with the Sweetened Whipped-Cream Frosting. Chill in the refrigerator till serving. Serves 12.

Tart Cherry Filling

Drain one 16-ounce can pitted *tart red cherries* (water pack), reserving ½ *cup* liquid. In a saucepan combine the liquid, 1 tablespoon *cornstarch,* and 1 tablespoon *sugar.* Add cherries. Cook and stir till mixture is thickened and bubbly. Cook and stir for 2 minutes more. Stir in 2 tablespoons *kirsch (cherry brandy).* Cool. Cover and chill in the refrigerator for at least 2 hours before using. *(Do not stir.)* Makes 1¾ cups.

SPECIAL TOUCH
▼ ▼ ▼
Create a topping that befits this luscious cake. Use a decorating bag and a small star tip to pipe whipped cream stars all over the top of the cake. Then encircle the cake with a border of loose chocolate curls and dark sweet cherries with stems.

PER SERVING
776 CALORIES
8 g PROTEIN
76 g CARBOHYDRATES
53 g TOTAL FAT
23 g SATURATED FAT
252 mg CHOLESTEROL
207 mg SODIUM

Cream-and-Berry-Filled Pastry Cones

▼ SCANDINAVIA

2 egg whites
¼ cup butter
½ cup sugar
½ cup all-purpose flour
2 cups Sweetened Whipped Cream (see recipe, page 210)
1 14½-ounce can lingonberries, drained, or 1 cup fresh raspberries

In a medium mixing bowl let egg whites stand at room temperature for 30 minutes. Meanwhile, generously grease a cookie sheet. (Repeat greasing the cookie sheet for each batch.) Set the cookie sheet aside.

In a small saucepan heat butter over low heat *just till melted.* Set aside to cool.

Beat egg whites with an electric mixer on medium to high speed till soft peaks form (tips curl). Gradually add sugar, *1 tablespoon* at a time, beating on medium to high speed till stiff peaks form (tips stand straight). Fold about *half* of the flour into the egg white mixture. Gently stir in the butter. Fold in the remaining flour till thoroughly combined.

Drop batter from a *heaping tablespoon* about 3 inches apart on the prepared cookie sheet. (Bake only 3 cookies at a time.) Using a knife or narrow metal spatula spread batter into 4-inch circles. Bake in a 375° oven for 5 to 6 minutes or till the edges of the cookies begin to brown.

Immediately remove cookies from cookie sheet, one at a time. Roll each cookie, bottom side in, around a metal cone. *Or,* to form cookie cups, place each cookie over an inverted glass, then gently fold edges down to form ruffles or pleats. (If cookies harden before you can shape them, reheat them in the oven about 1 minute or till softened.) When cookie is firm, slide cookie off cone or remove from glass and cool completely on a wire rack.

Just before serving, spoon the Sweetened Whipped Cream into a decorating bag fitted with a medium star or round tip (about ¼-inch opening). Pipe some of the whipped cream into each cookie cone or cup. Sprinkle with lingonberries or raspberries. Makes 14.

Cool Sensations

Indulging in a bowl of ice cream or a piece of chiffon
pie can bring back memories from yesteryears . . .
waiting for the ice-cream man, enjoying dessert socials
on the town square, or riding your bike to Grandma's
for an afternoon treat. Desserts from the icebox are
sure to cool you on a hot summer day and make you
think of only the sweet memories. So why not
reminisce over a piece of Peanut Butter Chiffon Pie, a
spoonful of Spumoni Soufflé, or a scoop of Pecan Ice
Cream with Brandied Peach Sauce?

▼▼▼

Cappuccino Gelato with Crème Anglaise

SPECIAL TOUCH
▼ ▼ ▼
Scoop servings of this
Italian frozen custard into
glass goblets and place on
dessert plates lined with
plain or gold-paper doilies.

5 *cups milk*
1 *cup sugar*
10 *beaten egg yolks*
¼ *cup instant espresso coffee powder* **or** *instant coffee crystals*
1 *tablespoon finely shredded orange peel*
2 *cups Crème Anglaise (using orange liqueur) (see recipe, page 212)*
Candied Citrus Peel (using oranges) (see recipe, page 217) **or** *finely shredded orange peel (optional)*

In a large saucepan combine 2½ *cups* of the milk, the sugar, and beaten egg yolks. Cook and stir over medium heat till mixture *just coats* a metal spoon. Remove from heat.

Stir the remaining milk, the coffee powder or crystals, and 1 tablespoon orange peel into the egg yolk mixture.

Cover the surface with plastic wrap. Cool thoroughly by placing the saucepan in a sink of *ice water* or overnight in the refrigerator.

Freeze in a 4- or 5-quart ice-cream freezer according to manufacturer's directions.

To serve, scoop the gelato into dessert dishes. Top with Crème Anglaise. If desired, garnish with Candied Citrus Peel or additional finely shredded orange peel. Makes about 2½ quarts (about 15 servings).

PER SERVING
247 CALORIES
6 g PROTEIN
27 g CARBOHYDRATES
13 g TOTAL FAT
7 g SATURATED FAT
205 mg CHOLESTEROL
55 mg SODIUM

Pineapple Sherbet in Chocolate Praline Baskets

1½ cups sugar

1 envelope unflavored gelatin

3¾ cups unsweetened pineapple juice

1 cup milk

8 ounces semisweet or bittersweet chocolate, chopped

4 teaspoons shortening

16 Praline Baskets (see recipe, page 216)

½ cup coconut, toasted

For sherbet, in a medium saucepan stir together sugar and gelatin. Then stir in the *2 cups* of the pineapple juice. Cook and stir till the sugar and gelatin dissolve. Remove saucepan from the heat.

Stir in milk and remaining pineapple juice. (Mixture will look curdled.) Cool. Transfer mixture to a 9x9x2-inch baking pan. Cover and freeze for 2 to 3 hours or till *almost* firm. (*Or,* after combining ingredients, freeze in a 4- or 5-quart ice-cream freezer according to manufacturer's directions. Omit remaining steps for sherbet.)

Place a large mixing bowl in the refrigerator or freezer to chill. Break the frozen mixture into small chunks. Transfer the small chunks to the chilled bowl. Beat with an electric mixer on medium speed till mixture is smooth but not melted. Then return mixture to the baking pan. Cover and freeze till firm.

Meanwhile, for chocolate Praline Baskets, melt the semisweet or bittersweet chocolate with the shortening according to the directions on page 225. Crumble *two* of the Praline Baskets into small pieces; set aside. Place *twelve* of the Praline Baskets on waxed paper. Using a pastry brush, brush the insides of the baskets with a thin layer of the melted chocolate, completely coating the bottoms and sides. Then sprinkle with toasted coconut. Let stand for 3 to 4 hours or till chocolate is dry. (Store the remaining 2 Praline Baskets in an airtight container at room temperature for up to 10 days or in the freezer for longer storage; serve ice cream, fresh fruit, or pudding in the remaining baskets.)

To serve, use a small ice-cream scoop to scrape along the surface. Place several small scoops of sherbet in each of the chocolate Praline Baskets. Then top with the crumbled Praline Baskets. Makes about 2 quarts (about 12 servings).

SPECIAL TOUCH
▼ ▼ ▼

A tisket, a tasket, try a nut and chocolate basket! The chocolate Praline Baskets make delicious containers for this refreshing sherbet. For even more pizzazz, drizzle additional melted chocolate on the dessert plates. Then place the Praline Baskets on the plates, fill with sherbet, and garnish with fresh pineapple wedges.

PER SERVING
508 CALORIES
4 g PROTEIN
74 g CARBOHYDRATES
26 g TOTAL FAT
6 g SATURATED FAT
22 mg CHOLESTEROL
28 mg SODIUM

Red Plum Sorbet with Caramel Filigree

SPECIAL TOUCH

▼ ▼ ▼

For a truly impressive
touch, decorate heatproof
dessert goblets or dishes
with some of the caramel
filigree mixture. When
making the Caramel
Filigree Garnishes, drizzle
part of the mixture
randomly into glass goblets
or dishes, making a lacy
pattern. Let stand till set.
A cleanup hint—soak the
goblets in hot water to
loosen the caramel.

3 *cups diced, pitted red plums*
¼ *cup water*
1 *cup water*
¾ *cup sugar*
1 *tablespoon kirsch (cherry brandy)*
   (optional)
2 *egg whites (see tip, page 175)*
   Caramel Filigree Garnishes (see recipe,
   page 217) (optional)

In a medium saucepan combine the plums
and the ¼ cup water. Bring to boiling, then
reduce heat. Cover and simmer, stirring
occasionally, about 10 minutes or till plums
are tender. Pour the plum mixture into a
blender container or food processor bowl.
Cover and blend or process till plums are
almost smooth. Then return the plum
mixture to the medium saucepan or transfer
to a mixing bowl.

Meanwhile, in a small saucepan stir together
the 1 cup water and sugar. Bring to boiling.
Then boil for 5 minutes; remove from heat.
Stir in the sugar mixture and, if desired,
kirsch. Set plum mixture aside to cool.

Meanwhile, beat the egg whites with an
electric mixer on medium to high speed till
stiff peaks form (tips stand straight). Fold the
egg whites into the plum mixture. Transfer
mixture to a 9x9x2-inch baking pan. Cover
and freeze for 3 to 4 hours or till *almost* firm.
(*Or,* after combining the ingredients, freeze
in a 2- or 4-quart ice-cream freezer according
to the manufacturer's directions. Omit the
remaining steps.)

Place a large mixing bowl in the refrigerator
or freezer to chill. Break the frozen mixture
into small chunks. Transfer the small chunks
to the chilled bowl. Beat on medium speed
till mixture is smooth but not melted. Then
return mixture to the baking pan. Cover and
freeze for at least 6 hours or till firm.

To serve, use an ice-cream scoop to scrape
along the surface. Place scoops in dessert
goblets or dishes. If desired, top with
Caramel Filigree Garnishes. Makes about
1½ quarts (about 9 servings).

PER SERVING
91 CALORIES
1 g PROTEIN
23 g CARBOHYDRATES
0 g TOTAL FAT
0 g SATURATED FAT
0 mg CHOLESTEROL
13 mg SODIUM

Raspberry Ice with Chocolate Lace

1 *10-ounce package frozen red raspberries, thawed*
¼ *cup sugar*
3 *tablespoons crème de cassis or orange juice*
½ *teaspoon finely shredded orange peel*
   Chocolate lace garnishes (using semisweet or bittersweet chocolate and white baking bar) (see page 228)

Place the raspberries in a blender container or food processor bowl. Cover and blend or process till puréed. Then press berries through a fine-mesh sieve; discard seeds. (You should have about *1¼ cups* sieved raspberry purée.)

Return the puréed berries to the blender container or the food processor bowl. Add the sugar, crème de cassis or orange juice, and orange peel. Cover and blend or process till sugar dissolves. Transfer raspberry mixture to a 9x5x3-inch loaf pan. Cover and freeze for 3 to 4 hours or till *almost* firm.

Place a large mixing bowl in the refrigerator or freezer to chill. Break the frozen mixture into small chunks. Transfer the small chunks to the chilled bowl. Beat with an electric mixer on medium speed till mixture is smooth but not melted. Then return mixture to the loaf pan. Cover and freeze at least 6 hours or till firm before serving.

To serve, let raspberry mixture stand at room temperature about 5 minutes. Using a small ice-cream scoop, scrape along the surface of the ice. For each serving, place 3 scoops in a dessert dish. Then garnish each with 1 or 2 pieces of the chocolate lace. Makes about 2½ cups (about 4 servings).

SPECIAL TOUCH
▼ ▼ ▼
Let loose when making the two-tone chocolate lace garnishes. Drizzle the melted chocolate and white baking bar in any free-form design.

PER SERVING
378 CALORIES
4 g PROTEIN
59 g CARBOHYDRATES
17 g TOTAL FAT
1 g SATURATED FAT
0 mg CHOLESTEROL
2 mg SODIUM

▼ ▼ ▼
At your next celebration, toast to good cheer with this *Cherry-Champagne Ice.*

Cherry-Champagne Ice

2/3 *cup sugar*
1/2 *cup unsweetened cherry juice* or *white grape juice*
1 1/4 *pounds fresh tart red cherries, pitted, or one 16-ounce package frozen unsweetened pitted tart red cherries, slightly thawed*
2/3 *cup champagne* or *white grape juice*
1/2 *teaspoon finely shredded lemon peel*

In a medium saucepan stir together sugar and cherry juice or white grape juice. Cook and stir over medium-high heat till sugar dissolves. Remove from heat. Transfer mixture to a medium mixing bowl. Set sugar mixture aside to cool.

Meanwhile, in a blender container or food processor bowl place cherries, champagne or white grape juice, and lemon peel. Cover and blend or process till cherry mixture is almost smooth.

Stir cherry mixture into the cooled sugar mixture. Transfer mixture to a 9x5x3-inch loaf pan. Cover and freeze for 3 to 4 hours or till *almost* firm. (*Or,* after combining ingredients, freeze in a 1- or 2-quart ice-cream freezer according to manufacturer's directions. Omit the remaining steps.)

Place a large mixing bowl in the refrigerator or freezer to chill. Break the frozen mixture into small chunks. Transfer the small chunks to the chilled bowl. Beat with an electric mixer on medium speed till mixture is smooth but not melted. Then return mixture to the loaf pan. Cover and freeze at least 6 hours more or till firm before serving.

To serve, use a small ice-cream scoop to scrape along the surface of ice. Makes about 1 quart (6 to 8 servings).

SPECIAL TOUCH
▼ ▼ ▼
Combine this flavorful fruit ice with chocolate and champagne for an absolutely stunning dessert. Before serving the Cherry-Champagne Ice, pipe melted chocolate on the dessert dishes to form cherry stems. Then attach chocolate leaves and set the dishes aside until the chocolate is dry. Right before serving, place small scoops of the ice in the dishes. Pour champagne around the ice and set chocolate-dipped spoons beside the desserts.

PER SERVING
145 CALORIES
1 g PROTEIN
34 g CARBOHYDRATES
0 g TOTAL FAT
0 g SATURATED FAT
0 mg CHOLESTEROL
4 mg SODIUM

Cream Cheese and Apricot Ice Cream

2 tablespoons apricot brandy, apricot nectar, kirsch (cherry brandy), orange liqueur, or orange juice
¼ cup finely chopped dried apricots, dried cherries, or dried blueberries
1 8-ounce package cream cheese
1¼ cups sugar
2 eggs (see tip, page 175)
1 teaspoon vanilla
1½ cups milk
1 cup whipping cream
3 ounces white baking bar, semisweet chocolate, or bittersweet chocolate, chopped

In a small mixing bowl pour apricot brandy over the dried fruit. Cover and let stand for 4 to 24 hours. *Do not drain.*

In a large mixing bowl beat cream cheese with an electric mixer on medium speed about 30 seconds or till softened.

Add sugar to the cream cheese and beat till smooth. Then add eggs and vanilla. Beat till thoroughly combined, scraping sides of bowl occasionally. Stir in milk, whipping cream, white baking bar or chocolate, and undrained fruit.

Freeze in a 2- or 4-quart ice-cream freezer according to the manufacturer's directions. If desired, for a harder ice cream, transfer the ice cream to a covered container and freeze for 24 hours before serving. Makes about 1½ quarts (about 9 servings).

PER SERVING
385 CALORIES
6 g PROTEIN
38 g CARBOHYDRATES
23 g TOTAL FAT
14 g SATURATED FAT
114 mg CHOLESTEROL
129 mg SODIUM

Triple-Chocolate Ice Cream with Cherry Sauce

4 ounces white baking bar, chopped
2 cups half-and-half or light cream
¾ cup sugar
2 beaten egg yolks
3 cups whipping cream
1 tablespoon vanilla
2 ounces milk chocolate, chopped
2 ounces semisweet or bittersweet
    chocolate, chopped
16 Chocolate Ruffled Cups (see recipe,
    page 230) (optional)
    Cherry Sauce (see recipe, page 215)

Melt the white baking bar according to the directions on page 225; cool.

In a large saucepan combine the half-and-half or light cream and sugar. Cook and stir over medium heat just till sugar dissolves.

Gradually stir about *1 cup* of the warm mixture into beaten egg yolks. Then return all of the egg yolk mixture to the saucepan. Bring to a gentle boil, stirring constantly. Remove from heat.

Stir the melted white baking bar into the egg yolk mixture till combined. Then stir in whipping cream and vanilla. Cool thoroughly by placing the saucepan either in a sink of *ice-water* or overnight in the refrigerator.

Stir the milk chocolate and semisweet or bittersweet chocolate into the cooled cream mixture. Freeze in a 4- or 5-quart ice-cream freezer according to the manufacturer's directions.

If desired, serve small scoops of the ice cream in *twelve* of the Chocolate Ruffled Cups. (Store the remaining 4 cups in a tightly covered container in a cool, dry place for up to 1 month; serve ice cream, fresh fruit, or pudding in the remaining chocolate cups.) Top with Cherry Sauce. Makes about 2 quarts (about 12 servings).

SPECIAL TOUCH
▼ ▼ ▼
Easy does it. With three kinds of chocolate and the Cherry Sauce, just top each dessert with a few chocolate curls for a finishing look.

PER SERVING
461 CALORIES
4 g PROTEIN
40 g CARBOHYDRATES
33 g TOTAL FAT
19 g SATURATED FAT
133 mg CHOLESTEROL
54 mg SODIUM

Rum-Pistachio Ice Cream

1 tablespoon rum
⅔ cup raisins
2 cups milk
½ cup sugar
6 egg yolks
½ cup sugar
1 cup whipping cream
1 teaspoon finely shredded orange peel
⅓ cup coarsely chopped pistachio nuts

Play up the pistachios! For each serving, dip the rim of a stemmed dessert dish into melted white baking bar, semisweet chocolate, or bittersweet chocolate. Allow the excess baking bar or chocolate to drip off. Then dip the rim of the dish into finely chopped pistachio nuts. Let the dessert dishes stand till dry.

In a small mixing bowl pour rum over raisins; set aside.

Meanwhile, in a large saucepan stir together milk and ½ cup sugar. Cook and stir over medium heat till mixture *almost boils* and sugar dissolves. Remove from heat; set aside.

In a blender container or food processor bowl place egg yolks and ½ cup sugar. Cover and blend or process about 2 minutes or till mixture thickens. With the blender or food processor running, gradually add about *1 cup* of the warm milk mixture. (*Or,* in a medium mixing bowl beat egg yolks and the ½ cup sugar with an electric mixer on medium to high speed about 4 minutes or till thick. Gradually beat in about *1 cup* of the warm milk mixture.)

Return all of the egg yolk mixture to the remaining milk mixture in saucepan. Bring to boiling, stirring constantly. *Immediately* pour mixture into a large mixing bowl. Stir in whipping cream, orange peel, and *undrained* raisins. Cool thoroughly by placing the bowl either in a larger bowl or sink of *ice-water* or overnight in the refrigerator.

Stir the pistachio nuts into the cream mixture. Freeze in a 2-quart ice-cream freezer according to the manufacturer's directions. Makes about 1 quart (about 6 servings).

PER SERVING
453 CALORIES
8 g PROTEIN
52 g CARBOHYDRATES
25 g TOTAL FAT
12 g SATURATED FAT
273 mg CHOLESTEROL
65 mg SODIUM

Lemon Mint Ice Cream

2 eggs (see tip, page 175)
3 cups half-and-half **or** light cream
2 cups sugar
¼ cup finely snipped fresh mint
1 tablespoon finely shredded lemon peel
¼ cup lemon juice
4 cups whipping cream

In a large mixing bowl use a rotary beater or wire whisk to lightly beat eggs *just till mixed.* Then stir in half-and-half or light cream, sugar, mint, lemon peel, and lemon juice. Stir till sugar dissolves.

Stir whipping cream into egg mixture. Freeze in a 4- or 5-quart ice-cream freezer according to the manufacturer's directions. Makes about 3 quarts (about 18 servings).

Using Eggs Safely

Eggs can make desserts lighter in texture and richer in flavor. But to be on the safe side, always use clean, fresh eggs. When cracking eggs, avoid getting any eggshell in with the raw eggs. Also when separating eggs, don't pass the yolk from shell half to shell half. Instead, use an egg separator so that if bacteria is present on the shell, it won't contaminate the yolk or white.

Eating uncooked or slightly cooked eggs in foods such as sauces or frozen desserts may be harmful because of possible bacterial contamination from salmonella. The individuals most susceptible include the elderly, infants, pregnant women, and those who are already ill. Check with your doctor to see if you are at risk. If you are, you probably should avoid eating foods that contain raw or partially cooked eggs. Healthy people should eat raw eggs with discretion.

Or, if you like, replace whole eggs or egg yolks in desserts with a frozen or refrigerated egg substitute. Egg substitues are pasteurized to destroy salmonella bacteria. Use ¼ cup egg substitute for 1 whole egg and *2 tablespoons* egg substitute for 1 egg yolk.

PER SERVING
325 CALORIES
3 g PROTEIN
25 g CARBOHYDRATES
25 g TOTAL FAT
15 g SATURATED FAT
111 mg CHOLESTEROL
43 mg SODIUM

▼ ▼ ▼

No matter what the season, this *Pecan Ice Cream with Brandied Peach Sauce* is one of the most tantalizing delicacies imaginable.

Pecan Ice Cream with Brandied Peach Sauce

2 cups half-and-half, light cream, or milk
1 cup packed brown sugar
2 beaten egg yolks
3 cups whipping cream
1 tablespoon vanilla
1 cup chopped toasted pecans, almonds,
     or hazelnuts (filberts)
16 Praline Baskets (see recipe, page 216)
     (optional)
     Brandied Peach Sauce

In a large saucepan stir together the half-and-half, light cream, or milk and the brown sugar. (Mixture may look curdled.) Cook and stir over medium heat till mixture *almost boils* and brown sugar dissolves.

Gradually stir about *1 cup* of the warm mixture into the beaten egg yolks. Return all of the egg yolk mixture to the saucepan. Bring to boiling, stirring constantly. Reduce heat. Cook and stir for 2 minutes more, then remove from heat.

Stir whipping cream and vanilla into the hot mixture in the saucepan. Cool thoroughly by placing the saucepan either in a sink of *ice-water* or overnight in the refrigerator.

Stir the pecans, almonds, or hazelnuts into the cooled cream mixture. Freeze in a 4- or 5-quart ice-cream freezer according to the manufacturer's directions.

If desired, scoop the ice cream into *twelve* of the Praline Baskets. (Store the remaining 4 Praline Baskets in an airtight container at room temperature for up to 10 days or in the freezer for longer storage; serve ice cream, fresh fruit, or pudding in the remaining baskets.) Top the ice cream with the warm Brandied Peach Sauce. Makes about 2 quarts (about 12 servings).

Brandied Peach Sauce

In a large saucepan stir together 1 cup packed *brown sugar* and 2 tablespoons *cornstarch*. Add 1 cup *whipping cream* and 1 tablespoon *margarine* or *butter.* Cook and stir over medium heat till thickened and bubbly. Add 2 cups thinly sliced, peeled *peaches;* ⅓ cup chopped toasted *pecans, almonds,* or *hazelnuts (filberts);* and 1 to 2 tablespoons *peach brandy* or *brandy.* Cook and stir till bubbly. Cool slightly before serving. Makes 3 cups.

SPECIAL TOUCH
▼ ▼ ▼

Win a five-star rating by serving this creamy, rich ice cream in nut-lace cookie bowls. For an extra-fabulous treat, brush the edge of each bowl with melted chocolate and present the dessert on a bed of chocolate and gold-paper leaves.

PER SERVING
585 CALORIES
4 g PROTEIN
47 g CARBOHYDRATES
44 g TOTAL FAT
22 g SATURATED FAT
159 mg CHOLESTEROL
69 mg SODIUM

Orange Swirl Ice Cream Pie

¼ cup margarine or butter, melted
1 cup finely crushed gingersnaps
¾ cup finely chopped pecans or walnuts
1 teaspoon finely shredded orange peel
½ gallon (8 cups) vanilla ice cream
2 cups Citrus Curd (using orange peel and juice) (see recipe, page 215)

Chill an extra large mixing bowl in the refrigerator or freezer.

Meanwhile, for crust, in a small saucepan melt margarine or butter. Stir in crushed gingersnaps, pecans or walnuts, and orange peel. Spread mixture evenly into an 8- or 9-inch springform pan. Press the crumb mixture onto the bottom and about 1 inch up the sides to form a firm, even crust. Bake in a 375° oven for 4 minutes. Cool completely on a wire rack.

Place the ice cream in the chilled bowl. Use a wooden spoon to stir the ice cream to soften slightly. Gently fold in the Citrus Curd, swirling just enough to marble slightly. Turn the ice cream mixture into the cooled crust. Cover and freeze for at least 8 hours before serving.

To serve, loosen the crust from the sides of the springform pan. Then remove the sides of the springform pan. Cut into wedges. Makes 10 servings.

SPECIAL TOUCH
▼ ▼ ▼

The marbled filling in this frozen masterpiece is as attractive as it is delicious. For an added touch, top each piece of pie with an orange peel bow or knot. To make the peel garnishes, use a vegetable peeler or a knife to cut long thin strips of peel from oranges. Then cut the strips into very narrow strips. Tie the orange peel strips into bows or knots.

PER SERVING
518 CALORIES
6 g PROTEIN
59 g CARBOHYDRATES
30 g TOTAL FAT
11 g SATURATED FAT
175 mg CHOLESTEROL
260 mg SODIUM

Double-Decker Pumpkin Chiffon Pie

1 recipe for Flaky Pie Pastry for a single
  crust (see page 205)
¾ cup finely chopped pecans
1 3-ounce package cream cheese
⅔ cup whipping cream
1 tablespoon sugar
½ cup milk
1 envelope unflavored gelatin
3 slightly beaten egg yolks
1¼ cups canned pumpkin
¾ cup packed brown sugar
1 teaspoon ground cinnamon
½ teaspoon ground ginger
⅛ teaspoon ground cloves
3 egg whites (see tip, page 175)
¼ cup sugar
1 cup Sweetened Whipped Cream (see
  recipe, page 210) (optional)

For pastry shell, prepare the Flaky Pastry as directed, *except* stir ¼ cup of the finely chopped pecans into the flour mixture before adding the water. On a lightly floured surface, use your hands to slightly flatten dough. Roll dough from center to edges, forming a 12-inch circle. Wrap pastry around the rolling pin. Then unroll pastry onto a 9-inch pie plate. Ease pastry into pie plate, being careful not to stretch it.

Trim pastry to ½-inch beyond edge of pie plate. Fold under extra pastry. Crimp edge. Using the tines of a fork, prick bottom and sides of pastry generously. Line pastry shell with a double thickness of foil. Bake in a 450° oven for 8 minutes. Remove foil. Bake for 5 to 6 minutes more or till golden. Cool on a wire rack.

For cream cheese filling, in a medium mixing bowl beat the cream cheese with an electric mixer on medium speed about 30 seconds or till softened. Add the whipping cream and 1 tablespoon sugar. Beat for 1 to 2 minutes more or till soft peaks form. Spread cream cheese filling over the bottom of the cooled pastry shell. Sprinkle with the remaining ½ cup pecans. Cover; chill in the refrigerator.

For pumpkin filling, in a medium saucepan combine milk and gelatin. Let stand for 5 minutes. Cook and stir over low heat till gelatin dissolves. Gradually stir about *half* of the gelatin mixture into the egg yolks. Then return all of the egg yolk mixture to the saucepan. Cook and stir till mixture comes just to boiling. Remove from heat. Stir in pumpkin, brown sugar, cinnamon, ginger, and cloves. If necessary, chill the filling till it mounds when spooned, stirring occasionally.

In a medium mixing bowl *immediately* beat egg whites with an electric mixer on medium to high speed till soft peaks form (tips curl). Gradually add ¼ cup sugar, *1 tablespoon* at a time, beating on high speed till stiff peaks form (tips stand straight). Fold egg white mixture into pumpkin mixture. If necessary, chill the pumpkin filling in the refrigerator till it mounds when spooned. Spoon pumpkin filling on top of the cream cheese filling in pastry shell. Cover and chill in the refrigerator for at least 8 hours or till set. If desired, serve with Sweetened Whipped Cream. Makes 8 servings.

SPECIAL TOUCH
▼ ▼ ▼
Use the ever-popular Sweetened Whipped Cream to garnish the rim of this splendid pumpkin pie. When adding the whipped cream border, use a decorating bag fitted with a medium or large star tip to pipe stars around the edge of the pie. For an extra frill, sprinkle finely chopped pecans on top of the whipped cream.

PER SERVING
437 CALORIES
8 g PROTEIN
48 g CARBOHYDRATES
25 g TOTAL FAT
9 g SATURATED FAT
113 mg CHOLESTEROL
145 mg SODIUM

Peanut Butter Chiffon Pie

SPECIAL TOUCH

▼ ▼ ▼

To dress this scrumptious
pie in high fashion, pipe
small polka dots of the
Bittersweet Chocolate
Sauce on the dessert plate
around each serving of pie.

⅓ cup *margarine* or *butter*

¼ cup *sugar*

1½ cups *finely crushed chocolate wafers
(25 wafers)* or *vanilla wafers (36 to
40 wafers)*

¼ cup *finely chopped peanuts*

⅓ cup *sugar*

1 envelope *unflavored gelatin*

¾ cup cold *water*

¾ cup *milk*

⅔ cup *peanut butter*

3 *slightly beaten egg yolks*

3 *egg whites (see tip, page 175)*

3 *tablespoons sugar*

1 cup *whipping cream*

½ cup *Bittersweet Chocolate Sauce (see
recipe, page 212)*

¼ cup *chopped peanuts*

Chill a small mixing bowl in the refrigerator.

Meanwhile, for crumb crust, in a small
saucepan melt the margarine or butter. Stir
in the ¼ cup sugar. Then stir in crushed
chocolate or vanilla wafers and ¼ cup finely
chopped peanuts. Spread mixture evenly into
a 9-inch pie plate. Press onto bottom and
sides to form a firm, even crust. Chill in the
refrigerator while preparing the filling.

For filling, in a medium saucepan stir
together the ⅓ cup sugar and gelatin. Stir in
the cold water. Cook and stir over low heat
till gelatin is dissolved. Stir in milk and
peanut butter till smooth.

Gradually stir about *half* of the gelatin
mixture into egg yolks. Then return all the
egg yolk mixture to the saucepan. Cook and
stir over low heat just till mixture begins to
boil. Remove from heat. Cool to room
temperature, stirring occasionally.

In a medium mixing bowl beat the egg
whites with an electric mixer on medium to
high speed till soft peaks form (tips curl).
Gradually add the 3 tablespoons sugar,
1 tablespoon at a time, beating on high speed
till stiff peaks form (tips stand straight). Fold
the egg white mixture into the peanut butter
mixture.

Wash the beaters; rinse with cold water. In
the chilled mixing bowl beat the whipping
cream on low speed till soft peaks form. Fold
the whipped cream into the gelatin mixture.
If necessary, chill the filling in the
refrigerator till it mounds when spooned,
stirring occasionally.

Spoon the filling into the crumb crust. Cover
and chill in the refrigerator for 6 to 24 hours
or till set.

Just before serving, drizzle about *2 tablespoons*
of the Bittersweet Chocolate Sauce over the
pie. Sprinkle with ¼ cup chopped peanuts.
Serve with the remaining Bittersweet
Chocolate Sauce. Makes 8 servings.

PER SERVING

627 CALORIES

14 g PROTEIN

48 g CARBOHYDRATES

44 g TOTAL FAT

14 g SATURATED FAT

138 mg CHOLESTEROL

380 mg SODIUM

Margarita Pie

Flaky Pie Pastry for a single crust pie (see recipe, page 205)

½ cup sugar
½ cup water
1 teaspoon finely shredded lime peel (set aside)
¼ cup lime juice
1 envelope unflavored gelatin
4 slightly beaten egg yolks
2 tablespoons tequila
1 tablespoon orange liqueur
4 egg whites (see tip, page 175)
¼ cup sugar
½ cup whipping cream
1 cup Sweetened Whipped Cream (see recipe, page 210) (optional)

Chill a small mixing bowl in the refrigerator.

Meanwhile for pastry shell, on a lightly floured surface, use your hands to slightly flatten Flaky Pie Pastry dough. Roll dough from center to edges, forming a 12-inch circle. Wrap pastry around the rolling pin. Then unroll pastry onto a 9-inch pie plate. Ease pastry into pie plate, being careful not to stretch it.

Trim pastry to ½ inch beyond edge of pie plate. Fold under extra pastry. Crimp edge. Using the tines of a fork, prick bottom and sides of pastry generously. Line pastry shell with a double thickness of foil. Bake in a 450° oven for 8 minutes. Remove foil. Bake for 5 to 6 minutes more or till golden. Cool pastry on a wire rack.

For filling, in a medium saucepan combine ½ cup sugar, water, lime juice, and gelatin. Cook and stir over low heat till gelatin is *completely* dissolved. Gradually stir all of the gelatin mixture into the egg yolks. Then return all of the egg yolk mixture to the saucepan. Bring to a gentle boil. Cook and stir for 2 minutes more. Remove from heat. Stir in lime peel, tequila, and orange liqueur. Chill in the refrigerator about 30 minutes or till the consistency of corn syrup, stirring occasionally.

Remove the gelatin mixture from the refrigerator (it will continue to set). In a medium mixing bowl *immediately* beat the egg whites with an electric mixer on medium to high speed till soft peaks form (tips curl). Gradually add ¼ cup sugar, about *1 tablespoon* at a time, beating on medium to high speed till stiff peaks form (tips stand straight). When gelatin is partially set (consistency of unbeaten egg whites), fold in the egg white mixture.

Wash the beaters and rinse with cold water. In the chilled bowl beat whipping cream on low speed till soft peaks form. Fold the whipped cream into the gelatin mixture. Chill the filling about 1 hour or till it mounds when spooned. Spoon filling into the baked pastry shell. Cover and chill in the refrigerator for 4 to 24 hours or till set. If desired, serve with Sweetened Whipped Cream. Makes 8 servings.

SPECIAL TOUCH
▼ ▼ ▼
Whipped cream is a natural finish for this fluffy lime pie spiked with tequila and orange liqueur. For a lime garnish with a frosted look, dip lime slices in a little sugar and arrange them on the pie just before serving.

PER SERVING
297 CALORIES
6 g PROTEIN
34 g CARBOHYDRATES
15 g TOTAL FAT
6 g SATURATED FAT
127 mg CHOLESTEROL
106 mg SODIUM

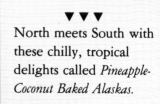

North meets South with these chilly, tropical delights called *Pineapple-Coconut Baked Alaskas*.

Pineapple-Coconut Baked Alaskas

1 *recipe for 1 layer Génoise* **or** *Chocolate Génoise (see page 207)*
1 *pint vanilla ice cream, softened*
¼ *cup frozen pineapple-coconut piña colada mix, thawed*
1 *8-ounce can crushed pineapple (juice pack), drained*
6 *egg whites (see tip, page 175)*
¾ *teaspoon vanilla*
¾ *cup sugar*
⅔ *cup grated* **or** *chopped flaked coconut, toasted*

Grease a 13x9x2-inch baking pan. Line the bottom of the baking pan with waxed paper parchment paper or plain brown paper; grease paper. Set pan aside.

Prepare batter for one 8- or 9-inch layer of Génoise or Chocolate Génoise as directed, *except* spread the batter into the prepared 13x9x2-inch pan. Bake in a 350° oven for 10 to 15 minutes or till a wooden toothpick inserted near the center of the cake comes out clean. Cool cake in pan on wire rack for 10 minutes. Then remove cake from pan and peel off paper. Cool completely on the rack.

Meanwhile, place the ice cream in a large mixing bowl. Stir in the thawed piña colada mix. Then freeze till firm.

To assemble, use a 4-inch round cutter to cut the cake into 6 circles. Place each cake circle on a piece of foil, then place each on a baking sheet. Equally divide the pineapple on top of each circle. Then top each with a scoop of the ice cream mixture. Place the baking sheet in the freezer till serving time.

About 30 minutes before serving, place egg whites in a medium bowl and let stand at room temperature. For meringue, add vanilla to egg whites. Beat with an electric mixer on medium to high speed till soft peaks form (tips curl). Gradually add sugar, *1 tablespoon* at a time, beating on high speed about 6 minutes or till stiff, glossy peaks form (tips stand straight) and sugar is *completely* dissolved. Fold in the toasted coconut.

If desired, spoon meringue into a decorating bag fitted with a large round tip (about ½-inch opening). Remove 1 cake circle from the freezer. Immediately pipe or spread the meringue over the sides and top of the cake circle and ice cream, carefully sealing edges to the foil. Return the meringue-topped cake on the foil to the baking sheet in the freezer. Repeat piping or spreading meringue on each of the remaining cakes.

To serve, bake the meringue-topped cakes in a 500° oven about 2 to 3 minutes or till meringue is lightly browned. Serve immediately. Makes 6 servings.

SPECIAL TOUCH
▼ ▼ ▼

For extra pizzazz create pineapple-shaped baked Alaskas.

Instead of cutting cake circles, cut egg-shaped ovals that are 2½ inches wide at the base and 4 inches long. Then assemble the desserts as directed in the recipe. For the pineapple leaves, draw a vegetable peeler across the meat of a fresh coconut to make thin strips. Then toast the strips and add them to the plates with the baked Alaskas. If you like, sprinkle the plates or baked Alaskas with toasted coconut.

PER SERVING
491 CALORIES
10 g PROTEIN
72 g CARBOHYDRATES
19 g FAT
9 g SATURATED FAT
147 mg CHOLESTEROL
148 mg SODIUM

Candy Bar Squares

⅓ cup *margarine* or *butter*
1½ cups *finely crushed chocolate wafers* (*25 wafers*)
24 *large marshmallows* or 2½ *cups tiny marshmallows*
⅓ cup *milk*
⅔ cup *caramel ice-cream topping*
1 cup *whipping cream*
1 *pint (2 cups) vanilla ice cream*
6 *ounces milk chocolate, coarsely chopped*
¾ cup *cocktail peanuts, coarsely chopped*
⅔ cup *fudge ice-cream topping*

Chill a small mixing bowl, a large mixing bowl, and the beaters of an electric mixer in the refrigerator. Line a 9x9x2-inch baking pan with foil, extending the foil over the edges of the pan. Set pan aside.

For crumb crust, in a small saucepan melt margarine or butter. Stir in crushed chocolate wafers. Spread mixture evenly into the prepared pan. Press onto bottom and 1 inch up sides to form a firm, even crust. Bake in a 375° oven for 8 minutes. Cool on a wire rack.

Meanwhile, for filling, in a heavy medium saucepan heat and stir marshmallows and milk over low heat just till marshmallows melt. Remove from heat; cool to room temperature.

Spread the caramel ice-cream topping on top of the cooled crust; set aside.

In the chilled small bowl beat the whipping cream with the chilled beaters on low speed till soft peaks form; set aside.

Place the ice cream in the chilled large bowl. Use a wooden spoon to stir the ice cream to soften slightly. Gently fold the whipped cream and cooled marshmallow mixture into the softened ice cream. Then fold in the chopped milk chocolate and peanuts. *Carefully* spread the ice-cream mixture evenly over the caramel topping in pan. Cover and freeze for at least 4 hours or till firm before serving.

To serve, cut into squares and place pieces on dessert plates. Then drizzle with the fudge ice-cream topping. Makes 8 servings.

Peanut Candy Bar Squares

Prepare Candy Bar Squares as directed above, *except* stir 1 cup *peanut butter* into the hot marshmallow mixture till melted; cool to room temperature. Omit the caramel ice-cream topping.

Per Serving: Same as main recipe, except 864 calories, 19 g protein, 79 g carbohydrate, 57 g fat, 16 g saturated fat, and 471 mg sodium.

▼ery Berry Sundaes

1 *pint (2 cups) strawberry ice cream*
1 *8-ounce carton dairy sour cream* **or**
   plain yogurt
2 *tablespoons orange liqueur*
1 *cup sliced strawberries*
2 *teaspoons sugar*
⅔ *cup chopped toasted almonds*
½ *cup Bittersweet Chocolate Sauce (see*
   recipe, page 212) or Raspberry Sauce
   (using strawberrries) (see recipe,
   page 213)

Chill a medium mixing bowl in the refrigerator or freezer.

Place the ice cream in the chilled mixing bowl. Use a wooden spoon to stir the ice cream to soften slightly. Gently fold the sour cream or yogurt and the orange liqueur into the softened ice cream. Cover and freeze for 4 to 5 hours or till firm.

Meanwhile, in a small mixing bowl stir together strawberries and sugar. Cover and chill strawberry mixture in the refrigerator till ready to serve.

Line a baking sheet with waxed paper. Then chill the the baking sheet in the refrigerator.

Using a small ice-cream scoop, scoop the ice cream into 12 small balls. Place *four* of the ice-cream balls on the chilled baking sheet. Roll the remaining ice-cream balls in the chopped almonds, then place the almond-coated ice-cream balls on the chilled baking sheet. Freeze about 15 minutes or till firm.

To assemble, just before serving, spoon about *1 tablespoon* of the Bittersweet Chocolate Sauce or Raspberry Sauce (using strawberries) into *each* of 4 ice-cream dishes, parfait glasses, or dessert dishes. Place an almond-coated ice-cream ball in each dish. Top each with some of the strawberry mixture. Then add a plain ice-cream ball and the remaining strawberry mixture to each. Finally, add a remaining almond-coated ice-cream ball to each dish and top with the remaining sauce. Makes 4 servings.

SPECIAL TOUCH
▼ ▼ ▼

Both kids and adults will enjoy extra toppings on these sophisticated sundaes. Complement the sundaes with dollops of whipped cream and sprinkles of chopped chocolate and toasted almonds on top.

PER SERVING
572 CALORIES
10 g PROTEIN
47 g CARBOHYDRATES
41 g TOTAL FAT
13 g SATURATED FAT
71 mg CHOLESTEROL
81 mg SODIUM

Strawberry-Melon Soup with Melon Balls

Ladle this refreshing fruit
dessert into shallow china
or cut-glass bowls and place
the bowls on dessert plates.
For a splash of color as well
as a simple party favor,
nestle a fresh flower on
each plate next to the bowl.

1 *small cantaloupe*
½ *of a small honeydew melon*
½ *cup unsweetened pineapple juice*
⅓ *cup sugar*
1 *tablespoon grated gingerroot*
4 *cups fresh or frozen unsweetened whole
    strawberries*
1 *8-ounce carton vanilla yogurt*
1 *8-ounce carton dairy sour cream*
2 *cups milk*

Using a small melon baller, scoop the
cantaloupe and the honeydew melon into
balls. *Or,* use a knife to cut melon into cubes.
(You should have about *4 cups* cantaloupe
pieces and *2 cups* honeydew pieces.) Set
2 cups of the cantaloupe aside.

In a small saucepan combine pineapple juice,
sugar, and gingerroot. Bring to boiling,
stirring till sugar dissolves. Reduce heat.
Simmer, uncovered, over medium heat for 5
to 7 minutes or till the mixture is the
consistency of a thin syrup. Then remove the
saucepan from heat and cool syrup to room
temperature.

Transfer the syrup to a storage container or
bowl. Add the remaining 2 cups cantaloupe
balls and all of the honeydew balls. Cover
and chill in the refrigerator for 4 to 24 hours
before serving.

Meanwhile, place the strawberries in a
blender container or food processor bowl.
Cover and blend or process till smooth;
remove berries and set aside.

Place the reserved 2 cups cantaloupe balls in
the blender container or food processor
bowl. Cover and blend or process till
smooth; set aside.

For soup, in a large mixing bowl stir
together yogurt and sour cream. Add the
puréed strawberries, puréed cantaloupe, and
milk. Stir till combined. Cover and chill the
soup in the refrigerator for 4 to 24 hours
before serving.

Just before serving, drain melon balls,
reserving syrup. Stir the reserved syrup into
the soup. To serve, ladle the soup into
bowls. Top with melon balls. Serves 8 to 10.

PER SERVING
224 CALORIES
6 g PROTEIN
36 g CARBOHYDRATES
8 g TOTAL FAT
5 g SATURATED FAT
18 mg CHOLESTEROL
75 mg SODIUM

Amaretto Cheesecake Pudding Parfaits

⅓ cup sugar

2 tablespoons all-purpose flour

1¾ cups milk

1 beaten egg

½ of an 8-ounce container soft-style cream
    cheese

⅓ cup dairy sour cream

2 tablespoons amaretto or hazelnut,
    coffee, or orange liqueur

1 teaspoon vanilla

2 tablespoons margarine or butter

⅔ cup crushed chocolate wafers
    (12 wafers)

2 tablespoons chopped toasted almonds or
    hazelnuts (filberts)

1 cup Sweetened Whipped Cream (see
    recipe, page 210) (optional)

For pudding, in a heavy medium saucepan
stir together sugar and flour. Stir in milk.
Cook and stir over medium heat till
thickened and bubbly. Cook and stir for
1 minute more. Remove from heat.

Gradually stir about *half* of the hot mixture
into egg. Then return all of the egg mixture
to the saucepan. Bring to a gentle boil, then
reduce heat. Cook and stir for 2 minutes
more. Add cream cheese; stir till melted.
Remove from heat. Stir in sour cream,
amaretto or liqueur, and vanilla. Cover
surface with plastic wrap. Chill in the
refrigerator for 2 to 24 hours. *(Do not stir.)*

Meanwhile, in a small saucepan melt
margarine or butter. Stir in crushed
chocolate wafers and nuts.

To assemble, in *each* of 4 parfait glasses, layer
a *scant ¼ cup* of the pudding, then about
1 tablespoon of the chocolate-wafer mixture.
Repeat layers 2 more times, ending with the
chocolate-wafer mixture. Serve immediately
or chill in the refrigerator for up to 30
minutes before serving. If desired, serve with
Sweetened Whipped Cream. Serves 4.

SPECIAL TOUCH
▼ ▼ ▼

For a stunning finish, pipe a
whipped cream star on top
of each parfait. Then top
each with a chocolate-
dipped almond or hazelnut
and a small edible leaf
(such as lemon balm
or mint).

PER SERVING
468 CALORIES
10 g PROTEIN
42 g CARBOHYDRATES
28 g TOTAL FAT
10 g SATURATED FAT
102 mg CHOLESTEROL
380 mg SODIUM

Entice your dear ones
with this sweet, light,
and luscious *Twin-Fruit
Parfait.*

Twin-Fruit Parfait

1 *recipe for Marzipan Treasures (see page*
    104) or 10 ounces purchased
    marzipan
½ *cup small fresh or frozen strawberries*
½ *of a medium papaya, seeded, peeled,*
    and cubed (about 1 cup) or one 15-
    ounce can papaya chunks, drained
¼ *cup sugar*
1 *tablespoon orange liqueur or orange*
    juice
1 *drop red food coloring*
1 *egg white (see tip, page 175)*
¼ *cup sifted powdered sugar*
1 *cup whipping cream*
2 *recipes for White Chocolate Sauce (see*
    page 12)
1 *cup Raspberry Sauce (using*
    strawberries) (see recipe, page 213)
    (optional)

Line bottom and sides of a 10x3½x2½-inch
loaf dessert pan or an 8x4x2-inch loaf pan
with plastic wrap, extending plastic wrap
over edges of the pan. Set pan aside.

If using, prepare Marzipan Treasures as
directed, *except* do not tint or shape it. Roll
half of the homemade marzipan or all the
purchased marzipan to ⅛-inch thickness as
directed for sheets (see page 232). (Reserve
remaining homemade marzipan for another
use. Wrap the marzipan in plastic wrap or
foil and refrigerate for up to 1 week.)
Measure the inside bottom of the loaf pan.
Cut 2 pieces of marzipan the size of the
bottom. Place 1 marzipan piece in the pan.
Cover remaining piece with plastic wrap. Set
the pan and marzipan aside.

Place strawberries in a blender container or
food processor bowl. Cover and blend or
process till smooth. Press berries through a
sieve; discard seeds, Set purée aside. Then
blend or process the papaya till smooth. Stir
2 tablespoons sugar and *1½ teaspoons* liqueur or
orange juice into *each* puréed fruit. Stir red
food coloring into puréed berries. Set aside.

Beat egg white with an electric mixer on
medium to high speed or till soft peaks form
(tips curl). Gradually add the powered sugar,
1 tablespoon at a time, beating on high speed
till very stiff peaks form (tips stand straight).
Transfer to a large mixing bowl.

In a bowl beat whipping cream on low speed
till soft peaks form. Fold whipped cream into
egg white mixture. Then fold *half* of the
whipped cream mixture into *each* of the
puréed fruit mixtures.

Spoon the strawberry mixture on top of the
marzipan in pan. Spread to smooth top.
Freeze about 2 hours or till set, but not firm.
Meanwhile, cover and refrigerate the papaya
mixture. Spoon papaya mixture on top of the
frozen strawberry mixture. Smooth top. Top
with the remaining marzipan piece; lightly
press mazipan onto the papaya mixture so it
adheres. Freeze for 8 to 24 hours or till firm.

Invert pan on cutting board. Remove pan
and plastic wrap. Let stand at room
temperature 20 minutes. Cut into slices.
Serve with White Chocolate Sauce and, if
desired, strawberry sauce. Serves 12 to 14.

SPECIAL TOUCH
▼ ▼ ▼
Make this sweet Twin-Fruit
Parfait a bit sweeter by
lining each dessert plate
with the White Chocolate
Sauce. Then add the
strawberry sauce in a
bleeding-heart design
around the outer edge of
the plate. Arrange two thin
slices of this frozen delight
in the center and add a
strawberry fan for a
finishing touch.

PER SERVING
527 CALORIES
5 g PROTEIN
63 g CARBOHYDRATES
30 g TOTAL FAT
15 g SATURATED FAT
109 mg CHOLESTEROL
74 mg SODIUM

Gingerbread-Lemon Terrine

¾ cup sugar
1 envelope unflavored gelatin
¾ cup cold water
1 teaspoon finely shredded lemon peel
¼ cup lemon juice
½ teaspoon finely shredded orange peel
 Few drops yellow food coloring
1 cup whipping cream, whipped
 Gingerbread Pound Cake
 Powdered sugar
1 cup Raspberry Sauce (see recipe, page 213)
1 cup Kiwi Sauce (see recipe, page 214)

In a medium saucepan combine sugar and gelatin. Stir in cold water, lemon peel, lemon juice, and orange peel. Cook and stir till gelatin is *completely* dissolved. Stir in food coloring. Chill in the refrigerator about 30 minutes or till the consistency of corn syrup.

Remove gelatin mixture from the refrigerator (it will continue to set). When gelatin mixture is partially set (consistency of unbeaten egg whites), fold in *one-fourth* of the whipped cream. Then fold all of the gelatin mixture into the remaining whipped cream. Chill in refrigerator about 20 minutes or till mixture mounds when spooned.

To assemble terrine, line a 9x5x3-inch loaf pan with plastic wrap; set aside. Trim crusts from the Gingerbread Pound Cake. Slice the cake horizontally into *four* slices. Place a slice on the bottom of prepared pan. Cut another slice in half lengthwise. Place the 2 half slices along either side of pan. Spoon in *half* of the lemon filling. Then place a cake slice on top

of the filling, cutting to fit pan. Finally, spoon in the remaining lemon filling. Top with the remaining cake slice. Cover and chill in the refrigerator for at least 4 hours or till firm before serving.

To serve, unmold terrine onto a serving plate; sift powdered sugar over top. Then cut into slices and serve with Raspberry Sauce and Kiwi Sauce. Makes 12 servings.

Gingerbread Pound Cake

Let 1 cup *margarine* or *butter* and 4 *eggs* stand at room temperature for 30 minutes. Grease and flour a 9x5x3-inch loaf pan. Stir together 2 cup *all-purpose flour,* 1 teaspoon *baking powder,* 1 teaspoon ground *ginger,* and 1 teaspoon ground *cinnamon.* Set aside.

In a large bowl beat margarine with an electric mixer on medium speed for 30 seconds. Gradually add ¾ cup packed *brown sugar,* 2 tablespoons at a time, beating on medium to high speed about 6 minutes total or till light and fluffy. Add *eggs,* one at a time, beating 1 minute after each addition; scraping bowl often. Beat in ¼ cup *molasses.* Gradually add flour mixture, beating on low speed *just till combined.*

Pour batter into the prepared pan. Bake in a 325° oven for 55 to 65 minutes or till a wooden toothpick inserted near the center comes out clean. Cool cake in pan on a wire rack for 10 minutes. Then remove cake and cool completely on the rack. Serves 12.
Per Serving: 303 calories, 4 g protein, 33 g carbohydrate, 17 g fat, 3 g saturated fat, 71 mg cholesterol, and 231 mg sodium.

Chocolate Terrine

3/4 cup sugar
1 envelope unflavored gelatin
3/4 cup cold water
4 beaten egg yolks
6 ounces semisweet or bittersweet
    chocolate, chopped
4 egg whites (see tip, page 175)
3/4 cup whipping cream
2 tablespoons orange liqueur
    Rhubarb-Strawberry Sauce

In a medium saucepan combine sugar and unflavored gelatin. Stir in the cold water. Cook and stir over medium heat till gelatin is *completely* dissolved. Gradually stir about *half* of the hot mixture into the egg yolks. Then return all of the egg yolk mixture to the saucepan. Bring to a gentle boil, then reduce heat. Cook and stir for 2 minutes more. Remove from heat. Cover surface with plastic wrap. Cool about 1 hour or till mixture reaches room temperature.

Meanwhile, melt chocolate according to the directions on page 225; set aside to cool. Chill a small mixing bowl in the refrigerator. Place egg whites in a large mixing bowl; let stand at room temperature for 30 minutes.

Beat egg whites with an electric mixer on high speed about 4 minutes or till stiff peaks form (tips stand straight). Then fold in the gelatin mixture.

Wash beaters and rinse with cold water. In the chilled bowl beat the whipping cream on low speed just till soft peaks form. Fold the whipped cream into gelatin mixture. Divide into 2 equal portions (about *2 cups* each).

Lightly fold the melted chocolate into 1 portion; cover and let stand at room temperature. Fold orange liqueur into remaining portion. Pour the liqueur portion into an 8x4x2-inch loaf pan, spreading evenly in pan. Cover and chill liqueur layer in the refrigerator for 20 to 30 minutes or till *almost* firm (mixture will look set but flows if tipped to one side). Carefully spoon the chocolate mixture on top of the liqueur layer. Cover and chill in the refrigerator about 6 hours or till firm before serving.

To serve, unmold the terrine onto a large serving plate. Cut into slices. Serve with Rhubarb-Strawberry Sauce. Make 6 servings.

Rhubarb-Strawberry Sauce

In a medium saucepan combine 2 cups *fresh rhubarb* cut into 1-inch pieces *or* 1/2 of a 16-ounce package *frozen unsweetened sliced rhubarb, thawed;* 1 cup sliced *strawberries;* and 1/4 cup *water.* Bring to boiling; reduce heat. Cover and simmer for 5 to 8 minutes or till fruit is tender. Press mixture through a seive; discard pulp. Add enough *water* to seived mixture to equal *1 1/4 cups.* Return seived mixture to the saucepan.

Stir together 1/2 cup *sugar* and 4 teaspoons *cornstarch;* stir into mixture in saucepan. Cook and stir till thickened and bubbly. Cook and stir for 2 minutes more. Cool. Cover and chill in the refrigerator. Makes about 1 cup.

SPECIAL TOUCH
▼ ▼ ▼

For each serving, place two slices of this luscious chocolate-and-orange-layered dessert on a plate lined with the Rhubarb-Strawberry Sauce. Decorate the edge of each plate with two or three mandarin orange sections.

PER SERVING
478 CALORIES
8 g PROTEIN
65 g CARBOHYDRATES
24 g TOTAL FAT
8 g SATURATED FAT
183 mg CHOLESTEROL
58 mg SODIUM

Café à la Crème Torte

1½ *to 2 teaspoons instant espresso powder or instant coffee crystals*
1   *tablespoon* hot *water*
¾   *cup half-and-half or light cream*
1   *cup butter*
1   *cup packed brown sugar*
30 *ladyfingers*
2   *tablespoons anisette liqueur*
2   *cups Sweetened Whipped Cream (see recipe, page 210)*

For filling, dissolve the instant espresso powder or instant coffee crystals in the hot water. Then stir coffee into half-and-half or light cream. Set coffee mixture aside.

In a large mixing bowl beat butter with an electric mixer on medium to high speed about 30 seconds or till softened. Add brown sugar and beat till combined. Gradually add the coffee mixture to the butter mixture, beating thoroughly after each addition. Set filling aside.

Split ladyfingers in half horizontally. Using a pastry brush, lightly brush cut sides of

ladyfingers with liqueur. Line a 2½-quart bowl with enough ladyfingers to completely cover the inside of the bowl up to 1 inch from the top of the bowl, cutting ladyfingers as necessary to fit. *Or,* line the bottom and the sides of an 8- to 9-inch springform pan with the ladyfingers.

In the ladyfinger-lined bowl or pan, alternately layer the filling and the remaining ladyfingers, starting with the filling and finishing with the ladyfingers. (You will have 4 to 6 layers, depending on the depth of the bowl or pan.) Cover and chill in the refrigerator for 4 to 24 hours before serving

Just before serving, invert a serving plate over the bowl, and turn bowl and plate over together. Lift off the bowl. *Or,* remove sides from the springform pan. Spoon the Sweetened Whipped Cream into a decorating bag fitted with a medium star tip (about ¼-inch opening). Pipe stars over torte to cover. *Or,* use a narrow metal spatula to spread whipped cream over torte. Serves 12.

Raspberry Charlotte

4 cups fresh or frozen raspberries
¾ cup peach or apricot nectar
⅓ cup sugar
1 envelope unflavored gelatin
1 tablespoon lemon juice
⅛ teaspoon almond extract
2 egg whites (see tip, page 175)
⅓ cup raspberry jam
20 ladyfingers
¾ cup whipping cream
⅓ cup raspberry jam

Chill a small mixing bowl in the refrigerator.

Thaw raspberries, if frozen; *do not drain.* In a blender container or food processor bowl place raspberries and peach or apricot nectar. Cover and blend or process till smooth. Press mixture through a fine-mesh sieve; discard seeds. (You should have *2 cups* of the sieved raspberry purée).

In a small saucepan combine sugar and gelatin. Stir in *¾ cup* of the purée. Cook and stir over low heat till gelatin is *completely* dissolved. Remove from heat. Stir in the remaining raspberry purée, lemon juice, and almond extract. Gradually stir in the unbeaten egg whites. Cool about 30 minutes or till mixture reaches room temperature.

Meanwhile, line a 9x5x3-inch loaf pan with waxed paper. Split ladyfingers in half horizontally. Spread ⅓ cup raspberry jam on the cut sides of *eleven* of the ladyfinger halves.

Top with 11 more ladyfinger halves, forming ladyfinger sandwiches. Arrange *seven* of the ladyfinger sandwiches crosswise on the bottom of the prepared pan. Set the remaining 4 sandwiches aside. Arrange the 18 remaining ladyfinger halves around the sides of the loaf pan with cut sides toward center of the pan.

Beat the cooled gelatin mixture with an electric mixer on medium speed for 4 or 5 minutes or till light; set aside.

Wash beaters; rinse with cold water. In the chilled bowl beat whipping cream on low speed till soft peaks form. Fold the whipped cream into the gelatin mixture. Chill in the refrigerator about 2 hours or till mixture mounds when spooned, stirring occasionally.

Carefully spoon *half* of the gelatin mixture into the ladyfinger-lined pan. Arrange the remaining 4 ladyfinger sandwiches lengthwise on top of the gelatin mixture. Top with the remaining gelatin mixture. Cover and chill in the refrigerator for 6 to 8 hours or till firm before serving.

Just before serving, invert a serving plate over the loaf pan, and turn pan and plate over together. Remove the pan and the waxed paper. In a small saucepan heat and stir ⅓ cup raspberry jam till melted. Spread the melted jam on the top of the charlotte. Makes 16 servings.

PER SERVING
142 CALORIES
2 g PROTEIN
24 g CARBOHYDRATES
5 g TOTAL FAT
3 g SATURATED FAT
38 mg CHOLESTEROL
37 mg SODIUM

▼ ▼ ▼
For an extra heavenly taste treat, try this fluffy *Passion Fruit Mousse* (page 196) served in pretty pink *Marbled-Chocolate Bowls* (page 197).

White Chocolate Mousse with Strawberry Purée

1 egg white (see tip, page 175)
2 beaten egg yolks
½ cup milk
1 teaspoon cornstarch
1 tablespoon sugar
3 ounces white baking bar, grated
½ teaspoon vanilla
⅛ teaspoon cream of tarter
2 tablespoons sugar
1 cup whipping cream
   Strawberry Purée

In a small mixing bowl let the egg white stand at room temperature for 30 minutes. Chill another small mixing bowl in the refrigerator.

In a heavy small saucepan combine the egg yolks, milk, cornstarch, and 1 tablespoon sugar. Cook and stir over medium heat till slightly thickened and bubbly. Cook and stir for 2 minutes more. Remove from heat. Stir in the grated white baking bar and the vanilla. Stir till the baking bar is melted. Cool to room temperature.

Add the cream of tartar to the egg white. Beat with an electric mixer on medium to high speed till soft peaks form (tips curl).

Gradually add the 2 tablespoons sugar, 1 tablespoon at a time, beating till stiff peaks form (tips stand straight). Gently fold the cooled white baking bar mixture into the beaten egg white mixture.

Wash the beaters; rinse with cold water. In the chilled bowl beat the whipping cream on low speed till soft peaks form. Fold whipped cream into the egg white mixture. Gently spoon the mixture into a 7½x3½x2-inch loaf pan. Chill in the refrigerator for 4 to 24 hours or till firm before serving.

To serve, spoon mixture onto dessert plates. Serve with Strawberry Purée. Serves 6.

Strawberry Purée

In a blender container or food processor bowl combine 3 cups fresh small strawberries or frozen unsweetened whole strawberries, partially thawed, and 2 tablespoons orange liqueur. Cover and blend or process till smooth. Press the strawberry mixture through a fine-mesh sieve; discard seeds. If desired, stir in 2 to 3 teaspoons sugar. Cover and chill the purée in the refrigerator till serving time. Makes about 1⅔ cups.

SPECIAL TOUCH
▼ ▼ ▼

Give this creamy mousse a look of distinction by using an ice-cream scoop to dish it up. Place the scoops of mousse on dessert plates lined with the Strawberry Purée. For the crowning touch, generously top each serving with large, loose curls made from a white baking bar.

PER SERVING
181 CALORIES
4 g PROTEIN
24 g CARBOHYDRATES
7 g TOTAL FAT
4 g SATURATED FAT
73 mg CHOLESTEROL
37 mg SODIUM

Passion Fruit Mousse

This sweet and tangy
dessert showcases a palette
of pastels. Use pink candy
coating and white baking
bar to make the marbled
bowls or ruffled cups and
chocolate cutouts. Then
arrange each dessert in a
pool of strawberry sauce
and float a few thin strips
of lime peel on top.

Pictured on page 194

PER SERVING
240 CALORIES
5 g PROTEIN
18 g CARBOHYDRATES
17 g TOTAL FAT
10 g SATURATED FAT
161 mg CHOLESTEROL
54 mg SODIUM

8 *passion fruit*
¼ *cup water*
1½ *teaspoons unflavored gelatin*
3 *eggs*
⅓ *cup sugar*
1 *teaspoon finely shredded lemon peel*
1 *cup whipping cream*
6 *Marbled-Chocolate Bowls (using pink vanilla-flavored candy coating)* **or** *Chocolate Ruffled Cups (see recipes, pages 197 and 230) (optional)*
2 *cups Raspberry Sauce (using strawberries) (see recipe, page 213) (optional)*

Chill a small mixing bowl in the refrigerator.

Cut passion fruit in half. Using a spoon, scoop out seeds and pulp. Discard the shells. Press the seeds, pulp, and juices through a sieve. Measure the sieved fruit; if necessary, add enough *water* to equal ⅓ *cup.*

In a small saucepan combine ¼ cup water and the gelatin. Cook and stir over low heat till gelatin is *completely* dissolved. Cool slightly.

In the top of a double boiler combine the sieved passion fruit, eggs, sugar, and lemon peel. Beat with an electric mixer on low speed for 30 seconds. Then place the top of

the double boiler over, but not touching, gently boiling water. Clip a candy thermometer to the side of the top of the double boiler. Heat, beating constantly on high speed till thermometer reaches 160° or till mixture is thick and light in color. This should take 6 to 8 minutes.

Stir the gelatin mixture into passion fruit mixture. Then transfer the mixture to a large mixing bowl. Cool to room temperature.

Meanwhile, wash beaters; rinse with cold water. In the chilled bowl beat the whipping cream on low speed till soft peaks form. Gently fold the whipped cream into the cooled gelatin mixture. Chill till mixture mounds when spooned, stirring occasionally.

Spoon mousse into dessert dishes. *Or,* if desired, spoon mousse into *six* Marbled-Chocolate Bowls or Chocolate Ruffled Cups. (If necessary, store any remaining chocolate bowls or cups in a tightly covered container in a cool, dry place for up to 1 month; serve fresh berries or pudding in the remaining chocolate bowls or cups.) Then cover and chill the mousse in the refrigerator for 4 to 24 hours or till firm before serving.

If desired, serve with the strawberry sauce. Makes 6 servings.

Marbled-Chocolate Bowls

6 *to 8 small round* **or** *oval balloons*
6 *ounces white baking bar, chopped*
2 *teaspoons shortening*
4 *ounces semisweet* **or** *bittersweet*
   chocolate **or** *desired color of vanilla-*
   flavored candy coating, chopped
1½ *teaspoons shortening*

Inflate the balloons till they measure about 3 inches at their widest points. Tie knots in the balloons to secure close. Line a baking sheet with waxed paper. Set balloons and baking sheet aside.

Melt the white baking bar with the 2 teaspoons shortening according to the directions on page 225. Set aside.

If using semisweet or bittersweet chocolate, quick-temper the chocolate with the 1½ teaspoons shortening according to the directions on page 226. *Or,* if using candy coating, melt it with the 1½ teaspoons shortening according to the directions on page 225.

In a 9-inch pie plate pour the melted white baking bar in four or five 1-inch-wide strips about 1 inch apart. Then between the white strips, pour the quick-tempered chocolate or melted candy coating. If desired, gently swirl the strips with a knife.

Place the pie plate in a 15x10x1inch baking pan. Carefully pour *very warm tap water* (100° to 110°) into the pan around the pie plate to a depth of about ½ inch. (Be very careful not to splash any water into the pie plate.)

Holding a balloon by its knot, place balloon in an upright position in the mixture in the pie plate. Then tip the balloon over on its side into the mixture to coat about 1 to 2 inches of the balloon. Bring the balloon back to an upright position. Lift the balloon and repeat to coat all sides of the ballon, each time moving the balloon to coat another 1 to 2 inches of the surface. Place the balloon, in an upright position, on the baking sheet. Repeat with the remaining balloons. Let stand till dry.

Use scissors to snip a *very small* opening near the knot of the balloon. Quickly pinch the hole with your fingers and *slowly* deflate the balloon as you gently pull the balloon away. Tightly cover the bowls and store in a cool, dry place for up to 1 month. Makes 6 to 8.

Pictured on page 194

PER SERVING
263 CALORIES
3 g PROTEIN
29 g CARBOHYDRATES
17 g TOTAL FAT
6 g SATURATED FAT
0 mg CHOLESTEROL
26 mg SODIUM

Curaçao-Ginger Mousse

SPECIAL TOUCH
▼ ▼ ▼
To create a unique look,
allow the layers of mousse
to set up at an angle. Just
place a wire rack in the
refrigerator. Then place the
goblets containing the rum
mixture on the rack,
slightly tilting them to one
side and leaning the tops
against the refrigerator
wall. Chill as directed.
Then spoon on the blue
curaçao layer and chill.

½ cup sugar
1 envelope unflavored gelatin
1¼ cups milk
3 beaten egg yolks
3 egg whites (see tip, page 175)
1 cup whipping cream
2 tablespoons light rum
3 tablespoons finely chopped crystallized ginger
3 tablespoons blue curaçao liqueur or orange liqueur plus a few drops of blue food coloring

Chill a small mixing bowl in the refrigerator.

In a medium saucepan stir together sugar and gelatin. Stir in milk. Cook and stir over medium heat till gelatin and sugar are *completely* dissolved.

Gradually stir about *half* of the gelatin mixture into the beaten egg yolks. Then return all of the egg yolk mixture to the saucepan. Bring to a gentle boil, then reduce heat. Cook and stir for 2 minutes more. Remove from heat. Cover and chill in the refrigerator about 2 hours or till mixture is the consistency of corn syrup, stirring occasionally.

Remove gelatin mixture from the refrigerator (it will continue to set). Meanwhile, in a medium mixing bowl beat egg whites with an electric mixer on medium to high speed till stiff peaks form (tips stand straight). Set egg whites aside.

Wash beaters; rinse with cold water. In the chilled mixing bowl beat whipping cream on low speed till soft peaks form. Fold beaten egg whites into the gelatin mixture. Then fold whipped cream into the gelatin mixture.

Divide gelatin mixture in half. Stir rum and crystallized ginger into 1 portion. Then spoon the rum mixture into 6 stemmed dessert dishes or a 1½-quart clear glass serving bowl with straight sides or soufflé dish. Chill in the refrigerator for 15 to 20 minutes or till *almost* firm (mixture will be sticky to the touch and will look set but flows if tipped to one side).

Meanwhile, stir curaçao or orange liqueur plus food coloring into the remaining gelatin mixture. Let stand at room temperature while rum mixture is chilling.

Carefully spoon curaçao mixture on top of the partially set rum mixture. Cover and chill in the refrigerator for 4 to 24 hours or till firm before serving. Makes 6 servings.

PER SERVING
305 CALORIES
7 g PROTEIN
25 g CARBOHYDRATES
18 g TOTAL FAT
11 g SATURATED FAT
165 mg CHOLESTEROL
73 mg SODIUM

Cranberry Mousse

½ cup sugar
1 envelope unflavored gelatin
¼ teaspoon finely shredded orange peel
½ cup orange juice
2 cups cranberries
2 egg whites (see tip, page 175)
2 tablespoons sugar
½ cup whipping cream
1 cup Raspberry Sauce (see recipe, page 213)

In a medium saucepan combine the ½ cup sugar and gelatin. Stir in orange juice. Cook and stir over medium heat till gelatin is *completely* dissolved. Stir in the orange peel and cranberries. Bring to boiling; reduce heat. Cover and simmer about 5 minutes or till cranberry skins pop. Remove from heat.

Transfer the cranberry-gelatin mixture to a medium mixing bowl. Chill in the refrigerator till the mixture is the consistency of corn syrup, stirring occasionally. Meanwhile, chill a small mixing bowl in the refrigerator.

Remove gelatin mixture from the refrigerator (it will continue to set). Meanwhile, in a small mixing bowl *immediately* beat egg whites with an electric mixer on medium to high speed till soft peaks form (tips curl). Gradually add the 2 tablespoons sugar, *1 tablespoon* at a time, beating on high speed till stiff peaks form (tips stand straight).

When gelatin mixture is partially set (the consistency of unbeaten egg whites), fold in the beaten egg white mixture.

Wash the beaters; rinse with cold water. In the chilled mixing bowl beat the whipping cream on low speed till soft peaks form. Fold whipped cream into the gelatin mixture. Chill in the refrigerator till mixture mounds when spooned.

Spoon the mousse into a 1-quart glass bowl. Chill in the refrigerator for 4 to 24 hours or till firm before serving. Serve the mousse with Raspberry Sauce. Makes 6 servings.

SPECIAL TOUCH
▼ ▼ ▼
Begin a new Thanksgiving tradition by ending dinner with this refreshing mousse. Spoon the mousse into your best dessert dishes, pour Raspberry Sauce over each, and garnish with fresh mint leaves.

PER SERVING
252 CALORIES
3 g PROTEIN
46 g CARBOHYDRATES
8 g TOTAL FAT
5 g SATURATED FAT
27 mg CHOLESTEROL
28 mg SODIUM

*S*pumoni Soufflé

SPECIAL TOUCH
▼ ▼ ▼

To make an elegant impression on your guests, use a decorating bag fitted with a large star tip (about ½-inch opening) to pipe a whipped cream border of stars around the soufflé. Then place one or two chocolate leaves in each star of whipped cream.

PER SERVING
364 CALORIES
9 g PROTEIN
28 g CARBOHYDRATES
24 g FAT
11 g SATURATED FAT
202 mg CHOLESTEROL
99 mg SODIUM

Margarine or butter
Sugar
¼ cup sugar
1 envelope unflavored gelatin
1¼ cups milk
4 beaten egg yolks
1 teaspoon vanilla
2 ounces milk chocolate, melted (see page 225) and cooled
4 egg whites (see tip, page 175)
2 tablespoons sugar
½ cup whipping cream, whipped
1 tablespoon crème de cacao (optional)
2 tablespoons chopped pistachio nuts
1 tablespoon light rum or ¼ teaspoon rum flavoring
Few drops green food coloring
½ cup chopped fresh or thawed, frozen pitted tart red cherries
1 tablespoon kirsh (cherry brandy) or ½ teaspoon cherry flavoring
Few drops red food coloring
1 cup Sweetened Whipped Cream (see recipe, page 210)

Grease the sides of a 1-quart soufflé dish with margarine or butter. For a collar on the soufflé dish, measure enough foil to wrap around the top of the dish; add 3 inches. Fold foil in thirds lengthwise. Lightly grease 1 side with margarine; sprinkle with sugar. Attach foil, sugar side in, around outside of dish so foil extends about 2 inches above dish. Tape ends of foil together. Sprinkle sides of dish with sugar; set dish aside.

In a small saucepan stir together the ¼ cup sugar and gelatin. Sir in milk. Cook and stir over medium heat till gelatin is *completely*

dissolved. Remove from heat. Gradually stir about *half* of the hot mixture into egg yolks. Return all the egg yolk mixture to the pan. Bring to a gentle boil, then reduce heat. Cook and stir for 2 minutes more. Stir in vanilla. Refrigerate about 30 minutes or till the consistency of corn syrup, stirring often.

Remove mixture from the refrigerator. In a medium mixing bowl beat egg whites with an electric mixer on medium to high speed till soft peaks form (tips curl). Gradually add *2 tablespoons* sugar, beating on high speed till stiff peaks form (tips stand straight). Fold egg whites into the partially set gelatin mixture. Then fold in the whipped cream. Divide gelatin mixture into thirds.

Fold chocolate and, if desired, crème de cacao into 1 portion. Spoon chocolate mixture into prepared dish. Chill in the refrigerator 30 minutes or till *almost* firm (mixture will be sticky to the touch and will look set but flows if tipped to one side).

Meanwhile, fold pistachio nuts, rum, and green food coloring into second portion. Fold cherries, kirsh, and red food coloring into the remaining portion. Let pistachio and cherry mixtures stand at room temperature while chocolate layer is chilling.

Spoon pistachio mixture on top of the chocolate layer. Refrigerate till *almost* firm. Spoon cherry mixture on top of nut layer. Cover and chill in refrigerator for 6 to 24 hours or till firm before serving. To serve, carefully remove foil collar. Serve with Sweetened Whipped Cream. Serves 6.

Dessert Party Menus

Chocolate and Cabernet Extravaganza

Double-Chocolate and Orange Torte,
page 22
Bittersweet Chocolate Pâté, page 39
Duo Chocolate Fondue, page 41
Chocolate truffles
Cabernet sauvignon

For an exquisite dessert party, bring two great tastes together. Sweet, rich chocolate is the ultimate complement to dry red wine.

Tree-Trimming Party

Creamy, Fudgy, and Nutty Brownies,
page 28
Fig Bars, page 69
Coconut Tassies, page 85
Assorted candies
Almond Biscotti Bites, page 93
Holiday Cutout Cookies,
page 123
Hot chocolate
Cranberry juice cocktail

Need an excuse to indulge in a special dessert? Why not plan a gathering around a banquet of sweets.

Here are eight suggested themed party menus using recipes from this book with additional accompaniments. If you're in a time crunch, make just one or two of the suggested recipes and fill in with purchased items.

To create other unique party menus, all you have to do is replace these recipes with favorites of your own.

Progressive International Dessert Party

Sacher Torte, page 136
Spanish Caramel Flan, page 153
Baklava, page 155
English Trifle, page 160
Cappuccino or espresso
Assorted teas

Set an afternoon or evening aside to be with friends. Then spend it by traveling from house to house sampling specialty desserts from various countries.

Fall Harvest Brunch

Gingered Fruit en Papillote, page 77
Baked ham slices
Scrambled eggs
Orange-Walnut Madeleines, page 89
Assorted muffins, bagels, or other
breads
Poached Pears with Almonds, page 73
Coffee or hot tea
Fruit juices

Usher in fall's glorious bounty with a salute to some of its precious fruits.

Valentine's Toast

Bittersweet Chocolate Torte with
Raspberries, page 21
Strawberries
Chocolate Cookie Hearts with
Raspberry Sauce, page 31
White Chocolate Lemon-Almond
Truffles, page 34
Champagne

Invite special friends over for dessert
and toast to all of the sweethearts.

After-the-Movie Gathering

Fudgy Brownies with Chocolate-Orange Glaze,
page 29
Triple-Chocolate Chunk Cookies,
page 30
Vanilla ice cream with assorted
toppings

Instead of heading for the ice cream
shop after the show, have a make-your-
own-sundae party at home.

Mother's Day Tea

Berries-and-Cream Tartlets, page 83
Chocolate Truffle Tartlets, page 84
Lemon Tea Cakes, page 87
Orange-Walnut Madeleines, page 89
Strawberries la Crème Fraîche, page 96
Assorted teas
Lemonade

Gather your linens, crystal, and silver
and set your table for tea in honor of
this special day.

Summertime Dessert Social

Almond Tile Wafers,
page 154
Cream Cheese and Apricot Ice Cream,
page 172
Rum-Pistachio Ice Cream, page 174
Candy Bar Squares, page 184
Root beer floats
Pink lemonade

Grab your lawn chairs, treats, and kids
and meet all your neighbors for a
summer block bash.

Dessert Artistry

Add some glamour and glitz to any dessert with a
drizzling of chocolate, a piping of frosting, a stenciling
of powdered sugar, or a swirling of sauce. All you
need to know about creating fancy presentations is right
here in this special section. Plus you'll find the
basic recipes that are used over and over throughout
the book, such as Génoise, Flaky Pie Pastry, and Crème
Fraîche, on these pages.

▼▼▼

Quick-Method Puff Pastry

BASIC RECIPES

▼ ▼ ▼

Wonderful desserts
begin with flaky
pastries, tender
cakes, and luscious
sauces. The
following recipes
provide the
foundations for many
of the beautiful
desserts featured in
this book.

4   *cups all-purpose flour*
1   *teaspoon salt*
2   *cups* cold *butter (1 pound)*
1¼ *cups* ice *water*

In a large mixing bowl stir together flour
and salt. Cut the cold butter into ½-inch
thick *slices* (not cubes). Add the butter slices
to the flour mixture. Then toss till the butter
slices are coated with the flour mixture and
are separated.

Pour the ice water over the flour mixture.
Using a spoon, quickly mix (butter will
remain in large pieces and flour will not be
completely moistened).

Turn dough out onto a lightly floured pastry
cloth. Knead the dough 10 times by pressing
and pushing dough together to form a
rough-looking ball, lifting the pastry cloth if
necessary to press dough together. Shape
dough into a rectangle (dough still will have
some dry-looking areas). Make the corners as
square as possible. Slightly flatten dough.

Working on a well-floured pastry cloth, roll
the dough into a 15x12-inch rectangle. Fold
dough crosswise into thirds to form a 12x5-
inch rectangle. Give dough a quarter turn,
then fold crosswise into thirds to form a 5x4-
inch rectangle and to create 9 layers.

Repeat the rolling and folding process once
more, forming a 5x4-inch rectangle. Wrap
the dough with plastic wrap. Chill the dough
in the refrigerator for 20 minutes. Repeat
the rolling and folding process 2 more times.
Then chill the dough in the refrigerator for
20 minutes more.

Using a sharp knife, cut the puff-pastry
dough in half *crosswise* into 2 equal portions.
Makes 2 portions.

To store: Wrap each dough portion in
plastic wrap and refrigerate till ready to use
or for up to 3 days. For longer storage, wrap
each dough portion in *heavy* foil. Seal well,
label, and freeze dough for up to 3 months.
Thaw the dough, covered, in the refrigerator
about 24 hours before using.

Cream Puff Pastry

½ cup margarine or butter
1 cup water
¼ teaspoon salt
1 cup all-purpose flour
4 eggs

Place margarine or butter in a medium saucepan. Add water and salt. Bring mixture to boiling, stirring till margarine or butter melts. Then add flour all at once, stirring vigorously. Cook and stir till mixture forms a ball that doesn't separate. Remove from heat and cool for 10 minutes.

Add eggs, one at a time, to margarine mixture, beating with a wooden spoon after each addition about 1 minute or till smooth.

▼Chocolate Cream Puff Pastry: Prepare Cream-Puff Pastry as directed at left, *except* stir together the flour, 3 tablespoons *unsweetened cocoa powder,* and 2 tablespoons *sugar.* Then add the flour mixture all at once to the boiling mixture, stirring vigorously. Continue as directed above.

To keep cream puffs, éclairs, and other pastries from becoming soggy, fill the pastries no more than 2 hours before serving. Then chill the pastries in the refrigerator until serving time.

Flaky Pie Pastry

▼ FOR A SINGLE CRUST:	▼ FOR A DOUBLE CRUST:

1¼ cups all-purpose flour	2 cups all-purpose flour
¼ teaspoon salt	½ teaspoon salt
⅓ cup shortening	⅔ cup shortening
3 to 4 tablespoons cold water	6 to 7 tablespoons cold water

In a mixing bowl stir together flour and salt. Cut in shortening till pieces are the size of small peas.

Sprinkle *1 tablespoon* of the water over part of mixture, then gently toss with a fork. Push moistened dough to side of the bowl. Repeat, using 1 tablespoon of water at a time, till all of the dough is moistened. Form dough into a ball (for a double-crust, divide dough in half and form *each* half into a ball).

This tried-and-true, traditional pie pastry is perfect with any kind of filling.

Rich Tart Pastry

Butter and egg yolk enrich this pastry to make a crisp, flavorful shell for fruit tarts.

½ cup cold *butter*
1¼ cups *all-purpose flour*
1 *beaten egg yolk*
2 *to 3 tablespoons* ice *water*

In a medium mixing bowl cut butter into flour till pieces are the size of small peas.

In a small mixing bowl combine the egg yolk and *1 tablespoon* of the ice water.

Gradually stir egg yolk mixture into flour mixture. Add remaining water, 1 tablespoon at a time, till all of the dough is moistened. Using your fingers, gently knead the dough just till a ball forms. If necessary, cover dough with plastic wrap and chill in the refrigerator for 30 to 60 minutes or till dough is easy to handle.

Sweet-Tart Pastry

Sweetened with sugar, this crust tastes like a buttery sugar cookie.

1¼ cups *all-purpose flour*
¼ cup *sugar*
½ cup cold *butter*
2 *beaten egg yolks*
1 *tablespoon water*

In a medium mixing bowl stir together flour and sugar. Cut in butter till pieces are the size of small peas.

In a small mixing bowl stir together egg yolks and water. Gradually stir egg yolk mixture into flour mixture. Using your fingers, gently knead the dough just till a

ball forms. If necessary, cover with plastic wrap and chill for 30 to 60 minutes or till dough is easy to handle.

▼Nut Sweet-Tart Pastry: Prepare Sweet-Tart Pastry as directed above, *except* stir ½ cup ground toasted *almonds, hazelnuts (filberts), pecans,* or *walnuts* into the flour mixture. If dough appears dry after adding yolk mixture, add 1 to 2 teaspoons additional *water* till all of the dough is moistened. Continue as directed above.

Génoise

½ *cup sugar*	1 *cup sugar*
3 *slightly beaten eggs*	6 *slightly beaten eggs*
1 *teaspoon vanilla*	2 *teaspoons vanilla*
½ *cup all-purpose flour*	1 *cup all-purpose flour*
¼ *cup unsalted butter, melted and cooled*	½ *cup unsalted butter, melted and cooled*

Grease one or two 9x1½-inch or 8x1½-inch round baking pan(s). Line with waxed paper, parchment paper, or plain brown paper; grease paper. Set pan(s) aside.

Place sugar and eggs in a heat-proof mixing bowl (use a 1½- to 2-quart bowl for 1 layer of cake and a 3- to 4-quart bowl for 2 layers of cake). Place bowl over 1 to 2 inches *hot water* in a large saucepan (bowl should not touch water). Heat over low heat, stirring occasionally, for 5 to 10 minutes or till egg mixture is lukewarm (105° to 110°). Remove bowl from saucepan. Stir in vanilla.

Beat egg mixture with an electric mixer on high speed for 6 minutes for 1 layer of cake and 15 minutes for 2 layers of cake. Sift about *one-third* of the flour over the egg

mixture, then gently fold in the flour. Repeat sifting and folding in one-third of the flour at a time. Gently fold in melted butter.

Spread batter into the prepared pan(s). Bake in a 350° oven for 25 to 30 minutes or till a wooden toothpick inserted near the center of each cake comes out clean. Cool cake(s) in pan(s) on wire rack(s) for 10 minutes. Then remove cake(s) and peel off paper. Cool cake(s) completely on the wire rack(s).

Chocolate Génoise

Prepare Génoise as directed at left, *except* melt *semisweet* or *bittersweet chocolate* (use *1½ ounces* for 1 layer of cake or *3 ounces* for 2 layers of cake) according to the directions on page 225; cool chocolate. Fold the chocolate into the batter with the melted butter.

This firm-textured sponge cake is the basis for many classic French desserts.

Traditionally, the sugar and eggs are warmed over hot water to help the sugar dissolve and to enable the eggs to be whipped to a greater volume.

Hot Milk Sponge Cake

▼ FOR 1 LAYER: ▼ FOR 2 LAYERS:

This foolproof sponge cake provides an excellent base for a variety of fillings and frostings.

FOR 1 LAYER:	FOR 2 LAYERS:
½ cup all-purpose flour	1 cup all-purpose flour
½ teaspoon baking powder	1 teaspoon baking powder
Dash salt	Dash salt
1 egg	2 eggs
½ cup sugar	1 cup sugar
¼ cup milk	½ cup milk
1 tablespoon margarine or butter	2 tablespoons margarine or butter

Grease and lightly flour one or two 9x1½-inch or 8x1½-inch round baking pan(s). In a small mixing bowl stir together flour, baking powder, and salt. Set pan(s) and flour mixture aside.

In a medium mixing bowl beat egg(s) with an electric mixer on high speed for 3 to 4 minutes or till thick and lemon-colored. Gradually add the sugar, beating on medium speed for 4 to 5 minutes or till sugar is *almost* dissolved. Add flour mixture. Beat on low to medium speed *just till combined.*

In a small saucepan heat the milk and margarine or butter just till margarine melts. Stir warm milk mixture into the egg mixture.

Pour batter into the prepared pan(s). Bake in a 350° oven about 18 minutes or till each cake top springs back when touched. Cool cake(s) in pan(s) on wire rack(s) for 10 minutes. Then remove cake(s) and cool completely on the rack(s).

Crème Fraîche

▼ FOR ½ CUP: ▼ FOR 1 CUP: ▼ FOR 2 CUPS:

More tangy than whipped cream and milder than sour cream, this flavorful cream enhances any fresh fruit, as well as many desserts.

FOR ½ CUP:	FOR 1 CUP:	FOR 2 CUPS:
¼ cup whipping cream (not *ultrapasteurized*)	½ cup whipping cream (not *ultrapasteurized*)	1 cup whipping cream (not *ultrapasteurized*)
¼ cup dairy sour cream	½ cup dairy sour cream	1 cup dairy sour cream

In a mixing bowl stir together the whipping cream and sour cream. Cover with plastic wrap. Let stand at room temperature for 2 to 5 hours or till mixture thickens. When thickened, cover and chill in the refrigerator till serving time or for up to 1 week. Stir before serving.

Pastry Cream

FOR I CUP:	FOR 2 CUPS:
¼ *cup sugar*	½ *cup sugar*
2 *tablespoons all-purpose flour*	¼ *cup all-purpose flour*
⅛ *teaspoon salt*	¼ *teaspoon salt*
1 *cup half-and-half* or *light cream*	2 *cups half-and-half* or *light cream*
½ *of a vanilla bean, split lengthwise* or ½ *teaspoon vanilla*	1 *vanilla bean, split lengthwise* or *1 teaspoon vanilla*
2 *beaten egg yolks*	4 *beaten egg yolks*

In a heavy saucepan stir together sugar, flour, and salt. Gradually stir in the half-and-half or light cream. Add vanilla bean, if using. Cook and stir over medium heat till thickened and bubbly. Cook and stir for 1 minute more.

Gradually stir about *half* the hot mixture into the beaten egg yolks. Then return all of the egg yolk mixture to the saucepan. Bring to a gentle boil, then reduce heat. Cook and stir for 2 minutes. Remove from heat. Remove and discard vanilla bean or stir in liquid vanilla, if using. Cover surface with plastic wrap. Cool slightly or chill in the refrigerator till serving time. *(Do not stir.)*

Chocolate Pastry Cream

Prepare Pastry Cream as directed at left, *except* add chopped *semisweet* or *bittersweet chocolate* to the half-and-half mixture before cooking it (use *1 ounce* chocolate for 1 cup of Pastry Cream or *2 ounces* chocolate for 2 cups of Pastry Cream).

Frequently, this thick filling is lightened with whipped cream or sour cream before using. Be sure to fold in these ingredients before the Pastry Cream cools completely.

Sweetened Whipped Cream

▼ FOR 1 CUP:	▼ FOR 2 CUPS:

Because cream whips best when it's very cold, our Test Kitchen recommends chilling the mixing bowl and beaters in the refrigerator about 15 minutes before whipping the cream. Then beat the cream on low speed of your electric mixer, so it doesn't turn to butter.

½ cup whipping cream
1 tablespoon powdered sugar
¼ teaspoon vanilla

1 cup whipping cream
2 tablespoons powdered sugar
½ teaspoon vanilla

Chill a mixing bowl and the beaters of an electric mixer in the refrigerator. In the chilled bowl combine cream, powdered sugar, and vanilla. Beat with the chilled beaters on low speed till soft peaks form.

▼Flavored Whipped Cream: Prepare Sweetened Whipped Cream as directed above, except beat in one of the following flavorings:

For 1 cup: Beat in 1 tablespoon unsweetened cocoa powder plus 2 teaspoons sugar; 1 tablespoon liqueur; ½ teaspoon instant coffee crystals; ¼ teaspoon almond extract; ¼ teaspoon finely shredded lemon, orange, or lime peel; or ⅛ teaspoon ground cinnamon, nutmeg, or ginger.

For 2 cups: Beat in double amounts of the above flavorings.

Sweetened Whipped-Cream Frosting

▼ FOR 1 CUP:	▼ FOR 2 CUPS:	▼ FOR 4 CUPS:

After piping, this frosting retains its shape for up to 2 days. Also, you can keep this frosting on hand in your freezer. Thaw the frozen frosting for several hours in the refrigerator. Then before using, stir it vigorously till smooth.

2 teaspoons cold water
¼ teaspoon unflavored gelatin
½ cup whipping cream
1 tablespoon sugar

1 tablespoon cold water
½ teaspoon unflavored gelatin
1 cup whipping cream
2 tablespoons sugar

2 tablespoons cold water
1 teaspoon unflavored gelatin
2 cups whipping cream
¼ cup sugar

In a 1-cup glass measuring cup combine cold water and gelatin. Let stand 2 minutes. Place measuring cup in saucepan of boiling water. Cook and stir about 1 minute or till the gelatin is completely dissolved.

In a bowl beat cream and sugar with an electric mixer on medium speed while gradually drizzling the gelatin over the cream mixture. Continue beating the cream mixture till stiff peaks form.

▼Chocolate Whipped-Cream Frosting: Prepare Sweetened Whipped-Cream Frosting as directed at left, except increase the sugar and mix the sugar with unsweetened cocoa powder before beating with cream (use 4 teaspoons sugar for 1 cup of frosting, 3 tablespoons for 2 cups of frosting, or 8 teaspoons for 4 cups frosting; use 1 tablespoon cocoa powder for 1 cup of frosting, 2 tablespoons for 2 cups of frosting, or ¼ cup for 4 cups of frosting).

Buttercream

▼ FOR 2 CUPS:	▼ FOR 3 CUPS:

⅔ cup sugar
¼ cup water*
4 slightly beaten egg yolks
1 tablespoon liqueur (optional)*
1 teaspoon vanilla
1 cup unsalted butter, softened

1 cup sugar
⅓ cup water*
6 slightly beaten egg yolks
2 tablespoons liqueur (optional)*
1½ teaspoons vanilla
1½ cups unsalted butter, softened

In a heavy saucepan combine sugar and water. Bring to boiling. Remove from heat. Gradually stir about *half* of the sugar mixture into the egg yolks. Return all of egg yolk mixture to saucepan. Bring to a gentle boil; reduce heat. Cook and stir for 2 minutes. Remove from heat. If desired, add liqueur. Stir in vanilla. Cool to room temperature.

In a large mixing bowl beat butter with an electric mixer on high speed till fluffy. Add cooled sugar mixture, beating till combined. If necessary, chill till spreading consistency.

▼**Chocolate Buttercream:** Prepare Buttercream at left, *except* melt *semisweet* or *bittersweet chocolate* (use *3 ounces* for 2 cups Buttercream or *4 ounces* for 3 cups buttercream) as directed on page 225; cool. Add chocolate to butter with sugar mixture.

*If using liqueur, decrease the *water* (use *3 tablespoons water* for 2 cups of frosting or *¼ cup* for 3 cups of frosting).

To quickly cool the sugar mixture, transfer it to a mixing bowl. Place the mixing bowl in a larger bowl filled with ice water. Then stir the sugar mixture frequently while cooling.

Chocolate Glaze

▼ FOR ½ CUP:	▼ FOR 1 CUP:	▼ FOR 2 CUPS:

2 ounces semisweet or
　bittersweet chocolate
1 tablespoon unsalted
　butter
¼ cup whipping cream
1 teaspoon light corn
　syrup

4 ounces semisweet or
　bittersweet chocolate
2 tablespoons unsalted
　butter
½ cup whipping cream
2 teaspoons light corn
　syrup

8 ounces semisweet or
　bittersweet chocolate
¼ cup unsalted butter
1 cup whipping cream
4 teaspoons light corn
　syrup

Melt chocolate with butter according to the directions on page 225. Set aside. In a heavy saucepan stir together cream and corn syrup. Bring to a gentle boil, then reduce heat.

Cook 2 minutes for ½ cup or 1 cup glaze and 3 minutes for 2 cups glaze. Remove from heat. Stir in chocolate mixture. Cool to room temperature before using.

For a flavor boost, stir rum, cognac, or orange or coffee liqueur into the hot glaze. Use 1½ teaspoons liqueur for ½ cup glaze, 1 tablespoon for 1 cup glaze, or 2 tablespoons for 2 cups glaze.

Crème Anglaise

As the vanilla bean cooks in this rich custard sauce, little flecks typically break off, giving a slightly speckled appearance to the sauce.

FOR I CUP:

⅔ *cup whipping cream*
½ *of a vanilla bean, split lengthwise*
    or *½ teaspoon vanilla*
1 *egg yolk*
⅓ *cup sugar*
2 *teaspoons amaretto, white crème de menthe, orange liqueur, coffee liqueur, raspberry liqueur,* **or** *other desired liqueur (optional)*

FOR 2 CUPS:

1⅓ *cups whipping cream*
1 *vanilla bean, split lengthwise*
    or *1 teaspoon vanilla*
2 *egg yolks*
⅔ *cup sugar*
1 *tablespoon amaretto, white crème de menthe, orange liqueur, coffee liqueur, raspberry liqueur,* **or** *other desired liqueur (optional)*

In a heavy saucepan bring cream and, if using, vanilla bean just to boiling, stirring frequently. Remove saucepan from heat.

In a mixing bowl combine a small amount of the hot cream, egg yolk(s), and sugar. Beat with an electric mixer on high speed for 2 to 3 minutes or till thick and lemon-colored.

Gradually stir about *half* of the remaining cream mixture into the egg yolk mixture.

Then return all of the egg yolk mixture to the saucepan. Cook and stir over medium heat just till mixture returns to boiling. Remove from heat. Remove and discard vanilla bean or stir in liquid vanilla, if using. If desired, stir in liqueur. Cover surface with plastic wrap. Chill in the refrigerator till serving time. *(Do not stir.)*

Bittersweet Chocolate Sauce

Ladle this satiny, smooth sauce over bowls of ice cream or poached fruit. Or, surround a piece of cake or pie with it.

FOR ½ CUP:

2 *ounces bittersweet* **or** *semisweet chocolate*
⅓ *cup whipping cream*
2 *tablespoons sugar*

FOR I CUP:

4 *ounces bittersweet* **or** *semisweet chocolate*
⅔ *cup whipping cream*
¼ *cup sugar*

FOR 2 CUPS:

8 *ounces bittersweet* **or** *semisweet chocolate*
1⅓ *cups whipping cream*
½ *cup sugar*

In a heavy saucepan heat and stir chocolate over low heat just till melted. Stir in whipping cream and sugar. Cook and stir over medium-low heat about 3 minutes or till mixture just boils around edges. Remove from heat. Cover and cool to room temperature.

Caramel Sauce

▼ FOR I CUP:	▼ FOR 2 CUPS:
¾ cup packed brown sugar	1½ cups packed brown sugar
4 teaspoons cornstarch	3 tablespoons cornstarch
⅔ cup whipping cream	1½ cups whipping cream
1 tablespoon margarine or butter	2 tablespoons margarine or butter

In a saucepan combine brown sugar and cornstarch. Add whipping cream and margarine or butter. Bring mixture to boiling, stirring constantly. Then reduce heat. Cook and stir for 2 minutes more. Cover and cool. Chill in the refrigerator till serving time. (Mixture will thicken as it chills.) Stir sauce before serving.

Top ice cream or your favorite crisps, cobblers, or baked fruits with this brown-sugar sauce.

Raspberry Sauce

▼ FOR ½ CUP:	▼ FOR I CUP:	▼ FOR 2 CUPS:
1½ cups fresh or frozen raspberries or strawberries	3 cups fresh or frozen raspberries or strawberries	6 cups fresh or frozen raspberries or strawberries
3 tablespoons sugar	⅓ cup sugar	¾ cup sugar
½ teaspoon cornstarch	1 teaspoon cornstarch	2 teaspoons cornstarch

Thaw berries, if frozen. Place *1½ cups* berries in a blender container or food processor bowl. Cover and blend or process till berries are puréed. Then press berries through a fine-mesh sieve; discard seeds. Repeat with remaining berries using 1½ cups each time. (You should have about ½ *cup* sieved purée from *each* 1½ cups berries.)

In a saucepan stir together sugar and cornstarch. Add sieved berries. Cook and stir over medium heat till thickened and bubbly. Then cook and stir for 2 minutes more. Remove from heat. Cool to room temperature before serving.

Both berry options give a bright red color and a fresh taste.

Kiwi Sauce

▼ FOR ½ CUP:	▼ FOR I CUP:	▼ FOR 2 CUPS:
2 *kiwi fruits (about 8 ounces total)*	4 *kiwi fruits (about 1 pound total)*	8 *kiwi fruits (about 2 pounds total)*
1 *tablespoon sugar*	2 *tablespoons sugar*	¼ *cup sugar*
Few drops green food coloring (optional)	*Few drops green food coloring (optional)*	*Few drops green food coloring (optional)*

Only blend or process the kiwi fruits till they are just smooth. If you blend or process them too long, the seeds will break up and give the sauce a muddy color.

Peel kiwi fruits and cut into chunks. Place the kiwi chunks and sugar in a blender container or food processor bowl. Cover and blend or process *just till smooth.*

Press kiwi mixture through a fine-mesh sieve. If desired, stir food coloring into the kiwi mixture. Cover and chill in the refrigerator till serving time.

Citrus Sauce

▼ FOR ½ CUP:	▼ FOR I CUP:	▼ FOR 2 CUPS:
3 *tablespoons sugar*	⅓ *cup sugar*	⅔ *cup sugar*
2 *teaspoons cornstarch*	4 *teaspoons cornstarch*	8 *teaspoons cornstarch*
¼ *teaspoon finely shredded orange, tangerine,* **or** *lemon peel*	½ *teaspoon finely shredded orange, tangerine,* **or** *lemon peel*	1 *teaspoon finely shredded orange, tangerine,* **or** *lemon peel*
½ *cup orange* **or** *tangerine juice* **or** *⅓ cup water* plus *1 tablespoon lemon juice*	1 *cup orange* **or** *tangerine juice* **or** *¾ cup water* plus *2 tablespoons lemon juice*	2 *cups orange* **or** *tangerine juice* **or** *1½ cups water* **plus** *¼ cup lemon juice*
1 *teaspoon margarine* **or** *butter*	1 *tablespoon margarine* **or** *butter*	2 *tablespoons margarine* **or** *butter*

When you want a tangy sauce, make the lemon variation. For a sweeter, milder flavor try the orange or tangerine option.

In a saucepan stir together sugar and cornstarch. Stir in citrus peel and juice. (Pair flavors of peel with juice.) Cook and stir till mixture is thickened and bubbly. Cook and stir for 2 minutes more. Remove from heat. Stir in margarine or butter. Cool to room temperature before serving.

Cherry Sauce

½ cup sugar
2 tablespoons cornstarch
½ cup water
2 cups fresh or frozen pitted tart red
   cherries
1 tablespoon orange or cherry liqueur,
   cherry brandy, or orange juice

In a medium saucepan stir together sugar and cornstarch. Then stir in water. Add fresh or frozen cherries. Cook and stir over medium heat till thickened and bubbly. Cook and stir for 2 minutes more. Remove saucepan from heat.

Stir in liqueur, brandy, or orange juice. Serve warm. *Or,* cool to room temperature before serving. Makes 2 cups.

Citrus Curd

▼ FOR ½ CUP:	▼ FOR I CUP:	▼ FOR 2 CUPS:
¼ cup sugar	½ cup sugar	1 cup sugar
1½ teaspoons cornstarch	1 tablespoon cornstarch	2 tablespoons cornstarch
1 teaspoon finely shredded lemon peel or 1½ teaspoons finely shredded orange or tangerine peel	2 teaspoons finely shredded lemon peel or 1 tablespoon finely shredded orange or tangerine peel	1 tablespoon finely shredded lemon peel or 2 tablespoons finely shredded orange or tangerine peel
¼ cup lemon juice or ¼ cup orange or tangerine juice plus 1 teaspoon lemon juice	½ cup lemon juice or ½ cup orange or tangerine juice plus 1 tablespoon lemon juice	1 cup lemon juice or 1 cup orange or tangerine juice plus 2 table-spoons lemon juice
1 tablespoon margarine or butter	2 tablespoons margarine or butter	¼ cup margarine or butter
1 beaten egg yolk	3 beaten egg yolks	6 beaten egg yolks

Spread this tart filling between yellow, white, or spice cake layers or use it to fill bite-size pastries.

In a saucepan stir together sugar and corn-starch. Stir in citrus peel and juice and margarine or butter. (Pair flavors of peel with juice.) Cook and stir over medium heat till thickened and bubbly.

Slowly stir about *half* of the citrus mixture into beaten egg yolks. Then return all of the egg yolk mixture to the saucepan. Bring to a gentle boil. Cook and stir for 2 minutes more. Cover surface with plastic wrap. Chill in the refrigerator till serving time.

Glazed Nuts

Margarine or *butter*
1½ cups blanched whole almonds,
    hazelnuts (filberts), macadamia nuts,
    walnut halves, or *pecan halves*
½ cup sugar
2 *tablespoons margarine* or *butter*
½ *teaspoon vanilla*

For *Individual Glazed Nuts,* prepare Glazed Nuts as directed at right *except,* after removing the skillet from the heat, use a well-buttered spoon to remove a few nuts at a time. Working quickly, separate the nuts on the foil. Cool and store as directed.

Line a baking sheet with foil. Grease foil with margarine; set aside. In a heavy 10-inch skillet combine nuts, sugar, 2 tablespoons margarine or butter, and vanilla.

Cook over medium-high heat, shaking skillet occasionally, till sugar begins to melt. *(Do not stir.)* Reduce heat to low; cook till sugar is melted and golden brown, stirring frequently. Remove from heat. Pour onto the prepared baking sheet. Cool completely. Break into clusters. Cover tightly; store in a cool, dry place for up to 1 month. Makes about 2 cups.

Praline Baskets

▼ FOR 4 BASKETS:	▼ FOR 8 BASKETS:
2 *tablespoons unsalted butter*	½ *cup unsalted butter*
¼ *cup sugar*	1 *cup sugar*
1 *tablespoon dark corn syrup*	¼ *cup dark corn syrup*
⅓ *cup finely chopped toasted pecans, almonds,* or *hazelnuts (filberts)*	1⅓ *cups finely chopped toasted pecans, almonds, or hazelnuts (filberts)*
1 *tablespoon all-purpose flour*	¼ *cup all-purpose flour*

Whether you line the cookie sheet with heavy foil or parchment paper, the baskets will be equally crisp and delicious. However, the cookies spread slightly more on the foil than on the paper. This will make the baskets a little thinner and give them slightly higher sides.

Line a large cookie sheet with parchment paper or *heavy* foil. *(Do not use plain brown paper.)* If using foil, grease it. Grease outside bottoms and sides of 4 inverted 6-ounce custard cups. Set cookie sheet and cups aside.

Melt butter in a saucepan. Stir in sugar and corn syrup. Stir in nuts and flour. For *each* basket, drop *2 tablespoons* of the batter 7 inches apart on the prepared cookie sheet; spread batter to 3-inch circles. (Bake only 2 cookies at a time.)

Bake in a 350° oven for 8 to 10 minutes or till a deep golden brown. Cool on cookie sheet about 2 minutes or just till cookies are

firm enough to hold their shape. Quickly remove cookies from cookie sheet and place each cookie over a prepared custard cup. Then use a wooden spoon to gently fold edges down to form ruffles or pleats. (If cookies harden before shaping, reheat them in the oven about 1 minute.) Cool on the custard cups. Then remove baskets from the cups. Repeat with remaining batter, wiping excess fat from baking sheet between batches. Tightly covered and store in a cool, dry place for up to 1 week or in freezer for up to 6 months.

Caramel Filigree Garnishes

Cooking oil
½ cup sugar
Few drops hot water

Line a baking sheet with foil. Lightly oil the foil. Set the baking sheet aside.

In a heavy 1-quart saucepan heat sugar over medium-high heat till sugar begins to melt, shaking skillet occasionally. Reduce heat and cook 5 minutes more or till sugar is melted and *medium* caramel in color. Remove skillet from heat. Stir in hot water. Let stand for 1 minute.

Using a spoon, *quickly* drizzle onto the baking sheet forming a small web design. Cool. Remove from foil. Store in layers separated with waxed paper in a tightly covered container for up to 3 weeks. Makes 8.

For different shapes, trace a diamond, heart, or other design on the foil. Drizzle the sugar mixture along the outline of the design. Then drizzle the mixture inside the design in a lacy pattern.

Candied Citrus Peel

2 *medium oranges* or *lemons, 4 medium tangerines,* or *1 grapefruit*
1⅓ cups sugar
⅓ cup water
Sugar (about ¼ cup)

Cut the peels of the fruit into quarters, cutting through the peels to the pulp. Then use a spoon to loosen the peel from the pulp, leaving the white membrane attached to the peel. (Reserve pulp for another use.)

Place the fruit peel in a 2-quart nonmetal bowl. Add enough *cold water* to cover. If necessary, place a plate in the bowl to keep the peel submerged. Let stand overnight.

Drain the peel. Rinse with cold water. Place peel in a 2-quart saucepan. Cover with *cold water.* Bring to boiling, then drain. Repeat boiling and draining the peel 3 more times. Drain peel; cool thoroughly.

Cut the peel into ⅛- to ¼-inch-wide strips. In the same saucepan combine the 1⅓ cups sugar and ⅓ cup water. Bring to boiling, stirring constantly to dissolve sugar. Add the peel. Return to boiling; reduce heat and cook over medium-low heat (mixture should boil at a moderate, steady rate over the entire surface), stirring occasionally, till peel is almost translucent. This should take 15 to 20 minutes. *(Do not overcook.)*

Using a slotted spoon, remove peel from syrup. Discard syrup. Cool till lukewarm on a wire rack with waxed paper underneath the rack. While peel is still slightly sticky, roll it in additional sugar to coat. Dry on the rack for 1 to 2 hours. Then tightly cover and store in a cool, dry place for up to 1 week or in the freezer for up to 6 months. Makes about 2 cups.

If you want a mildly flavored candied peel, use oranges or tangerines. For a sharper flavor, choose lemons or grapefruits.

DECORATIONS AND GARNISHES

▼ ▼ ▼

Decorations and garnishes turn a simply delicious dessert into a smashing success. For a finishing touch, pipe a whipped cream border on a chilled soufflé, stencil a cocoa powder design on a dessert plate, or top a cake with fresh flowers. On the following pages, you will find complete directions for these and many other decorations and garnishes.

Hints for Successful Decorating

Every artist, in every field of endeavor, begins with a few basic guidelines. To become an accomplished dessert artist keep these points in mind:

▼Choose garnishes and decorations with flavors that enhance the dessert. Fruit sauces usually pair well with chocolate desserts, and custard sauces make nice complements to fruit desserts.

▼Play it safe. A garnish or sauce that repeats a flavor or ingredient in the dessert is sure to be a success. For example, fresh raspberries are a perfect topping for a raspberry tart.

▼Choose just one main garnish. Although you may be tempted to top a cake with chocolate curls, fresh fruit, and candied flowers, any of these garnishes used alone generally will have more impact.

▼Consider the amount of time available. If you don't have enough time to create last-minute garnishes, select garnishes that you can make in advance.

▼Take some care in selecting plates and dishes that make the most of the dessert. A pedestal cake plate makes even the humblest cake seem special, while cut-glass goblets handsomely show off any ice cream.

▼Practice makes perfect. Don't be discouraged if your first attempts are less

than you expect. Many techniques such as swirling sauces require practice. Keep trying and soon you'll be trimming desserts like the world's greatest pastry chefs.

Marzipan

Marzipan, a creamy almond confection, can be formed into a variety of fanciful shapes and decorations. You can make your own marzipan (see recipe for Marzipan Treasures, page 104) or purchase marzipan from a gourmet, specialty, or grocery store.

To tint marzipan, break off a small portion and knead in a little liquid or paste food coloring. Add just a tiny bit of food coloring at a time until the marzipan becomes a shade you like.

For fruit or heart shapes, refer to the directions for shaping Marzipan Treasures. To make roses, cutouts, and ribbons, follow the directions for shaping Chocolate Modeling Clay (see pages 231 and 232).

Toasted Nuts

Add a simple and tasty finish by garnishing your dessert with toasted pecans, walnuts, hazelnuts, almonds, or another nut.

To toast nuts, spread them in a thin layer in a shallow baking pan. Bake the nuts in a 350° oven for 5 to 10 minutes or till the nuts are golden brown, stirring once or twice. If you like, toast more nuts than you need and store the extra toasted nuts in plastic bags in the freezer.

Garnishing with Edible Flowers

Top almost any dessert with naturally colorful, edible flowers. Scatter small flowers over cakes, tortes, mousses, or puddings. Or break off some petals and sprinkle them over the dessert.

Choose any edible flower to decorate your dessert. However, if you plan to actually eat the flower, select one with a flavor that is compatible with sweets. Some good dessert flowers are pansies, violets, rose petals, dianthus, and daylilies.

Be sure to use only *edible* flowers around food even if you don't plan to eat them. To be edible, the flower must be free of both naturally occurring and man-made toxins.

Not all flowers and not all parts of all flowering plants are edible. Choose only ones shown *(right)* or ones you know to be safe. If in doubt whether a variety of a flower's blossom, leaf, or stem is edible, check with your local poison control center or state extension service.

To find flowers for decorating food, look no farther than your own garden, provided that neither you nor your neighbors use chemical fertilizers or pesticides. Pick the flowers just before using, rinse, and gently pat dry.

And look for edible flowers in the produce sections of some supermarkets, at local herb gardens and some restaurant or produce suppliers, and through local or mail-order outlets. Flowers from a florist usually are treated with chemicals and should not be used with food.

Candied Flowers

With a luster all their own, candied flowers create a glistening garnish.

To make candied flowers, gently wash fresh edible flowers in water. Then place them on white paper towels and let air-dry or gently blot dry. For large flowers or flowers with petals that are tightly closed, break off the petals and candy the individual petals.

In a small bowl stir together 2 tablespoons *water* and 1 tablespoon thawed *frozen egg substitute.* Using a small, clean paintbrush, brush the egg mixture on each side of each petal in a thin, even layer. Sprinkle each flower evenly with *extra-fine-grain sugar.* To give the flowers a hint of gold color, mix ⅛ teaspoon *gold petal dust* with the sugar before sprinkling it over the flowers (see page 222). Shake each flower or petal to remove the excess sugar. Let the flowers dry on waxed paper for 2 to 4 hours.

Store candied flowers in an airtight container between layers of waxed paper for up to 4 weeks. For longer storage, freeze candied flowers for up to 6 months.

1) Marigolds (Tagetes species), 2) Borage (Borago officinalis), 3) Dianthus (Dianthus species), 4) Daylilies (Hemerocallis hybrids), 5) Geraniums (Pelargonium species), 6) Nasturtiums (Tropaeolum majus), 7) Pansies (Viola x wittrockiana) and Violets (viola species), 8) Roses (rosa species), 9) Calendulas (Calendula officinalis)

Holding the decorating bag

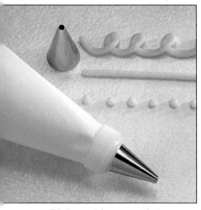

Piping with a round tip

Piping with a star tip

Piping

Add your signature to cakes, tortes, pastries, mousses, puddings, and many other desserts by piping frosting, whipped cream, or chocolate in a variety of designs. Pipe a border or a single special design, or completely cover your dessert with piped decorations. To start, all you need is a decorating bag and a few decorating tips.

▼**Decorating Bags:** Decorating bags are available in different sizes and materials. Or you can make your own from a heavy clear plastic bag.

To make a decorating bag from a plastic bag, simply snip off one of the bottom corners making a small whole in the bag. For dots, lines, and writing, just squeeze the frosting through the hole. For shells, leaves, and more intricate designs, fit the appropriate decorating tip into the plastic bag. If necessary, cut off a little more of the plastic bag to make a larger hole.

▼**Holding the Bag:** Fit the desired tip into the decorating bag. Fill the bag about half full of frosting. Then fold the corners over and roll the bag down to the frosting. With your writing hand, grip the bag near the roll above the frosting level. Then apply pressure from the palm of your hand, forcing frosting toward the tip. Use your other hand to guide the tip of the bag. With a little practice, you'll learn to control the flow of the frosting by changing pressure.

▼**Decorating Tips:** Decorating tips are available in many shapes and sizes. Although many specialty tips are available, you can make a beautifully decorated masterpiece with just three tips—a round tip, a star tip, and a leaf tip. Also, tips are available in different sizes. Most openings range from ⅛ inch to ½ inch. The size of the finished decoration increases with the size of the opening.

Try these ideas with your decorating tips.

Round tips have a simple round opening and are used for writing and making dots and lines.

To make dots, hold the bag at a 90-degree angle to the surface of the dessert (straight up and down) with the tip almost touching the surface. Squeeze out a dot of frosting till it's the size you want. Stop pressure and pull away.

For lines and writing, hold the bag at a 45-degree angle to the surface of the dessert. Guiding the tip just above the surface with your free hand, squeeze with your writing hand. To end each letter or line, gently touch the tip to the surface, release pressure, and pull away.

Star tips are used to make stars, shells, and zigzags.

For stars, hold the bag at a 90-degree angle to the surface of the dessert and with the tip just above the surface. Squeeze out some frosting, stop applying pressure, then pull away.

For shells, hold the bag at a 45-degree angle to the surface of the dessert. With the tip just above the surface, squeeze out some frosting till you've formed a mound. Then push the tip down and away from the mound till it touches the surface and forms a tail. Stop applying pressure and pull away. Start the next shell at the stopping point of the previous one (shells will overlap slightly).

For zigzags, hold the bag at a 45-degree angle to the dessert surface. Touch the tip to the surface; squeeze out frosting as you move the tip from side to side. Stop pressure and pull away.

Leaf tips are great for making leaves.

For leaves hold the bag at a 45-degree angle to the dessert surface and with the tip opening parallel to the dessert surface. Holding the point just above the surface, squeeze out some frosting to make the base of a leaf. Continue squeezing, but ease up on the pressure as you pull away. Stop the pressure and lift off.

▼Two-Tone Piping: Fill your decorating bag with two different colors of frosting or whipped cream to pipe marbled decorations or decorations with tinted edges. For these, use a decorating bag fitted with a medium or large star tip (about ¼- to ½-inch opening).

To make marbled stars, shells, or zigzags, carefully fill *each side of the bag* with a different color frosting or whipped cream.

To give tinted edges to stars, shells, or zigzags, use a long metal spatula to spread a thin layer of one color frosting or whipped cream onto the inside of the entire decorating bag. Then *carefully* spoon another color frosting or cream into the bag.

Dusting

Dusting is one of the easiest decorating techniques to master. You can dust over cakes, tortes, cheesecakes, cookies, and even puddings.

For toppings, try ground nuts; unsweetened cocoa powder; ground spices; coarse-grain or crystal sugar; extra-fine-grain sugar; cinnamon sugar; powdered sugar; or powdered sugar mixed with spices, unsweetened cocoa powder, or powdered food coloring.

Sift the topping through a sieve or sifter onto the top of the dessert. When selecting the utensil to use, consider the fineness of your topping. A sifter works well for powdered sugar or unsweetened cocoa powder. However, ground nuts will require a sieve with a coarser mesh.

To dust a dessert top, spoon the topping of your choice into a sieve or sifter. Hold the utensil over the dessert. With your free, hand gently tap the utensil so just a little of the topping comes out. Dust lightly, moving the sieve over the dessert to cover the whole surface. For a heavier coating, dust again.

Piping with a leaf tip

Two-tone piping

Painting with petal dust

Stenciling with a doily

Stenciling with a stencil

Painting

Paint a colorful design on desserts, like cookies, pastries, or frosted cakes. For paint, use powdered food coloring or petal dust. (Petal dust is a fine dusting powder that is available in many colors, including gold and silver. Use gold and silver petal dust to give a shimmery, glistening highlight to foods. Petal dust is available through mail-order sources or specialty stores.)

You can use powdered food coloring or petal dust either diluted with a little alcohol or in its dry form.

If you want a smooth finish on your designer desserts, mix a little powdered food coloring or petal dust with a few drops of 90- to 100-proof alcohol. *(Do not use rubbing alcohol.)* The alcohol will evaporate quickly, so you may need to add a few more drops of alcohol to the coloring while painting. With a clean, small paintbrush, paint designs on your dessert.

To give soft highlights to decorations made from marzipan or Chocolate Modeling Clay (see recipe, page 231) paint with the dry powdered coloring or petal dust. Use a dry, clean, small paintbrush to brush the coloring on the decoration. You may want to try brushing the powdered coloring or petal dust just along the edges of the decorations.

Stenciling

Personalize your dessert by stenciling a unique design. Stenciling works best on cakes, tortes, and pastries with flat surfaces. For other desserts, try stenciling a design directly on the serving plate.

For a stencil, use a purchased doily, a purchased stencil, or make your own stencil from lightweight cardboard. A doily can be cut into small pieces and you can use just part of the design.

To make your own stencil, draw a design on the cardboard (cardboard from a gift box or a manila folder works well). Then use a crafts knife to cut out the design.

Place the stencil on top of the dessert surface. Sift the desired topping over the stencil, as directed for Dusting (see page 221). If your stencil has large designs use a clean, dry brush to brush any topping left on the stencil into the holes. This keeps the edges of your design sharp and clean. Then, carefully lift off the stencil. If you like, brush any remaining topping off your stencil and save the stencil to use another time.

To stencil a design on a plate, choose a stencil with large holes. Place the stencil on the plate and lightly brush melted margarine or shortening in the holes (or spray the holes with nonstick spray coating). Sprinkle the desired topping over the stencil as directed for Dusting. Then carefully lift off the stencil.

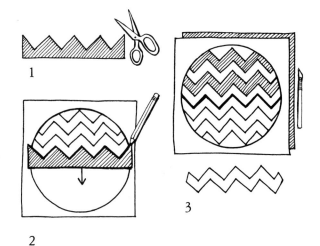

Making a cardboard stencil

Sauces

Sauces not only enhance the flavor of a dessert, but also add a splash of color. Although making the sauce requires some extra time and effort, decorating with sauces is easy. Sauces always add pizzazz when draped over a dessert. For a sophisticated look, try trimming the individual dessert plates with one or more sauces. Then place the dessert servings on top of the sauce.

▼**Pooling Sauces:** Spoon 1 to 2 tablespoons of a sauce onto each individual dessert plate. Then tilt the plate to spread the sauce into a an even layer.

If you like, pipe another sauce around the pooled sauce to make a border.

▼**Swirling Sauces:** You'll need two or three different sauces for this presentation. Choose sauces of different colors but compatible flavors. Spoon each sauce in a different pool near the edge of the plate. Then tilt the plate till the sauces run together. Or swirl the sauces together with a narrow metal spatula.

▼**Making Drawn Designs:** You will need one sauce to pool on the plate and another sauce (or you can use melted chocolate or Crème Fraîche) to draw the designs. To show off some designs, you may want to place the dessert off to one side of the plate. Start by drawing the following three designs. Once you master these, use your imagination to come up with your own designs.

Chevron stripes: Drizzle or pipe the second sauce onto the pooled sauce in parallel lines. Holding the edge of a narrow spatula or knife at a right angle to the parallel lines, draw the spatula through the lines at regular

intervals. If desired, draw every other line in the opposite direction.

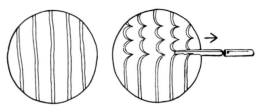

Spider web: Drizzle or pipe the second sauce onto the pooled sauce in a spiral. Holding the edge of a narrow spatula or a knife at a right angle to the circular lines, draw the spatula through the lines at regular intervals from the center to the edge.

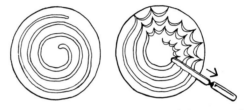

Bleeding hearts: Pipe drops of the second sauce on top of the pooled sauce or on top of an empty plate at regular intervals. Run the tip of a knife or skewer through each drop of sauce either into the pooled sauce or to the edge of the plate, creating a heart shape.

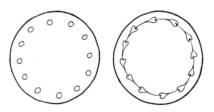

▼**Free-form designs:** For these, you will need two or three squeeze bottles. You can buy squeeze bottles at a specialty store or you can use catsup or mustard plastic squeeze bottles. Or use heavy plastic bags with one corner snipped off. Pour a different sauce, melted chocolate, or Crème Fraîche into each bottle or bag. Randomly squeeze or pipe the sauces onto dessert plates in any design you like.

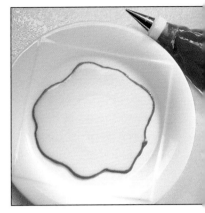

Pooling sauces

Swirling sauces

CHOCOLATE GARNISHES

▼ ▼ ▼

Sweet, seductive, and smooth—chocolate makes the ultimate dessert garnish. On the following pages, you will find everything you need to know to craft simple trims as well as stunning chocolate ornaments. Look for information on selecting, storing, melting, and quick-tempering chocolate, plus complete directions for making gorgeous chocolate garnishes.

Types of Chocolate

Grocery stores, candy stores, and gourmet shops sell many kinds of chocolate that can be used in cooking. When a recipe lists chocolate as an ingredient, it will specify one or more types of chocolate, such as unsweetened or semisweet. For best results, be sure to use only a type of chocolate that is listed in the recipe.

Even within types of chocolate, the flavor and sweetness vary from one manufacturer to another. Try several brands and settle on the one you like best.

▼**Unsweetened chocolate,** sometimes called baking or bitter chocolate, is pure chocolate. Since no sugar has been added to this chocolate, it has a strong, bitter taste. This type of chocolate is almost exclusively used for baking and cooking. Look for unsweetened chocolate in the baking section of your grocery store.

▼**Unsweetened cocoa powder** is pure chocolate with most of the cocoa butter removed. Some cocoa powders labeled Dutch-process or European-style have been treated to neutralize the naturally occurring acids. This gives the cocoa powder a more mellow flavor and a redder color.

All of the following chocolates have had sugar added to them, so they are referred to as sweet chocolates.

▼**Semisweet chocolate,** sometimes called bittersweet chocolate, is pure chocolate with added cocoa butter and sugar. Chocolate labeled as bittersweet is usually darker and less sweet than chocolate labeled as semisweet. However, since no legal

specifications for either term exist, this is not always the case. Some European bittersweet chocolates are labeled as dark chocolate and may be used as ingredients in recipes calling for semisweet or bittersweet chocolate. Look for these chocolates in both the candy and the baking aisles in your grocery store.

▼**Sweet baking chocolate** is pure chocolate with added cocoa butter and sugar. It is used primarily for baking and will be stocked in the baking section of your store.

▼**Milk chocolate** is pure chocolate with added cocoa butter, sugar, and milk solids. Most milk chocolates contain less pure chocolate than semisweet or bittersweet chocolates, so the chocolate flavor is milder. You most often will find milk chocolate in the candy aisle.

▼**Chocolate-like products** include candy coatings, white baking bars and pieces, and other products composed of sugar, milk solids, and vanillin or vanilla. Some manufacturers add cocoa butter for extra flavor. Look for these products in candy stores and in the baking aisle of some grocery stores.

White baking bars and pieces and vanilla-flavored candy coatings are often referred to as "white chocolate." However, this is a misnomer. Because these products lack pure chocolate, they can't legally be labeled chocolate in the United States.

Selecting Quality Chocolate

All quality chocolate will be glossy, break with a snap, and possess a chocolaty aroma. Also, it will melt on your tongue without waxiness or graininess.

Storing Chocolate

Store chocolate in a tightly covered container or a sealed plastic bag and place in a cool, dry place. Ideal storage conditions are between 60° and 78°, with less than 50 percent relative humidity.

Cocoa powder also should be stored in a tightly covered container in a cool, dry place. High temperatures and high humidity tend to cause cocoa powder to lump and lose its rich brown color.

Melting Chocolate

For most recipes, choose any of the methods below to melt chocolate. These methods work for melting white baking bars and pieces and candy coatings, too. Also, use one of these methods when a recipe instructs you to melt chocolate with another ingredient, such as margarine, butter, shortening, or whipping cream.

For some special cases, such as garnishes and dipped candies, chocolate must be melted by a special method called "tempering." This enables the chocolate to set up and hold its shape at room temperature. (See Quick-Tempering Chocolate, page 226.) Candy coatings and white baking bars and pieces will retain their shape without tempering.

Whether you melt or quick-temper chocolate, be careful to keep water from splashing on the chocolate. Even a small drop of water will cause the chocolate to stiffen.

For best results, coarsely chop chocolate bars and squares before melting them. Then choose the method that suits the equipment you have available.

▼**Direct Heat:** One of the most common and convenient methods for melting chocolate is using direct heat. Place the chocolate in a heavy saucepan over very low heat, stirring constantly till the chocolate begins to melt. Immediately remove the chocolate from the heat and stir till smooth.

▼**Double Boiler:** This method may take a little longer than the direct-heat method, but it avoids the possibility of scorching the chocolate. Place water in the bottom pan of a double boiler so that the top of the water is ½ inch below the upper pan. Place the chocolate in the upper pan. Then place the double boiler over low heat. Stir the chocolate constantly until it is melted. The water in the bottom of the double boiler should not come to boiling while the chocolate is melting.

▼**Microwave Oven:** Your microwave oven offers a handy way to melt chocolate. Place up to 6 ounces of chopped chocolate bars, chocolate squares, or chocolate pieces in a microwave-safe bowl, custard cup, or measure. Micro-cook, uncovered, on 100% power (high) for 1½ to 2 minutes or till soft enough to stir smooth. Stir every minute during heating. The chocolate will hold its shape after it starts to melt, so stir it to see how melted the chocolate is and to help it heat evenly.

Placing measure in water

Stirring the chocolate

Chocolate ready for dipping

Whichever method you choose to melt chocolate (either alone or with other ingredients), remember these points:

▼Make sure all the equipment is completely dry. Any moisture on the utensils or in the container may cause the chocolate to stiffen. If this happens, stir in ½ to 1 teaspoon of shortening for every ounce of chocolate.

▼To avoid scorching the chocolate, keep the heat low.

▼Always stir chocolate during melting because most chocolate will retain its shape as it melts.

Quick-Tempering Chocolate

Tempering chocolate is a method of slowly melting chocolate followed by carefully cooling it. This procedure stabilizes the cocoa butter so the chocolate holds its shape. Since tempering chocolate is a lengthy process, we use a method of melting chocolate that produces the same results in less time. We call this method "quick-tempering."

Quick-temper chocolate when you will be using it for decorations that must hold their shape at room temperature or for dipping. (White baking bars and candy coatings do not need to be tempered.)

Follow these step-by-step directions for quick tempering and your chocolate will set up crisp and glossy every time.

Step 1: Chop up to 1 pound of bars, squares, or large pieces of chocolate into small pieces. In a 4-cup glass measure or a 1½-quart glass mixing bowl, combine the amount of chocolate and shortening called for in the

recipe. (Or use 1 tablespoon of shortening for every 6 ounces of chocolate.)

Step 2: Pour very warm tap water (100° to 110°) into a large glass casserole or bowl to a depth of 1 inch. Place the measure or bowl containing the chocolate inside the casserole. Water should cover the bottom half of the measure or bowl containing the chocolate. Adjust the water level as necessary. *(Do not splash any water into the chocolate.)*

Step 3: Stir the chocolate mixture *constantly* with a rubber spatula until completely melted and smooth. This takes about 15 to 20 minutes. *(Do not rush the process.)*

Step 4: If the water begins to cool, remove the measure or bowl containing the chocolate. Discard the cool water and add warm water. Return the measure or bowl containing the chocolate to the bowl containing water.

Step 5: Do not allow any water or moisture to touch the chocolate. Just one drop can cause the chocolate to become thick and grainy. If water should get into the chocolate, stir in additional shortening, 1 teaspoon at a time, until the mixture becomes shiny and smooth.

Step 6: When melted and smooth, the chocolate is ready for dipping or shaping. If the chocolate becomes too thick during handling, repeat Step 4. Stir the chocolate constantly until it again reaches dipping consistency.

Step 7: Let your finished product set up in a cool, dry place. *Do not chill* your finished product or the chocolate will lose temper and become soft at room temperature.

Chocolate Garnishes

Chocolate garnishes make exquisite decorations for a variety of desserts. Choose a chocolate trim as simple as a sprinkling of grated chocolate. Or for a more elaborate ornament, shape a decoration from Chocolate Modeling Clay (see recipe, page 231). On the following pages you'll find instructions for these and many more chocolate creations.

▼**Grated Chocolate:** Sprinkle grated chocolate or white baking bar on the tops and sides of cakes or tortes. Or try sprinkling grated chocolate over a whipped cream garnish. To grate chocolate, rub a solid piece of chocolate across the grating section of a hand-held grater. Choose either the fine or the large grating section to obtain the size pieces you want.

Grating chocolate

▼**Shaved Chocolate:** Gently press shaved chocolate or white baking bar into the frosting or whipped cream on tortes and cakes. To shave chocolate, using a vegetable peeler, make short, quick strokes across the surface of a solid piece of chocolate.

Shaving chocolate

▼**Small Chocolate Curls:** Encircle a pie or cake with a border of small chocolate curls. Or add a few chocolate curls to an individual serving of mousse or pudding. Small chocolate curls are easiest to make with milk chocolate. To make small chocolate curls, carefully draw a vegetable peeler across a bar of chocolate. For narrower curls use the narrow side of the chocolate bar and for wide curls use the broad surface.

Making small chocolate curls

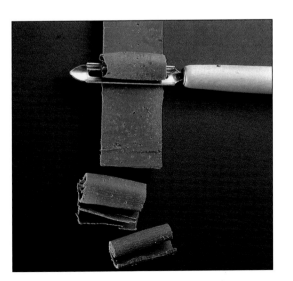

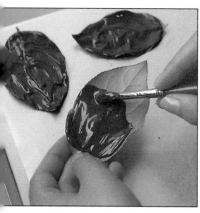

Brushing chocolate on a leaf

Removing leaf

▼**Chocolate Leaves:** Garnish individual servings of mousses with one or two chocolate leaves. For cakes, tortes, and pies, arrange clusters of chocolate leaves in the center. When making chocolate leaves, use nontoxic leaves such as mint, rose, lemon, or strawberry. For 12 small leaves, use 2 ounces of *quick-tempered* chocolate or melted white baking bar or candy coating. With a clean, small paintbrush, brush one or two coats of chocolate on the underside of each leaf. Wipe away any chocolate from the top side of the leaf. Then place the leaves, chocolate side up, on a curved surface (the bottom edge of a pie plate works well) or waxed paper-lined baking sheet until dry. Before using, peel the leaf away from the chocolate.

▼**Chocolate Cutouts:** Embellish frosted cakes by placing chocolate cutouts on the tops or sides. For chocolate cutouts, pour *quick-tempered* chocolate or melted white baking bar or candy coating onto a baking sheet lined with waxed paper and spread it ⅛ to ¼ inch thick. Let stand till almost dry. Firmly press hors d'oeuvre or small cookie cutters into the chocolate. Then carefully lift the cutouts from the waxed paper.

▼**Chocolate-Dipped Nuts:** These tiny morsels make one of the best-tasting garnishes. Dip nuts, one at a time, into *quick-tempered* chocolate or melted white baking bar or candy coating. Dip either the whole nut or half of the nut. For small nuts, such as hazelnuts, use a clean, small paintbrush to brush on the chocolate. Let the nuts stand on waxed paper until the chocolate is dry.

▼**Chocolate Lace Dishes and Garnishes:** Beautify ice creams and ices by serving them in lacy dishes. Make one large dish or several individual dishes. To start, press a piece of foil into a 1-quart shallow au gratin dish, an 8x8x2-inch baking pan, four shallow dessert bowls, or six 3½-inch muffin pan cups, covering the bottom and sides, and extending the foil over the edges. Chill while you *quick-temper* 6 ounces of chocolate with 1 tablespoon of shortening according to the directions on page 226. (Or use melted white baking bar or candy coating.)

Pipe or drizzle the chocolate in a random circular motion over the bottom and up the sides of the foil in the chilled container. Make the chocolate heaviest at the top rim and on the bottom to give your lace dish extra strength. Let stand until dry.

Making chocolate cutouts

Drizzling chocolate for a lace dish

Piping lace garnishes

To unmold, lift the foil from the container. *Carefully* peel the foil from the lace dish. Use a wide metal spatula to transfer the lace dish to a serving plate. Keep the dish in a cool, dry place till ready to serve or store it in a covered container kept in a cool, dry place for up to 1 week.

Make lace garnishes just as you make lace dishes, *except* pipe or drizzle small designs on waxed paper-lined baking sheets. Let stand until dry, then peel the garnishes from the waxed paper.

▼**Pencil Curls:** Mound pencil curls on top of cheesecakes, cakes, tortes, and chilled soufflés. To start making curls, *quick-temper* 2 ounces of chocolate with 1 teaspoon of shortening according to the directions on page 226. (Or use melted white baking bar or candy coating.) Set the chocolate aside.

Heat a 13x9x2-inch baking dish in a 350° oven for 2 minutes. Remove the dish from the oven and place the dish upside down on a thick towel to protect your work surface. Cool the dish until it is about the same temperature as the chocolate.

Using a narrow metal spatula (a spatula with an angled blade works best to spread the chocolate evenly), spread two 3-inch-wide bands of chocolate about 1 inch apart on the bottom of the inverted dish. Use about 1 tablespoon of the chocolate mixture for each band. Let stand until the chocolate comes to room temperature.

The chocolate is ready to scrape when it feels firm, but not hard. Also, the chocolate should be soft enough to scrape without breaking, yet firm enough that it will not melt. Steady the dish with one hand. With your other hand, hold the blade of a metal pancake turner or a clean paint scraper at a 45-degree angle and about 1 inch from the narrow edge of a chocolate band. With the blade of the turner, scrape the chocolate off the dish to form tight curls. Stop scraping when the curl is the size you want.

Use the turner or a long wooden skewer to lift the curl from the dish, being careful not to touch the curl with your fingers. Repeat scraping, making more tight curls.

▼**Large Loose Curls:** Top meringues, cakes and all kinds of desserts with large loose curls. For an extra touch, dust chocolate curls with powdered sugar and curls made from white baking bar or candy coating with unsweetened cocoa powder.

To make large loose curls, spread *quick-tempered* chocolate as directed for Pencil Curls (left), *except* spread the chocolate over the entire surface of the inverted dish. Let stand till the chocolate is firm, but not hard. Hold the blade of a metal pancake turner or a clean paint scraper at a 30-degree angle. Then push the blade of the turner away from you, scraping the chocolate off the dish. Use the turner or a long wooden skewer to remove the curls, being careful not to touch them with your fingers.

Making pencil curls

Large loose and pencil curls

Making large loose curls

Marbled chocolate curls

▼**Marbled Chocolate Curls:** To give your desserts extra style, try topping them with marbled chocolate curls.

To make the marbled chocolate, fill a decorating bag fitted with a medium plain round tip (about ¼-inch opening) or a heavy plastic bag with a snipped corner with 1 ounce of melted chocolate-flavored candy coating. Prepare the baking dish as directed for Pencil Curls or Large Loose Curls (see page 229). Pipe the candy coating in any pattern over the inverted dish. Then pour 1 ounce of melted white baking bar or white candy coating over the piped chocolate. Spread to a thin layer. Let stand till firm, but not hard. Scrape as directed for Pencil Curls or Large Loose Curls (see page 229).

▼**More Chocolate Garnishes:** The following two recipes offer more ways to enhance your desserts with spectacular chocolate decorations.

Chocolate Ruffled Cups

Chocolate Ruffled Cup

8   *ounces semisweet, bittersweet, or milk chocolate; white baking bar; or desired color of vanilla-flavored candy coating*
1   *tablespoon shortening*
8   *10-inch circles cut from smooth, heavy plastic bags*
8   *6- or 9-ounce paper or plastic drinking cups*

If using chocolate, quick-temper with the shortening according to the directions on page 226. If using white baking bar or candy coating, melt with shortening according to the directions on page 225. Cool slightly.

Spread about *1½ tablespoons* of chocolate in the center of *each* plastic circle to form a circle of chocolate 5 to 6 inches in diameter. Drape plastic, chocolate side up, over paper or plastic cups. Adjust plastic to make even ruffles. Let stand in a cool, dry place till dry.

To unmold, carefully lift chocolate cups from the cups. Turn right side up on waxed paper or plastic wrap. If desired, tightly cover and store in a cool, dry place for up to 1 month. *Or,* to serve, carefully peel plastic from inside the chocolate cups. If necessary, wear disposable gloves or use a plastic bag so your fingers do not melt the chocolate. Makes 8.

Chocolate Modeling Clay

▼ FOR 1 CUP:	▼ FOR 2 CUPS:

6 *ounces semisweet* or *bittersweet chocolate* or *white* or *desired color of vanilla-flavored candy coating*

3 *tablespoons light corn syrup*
  Sifted powdered sugar (optional)

12 *ounces semisweet* or *bittersweet chocolate, colored,* or *white* or *desired color of vanilla-flavored candy coating*

⅓ *cup light corn syrup*
  Sifted powdered sugar (optional)

Melt chocolate or candy coating according to the directions on page 225; cool. Stir in corn syrup *just till combined.*

Turn mixture out onto a large sheet of waxed paper. Let stand at room temperature for 6 to 24 hours or till dry to touch. If making 2 cups, divide chocolate clay into 2 portions. Gently knead each portion for 10 to 15 strokes or till clay is smooth and pliable. If clay is too soft, chill in the refrigerator about 15 minutes or till easy to handle. *Or,* if desired, knead in enough powdered sugar to make the clay stiff. Store unused clay in a sealed plastic bag at room temperature for 3 to 4 weeks. (Clay will stiffen with storage. Knead the clay till it is pliable before using.)

Note: To tint small portions of *white* Chocolate Modeling Clay, knead in *liquid* or *paste food coloring* to make desired color.

Here are some show-stopping garnishes that you can make with either Chocolate Modeling Clay (above) or homemade or purchased marzipan (see recipe, page 104).

Roses

Dust your work surface with powdered sugar. Press several ⅝-inch balls of clay or marzipan into ⅛-inch-thick circles. Cut the circles in half. For each rose, start at a corner of a half-circle and roll it up diagonally to form a cone shape for the rose center. Press on additional half-circles, curving the rounded edges outward and pressing them between your fingers to make thin petals. Add as many petals as you need to make a rose. Trim the bottom of the rose so it stands level on the dessert.

To give your rose a blush of color, let the rose dry about 15 minutes. Then using a dry, clean, small paintbrush, lightly brush the rose petals with petal dust or powdered food coloring (see page 222).

Cutouts

Shape a portion of clay or marzipan into a ball. Flatten slightly and place between two sheets of waxed paper dusted with powdered sugar. Roll to ⅛-inch thickness. Using small hors d'oeuvre or cookie cutters, cut the clay into desired shapes. Carefully lift the cutouts from the waxed paper.

Shaping roses

Sheets

Sheets made from Chocolate Modeling Clay or marzipan give a spectacular finish to cakes, tortes, cheesecakes, and terrines.

For a sheet that will cover an 8- or 9-inch round or square dessert, use the 1-cup option of Chocolate Modeling Clay or 8 ounces of marzipan. Shape the clay or marzipan into a ball. Dust one sheet of waxed paper with powdered sugar. Place the ball of clay on the waxed paper. Slightly flatten the ball and sprinkle with more powdered sugar. Place another sheet of waxed paper over the clay. Roll the clay from the center to the edge, forming a circle or a square about ⅛ inch thick. Trim the clay to fit the dessert. Wrap the clay sheet around the rolling pin. Then unroll the sheet onto the dessert.

▼**Two-Tone Sheets:** Give your dessert a personal touch by making a sheet that features hearts, stars, or other shapes.

For a two-tone sheet, prepare 1 cup of Chocolate Modeling Clay using white candy coating and 1 cup of modeling clay using chocolate or colored candy coating. (For marzipan, use 1 pound of marzipan and tint *half* of it with a little food coloring.)

Roll out the white clay as directed above for Sheets, *except* roll it to ¼-inch thickness. Roll out the chocolate clay as directed for Cutouts to ⅛-inch thickness and cut into shapes. Place the cutouts on the white sheet. Then roll to ⅛-inch thickness.

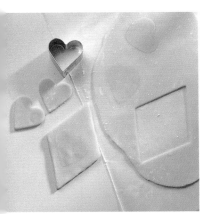

Making two-tone sheets

Ribbons

Ribbons made with Chocolate Modeling Clay or marzipan add a festive look to cakes and tortes. For a dessert that resembles a gift-wrapped package, arrange two ribbons over the sides and top of the dessert so they intersect in the middle. Or use several narrow ribbons to create a lattice top.

To make ribbons, roll out ¼ cup of chocolate clay or marzipan at a time, as directed for Sheets. Then use a fluted pastry wheel or a knife to cut the sheet into ribbons of desired width.

Or, use a pasta machine to make the ribbons. Set the machine at the widest opening and pass about ¼ cup of clay or marzipan through. If the clay begins to stick, dust it lightly with powdered sugar. Pass it through the same setting a second time to smooth the clay. Reset the machine on the next narrower opening. Pass the clay through the machine twice. Continue resetting the machine at narrower openings and passing the clay through twice at each setting until the clay is about ⅛ inch thick. If the length becomes too long, cut into shorter pieces. Trim the ragged edges. Then cut as desired to make ribbons. If ribbons are too soft for shaping, let stand for 2 to 4 hours or till ribbons are still pliable yet hold their shape.

▼**Two-Tone Ribbons:** Make 1 cup of clay with semisweet or bittersweet chocolate and another 1 cup of clay with white candy coating. (For marzipan, use 1 pound of marzipan and tint *half* of it with a little food coloring.) Roll out a small portion of chocolate clay and a small portion of white clay as directed above for ribbons, *except* roll it to ¼-inch thickness. Slightly overlap the two pieces of each clay. Roll out to ⅛-inch thickness. Cut into ribbons as desired.

Mail-Order Sources

If you're having difficulty in finding specialized ingredients or equipment used for making desserts, check the mail-order sources below. Many of the companies have catalogs for helping you to select the correct items.

American Spoon Foods
1668 Clarion Ave.
P.O. Box 566
Petoskey, MI 49770-0566
(616/347-9030 or
800-222-5886)
Carries dried cherries, blueberries, and cranberries; preserves and jellies; and nuts.

The Chef's Pantry
P.O. Box 3
Post Mills, VT 05058
(802/333-4141)
Carries chocolate, nuts, pure extracts, and crystallized flowers.

Country Cherry De-Lites—Country Ovens, Ltd.
123 Main St.
P.O. Box 195
Forestville, WI 54213
(414/743-2330)
Offers dried cherries and dried cranberries.

Country Kitchen Retail Mailorder
3225 Wells St.
Fort Wayne, IN 46808
(219/482-4835)
Carries baking, cake-decorating, and candy-making equipment and accessories. Nuts, food colorings, and flavorings also are offered.

Diamond Organics
P.O. Box 2159
Freedom, CA 95019
(408/662-9714 or
800-922-2396)
A source for edible flowers and a variety of fresh, organically grown produce.

Fiesta Nut Corporation
P.O. Box 366
75 Harbor Rd.
Port Washington, NY 11050
(516/883-1403 or
800-645-3296)
Carries nuts as well as sunflower seeds, pumpkin seeds, and dried fruits.

Maid of Scandinavia
3244 Raleigh Ave.
Minneapolis, MN 55416
(612/927-7996 or
800-328-6722)
Specializes in baking, cake-decorating, candy-making, and entertaining equipment and accessories. Different kinds of chocolate, candy coatings, food colorings, petal dusts, and flavorings also are offered.

Paradigm Foodworks, Inc.
5775 SW. Jean Rd, 106A
Lake Oswego, OR 97035
(503/636-4880 or
800-234-0250)
A source for different kinds of chocolate, jellies, and caramel and liqueur-fudge sauces.

Ruetenik Gardens
826 E. Schaaf Rd.
Brooklyn Heights, OH 44131
(216/741-1443)
Offers edible flowers and herb flowers.

Williams-Sonoma
P.O. Box 7456
San Francisco, CA 94120-7456
(415/421-4242 or
800-541-2233)
Specializes in cooking and baking equipment, small housewares, kitchenwares, and tablewares.

Wilton Enterprises, Inc.
2240 W. 75 St.
Woodridge, IL 60517
(708/963-7100)
Specializes in cake-decorating and candy-making supplies and tools.

Index

A-B

Nutrition Analysis
Keep track of your
daily nutrition needs by
using the information
we provide at the end
of each recipe. We've
analyzed the nutrition
content of each recipe
serving for you. When
a recipe gives an
ingredient substitution,
we used the first choice
in the analysis. If it
makes a range of
servings (such as 4 to
6), we used the smallest
number. Ingredients
listed as optional
weren't included in the
calculations.

234

Metric Cooking Hints

By making a few conversions, cooks in Australia, Canada, and the United Kingdom can use the recipes in Better Homes and Gardens® *Spectacular Desserts* with confidence. The charts on this page provide a guide for converting measurements from the U.S. customary system, which is used throughout this book, to the imperial and metric systems. There also is a conversion table for oven temperatures to accommodate the differences in oven calibrations.

Volume and Weight

Americans traditionally use *cup* measures for liquid and solid ingredients. The chart (bottom right) shows the approximate imperial and metric equivalents. If you are accustomed to weighing solid ingredients, here are some helpful approximate equivalents:

1 cup butter, caster sugar, or rice = 8 ounces = about 250 grams

1 cup flour = 4 ounces = about 125 grams

1 cup icing sugar = 5 ounces = about 150 grams

Spoon measures are used for smaller amounts of ingredients. Although the size of the teaspoon is the same, the size of the tablespoon varies slightly among countries. However, for practical purposes and for recipes in this book, a straight substitution is all that's necessary.

Measurements made using cups or spoons always should be *level,* unless stated otherwise.

Product Differences

Most of the ingredients called for in the recipes in this book are available in English-speaking countries. However, some are known by different names. Here are some common American ingredients and their possible counterparts:

▼ Sugar is granulated or caster sugar.
▼ Powdered sugar is icing sugar.
▼ All-purpose flour is plain household flour or white flour. When self-rising flour is used in place of all-purpose flour in a recipe that calls for leavening, omit the leavening (baking soda or baking powder) and salt.
▼ Light corn syrup is golden syrup.
▼ Cornstarch is cornflour.
▼ Baking soda is bicarbonate of soda.
▼ Vanilla is vanilla essence.

OVEN TEMPERATURE EQUIVALENTS

Fahrenheit Setting	Celsius Setting*	Gas Setting
300°F	150°C	Gas Mark 2
325°F	160°C	Gas Mark 3
350°F	180°C	Gas Mark 4
375°F	190°C	Gas Mark 5
400°F	200°C	Gas Mark 6
425°F	220°C	Gas Mark 7
450°F	230°C	Gas Mark 8
Broil		Grill

*Electric and gas ovens may be calibrated using Celsius. However, increase the Celsius setting 10 to 20 degrees when cooking above 160°C with an electric oven. For convection or forced-air ovens (gas or electric), lower the temperature setting 10°C when cooking at all heat levels.

Baking Pan Sizes

American	Metric
8x1½-inch round baking pan	20x4-centimetre sandwich or cake tin
9x1½-inch round baking pan	23x3.5-centimetre sandwich or cake tin
11x7x1½-inch baking pan	28x18x4-centimetre baking pan
13x9x2-inch baking pan	32.5x23x5-centimetre baking pan
12x7½x2-inch baking dish	30x19x5-centimetre baking pan
15x10x2-inch baking pan	38x25.5x2.5-centimetre baking pan (Swiss roll tin)
9-inch pie plate	22x4- or 23x4-centimetre pie plate
7- or 8-inch springform pan	18- or 20-centimetre springform or loose-bottom cake tin
9x5x3-inch loaf pan	23x13x6-centimetre or 2-pound narrow loaf pan or pâté tin
1½-quart casserole	1.5-litre casserole
2-quart casserole	2-litre casserole

USEFUL EQUIVALENTS

¼ cup = 2 fluid ounces = 50ml
⅓ cup = 3 fluid ounces = 75ml
½ cup = 4 fluid ounces = 125ml
⅔ cup = 5 fluid ounces = 150ml
¾ cup = 6 fluid ounces = 175ml
1 cup = 8 fluid ounces = 250ml
⅛ teaspoon = 0.5ml   2 cups = 1 pint
¼ teaspoon = 1ml   2 pints = 1 litre
½ teaspoon = 2ml   ½ inch = 1 centimetre
1 teaspoon = 5ml   1 inch = 2 centimetres